RADIO LUXEMBOURG
THE STATION OF THE STARS

RADIO LUXEMBOURG
THE STATION OF THE STARS

An Affectionate History of 50 Years of Broadcasting

BY RICHARD NICHOLS

A COMET BOOK
Published by the Paperback Division of
W.H. ALLEN & CO. LTD

A Comet Book
Published in 1983 by the Paperback Division of
W.H. Allen & Co. Ltd
A Howard & Wyndham Company
44 Hill Street, London W1X 8LB

Copyright © Richard Nichols, 1983

Printed and bound in Great Britain by
Hazell Watson & Viney Ltd, Aylesbury

ISBN 0 86379 035 6

Acknowledgements
A list of the names of all those who have helped would, at this juncture, be relatively pointless, since this book is itself a list of names, all of whom have been endlessly helpful. But otherwise without credit are a few people who have contributed enormously – Tony Fox, who has worked at least as hard as I have, Dave Atkey, as unselfishly generous as it's possible to be, and Lynn Cullen, who did all the tricky stuff with typewriters and photocopiers, plus licking the stamps.
Quotations from BBC internal memoranda on pages 15, 16, 19–22, 24, 30–33, 37, 61 and 62 are BBC copyright material reproduced by kind permission of The BBC Written Archive Centre, Caversham Park, Reading RG4 8TZ

This book is sold subject to the condition that it shall not, by way of trade or otherwise, be lent, re-sold, hired out or otherwise circulated without the publisher's prior consent in any form of binding or cover other than that in which it is published and without a similar condition including this condition being imposed on the subsequent purchaser.

CONTENTS

1: FOUNDATION	9
2: CONSOLIDATION	27
3: GAIRMANY CALLING...	49
4: 208	64
5: ROCK 'N' ROLL	83
6: FAB GEAR	103
7: JOLLY ROGER	123
8: LIVE, IF YOU WANT IT	138
9: TEENYBOPPER	166
INDEX	191

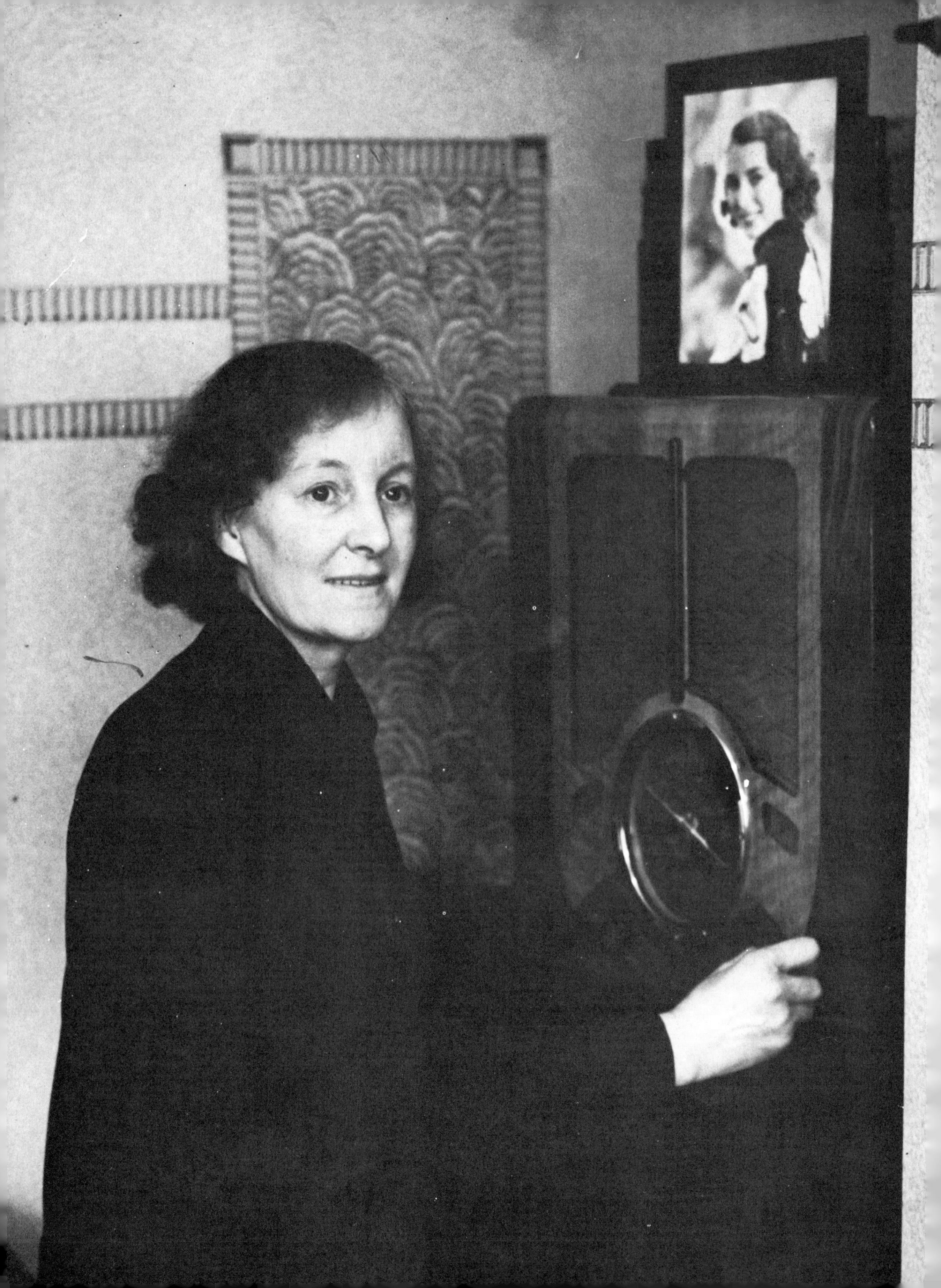

INTRODUCTION —

Writing books for a living is not what it's cracked up to be. There's more work, more anguish, and less fun than people would have you believe. And although all of that has been true of this book I am obliged to say that it has been both a pleasure and a privilege to write it.

This is solely and completely due to the fact that during its compilation I have come into contact with some of the nicest people you could hope to meet. Which probably sounds like a load of sycophantic drivel, but — as it happens — it's also completely true. Without exception large numbers of extremely busy people, all of whom have doubtless had 50 better things to do, have given freely their time and effort, racked their brains and searched their possessions in order to supply the material and photographs in these pages.

There was, however, for some considerable time one thing which was a source of continual sadness. Throughout all these interviews, meetings and discussions with people who had been involved with Radio Luxembourg during its 50-year history I constantly caught glimpses of an elusive and fleeting character who could never quite be pinned down. Because despite the facts and figures, despite the romance and glamour, the story of Radio Luxembourg is principally one of very charming, ordinary people — a fact which almost certainly accounts for the astounding record of this unique radio station.

However, somewhere in the background there was this other character; one who would account for the ease of access which a mention of Radio Luxembourg invariably granted in the close-knit media world. Someone who was responsible for the nostalgic and sometimes wistful smile which decorated the faces of everyone I spoke to. Without a single exception everybody remembered the radio station with great fondness — like people looking back on halcyon days at a school where they were never scolded or beaten.

Somewhere in this story there lurked a character who could inspire this emotion of deep affection mixed with youthful exuberance and tremendous warmth. As the days and weeks wore on I interviewed more and more people. Everyone I met said 'Oh, you *must* speak to so-and-so' and the list of people to see grew longer rather than shorter with each interview. And at every meeting the impression of this shadowy character grew stronger although no one ever named him or her, and I became more and more frustrated, despairing of ever making this most important acquaintance.

Until the day that realisation finally dawned; I had been staring it in the face for months. The character I was looking for was not a person, male or female, but a thing. It *was* Radio Luxembourg. Already I had regarded it as a unique radio station, but alone among radio stations this one imprints its own personality, style and charm upon the people who

Vera Lynn's mother tunes in to hear her daughter, whose picture stands on top of the wireless *(Pictorial Press).*

work there, the people who come into direct contact with it and the people who listen to it.

Radio Luxembourg's English Service has been broadcasting for 50 years, during which time that character has had more than ample opportunity to develop and grow, to the point at which it is not a personality radio station, but a radio station with a personality all its own. And a personality which does not impose upon its employees and its presenters, but one which gradually and slowly creeps under the skin, until the people who work there – behind the microphone or behind the scenes – have soaked it up and become part of a whole which is bigger and stronger than the sum of its component parts.

This is the radio station which gave you the Ovaltinies, the *Top Twenty Show*, the Beatles, Horace Batchelor and the Infra-Draw method, *Opportunity Knocks*, *Princess for a Day*, *Dance Party*, the *Teen and Twenty Disc Club*, *Jensen's Dimensions* and *Earthlink*. This is the radio station which made pop music radio in Europe, which began, styled and continues to influence music radio and the music industry in this country – and therefore the rest of the world.

Several years ago Radio Luxembourg ran a special two-hour programme, *This is how it all began*, briefly outlining their incredible story. This is that same story, in full. This is *where* it all began.

1: FOUNDATION

Although you may be forgiven for not realising it, 1896 was quite a year; there was trouble with the Boers, Kitchener was at war in the Sudan and the British Empire was rapidly expanding across East Africa. Against a seething historical backdrop people like Max Beerbohm, H G Wells and A E Housman were turning out their best works, while Gilbert and Sullivan set the antics of the Empire to music. The first copy of the *Daily Mail* was published in time to record the repealing of the Red Flag Act, the Klondyke gold rush and the establishment of the Nobel Prize. And almost insignificantly Italian engineer Guglielmo Marconi demonstrated the first ever practical application of the new science of Wireless Telegraphy (W/T) on Salisbury Plain. It was this apparently small happening which would have by far the widest impact out of all the events of that year.

By 1898 Marconi had established W/T communication by Morse Code between Bournemouth and the Isle of Wight, and had extended his range from Poldhu in Cornwall to St John's in Newfoundland before the end of 1901. In 1914, with the outbreak of the Great War, W/T was possible between ships at sea, and it was the military applications which were seen to be most exciting. It was also the possible military applications of Wireless which led to its use being stringently regulated in Britain: for the first time enemy forces were within easy communication of the homeland, and in fear of this its use was denied the public.

After the war was over these restrictions were lifted, and in 1919 Marconi successfully transmitted the human voice across the Atlantic. It was this which led him to establish a public broadcasting station of 6 kilowatts in a shed at Writtle near Chelmsford, putting out two half-hour programmes every day.

Existing laws covering this new technology had been specifically designed to regulate maritime Wireless Telegraphy, and were insufficient to cope with Marconi's advances; despite the war's end pressure from the armed services forced the Post Office to step in and ban further broadcasts until more relevant laws could be introduced.

Marconi and the 3000 members of the 63 societies which already existed in Britain to enjoy and exploit the science of radio applied pressures of their own. In 1921 the Post Office issued 4000 licences to private individuals to receive wireless broadcasts and 150 to operators of transmitting stations. Marconi was one of the 150, and station 2MT went on the air on 14 February 1922 from Chelmsford, even though the terms of the licence permitted a mere 15 minutes of broadcasting each week.

2MT was followed by an experimental station at Marconi House in London and it was clear that unless the government took firm action to bring radio properly under its wing then developments would get beyond

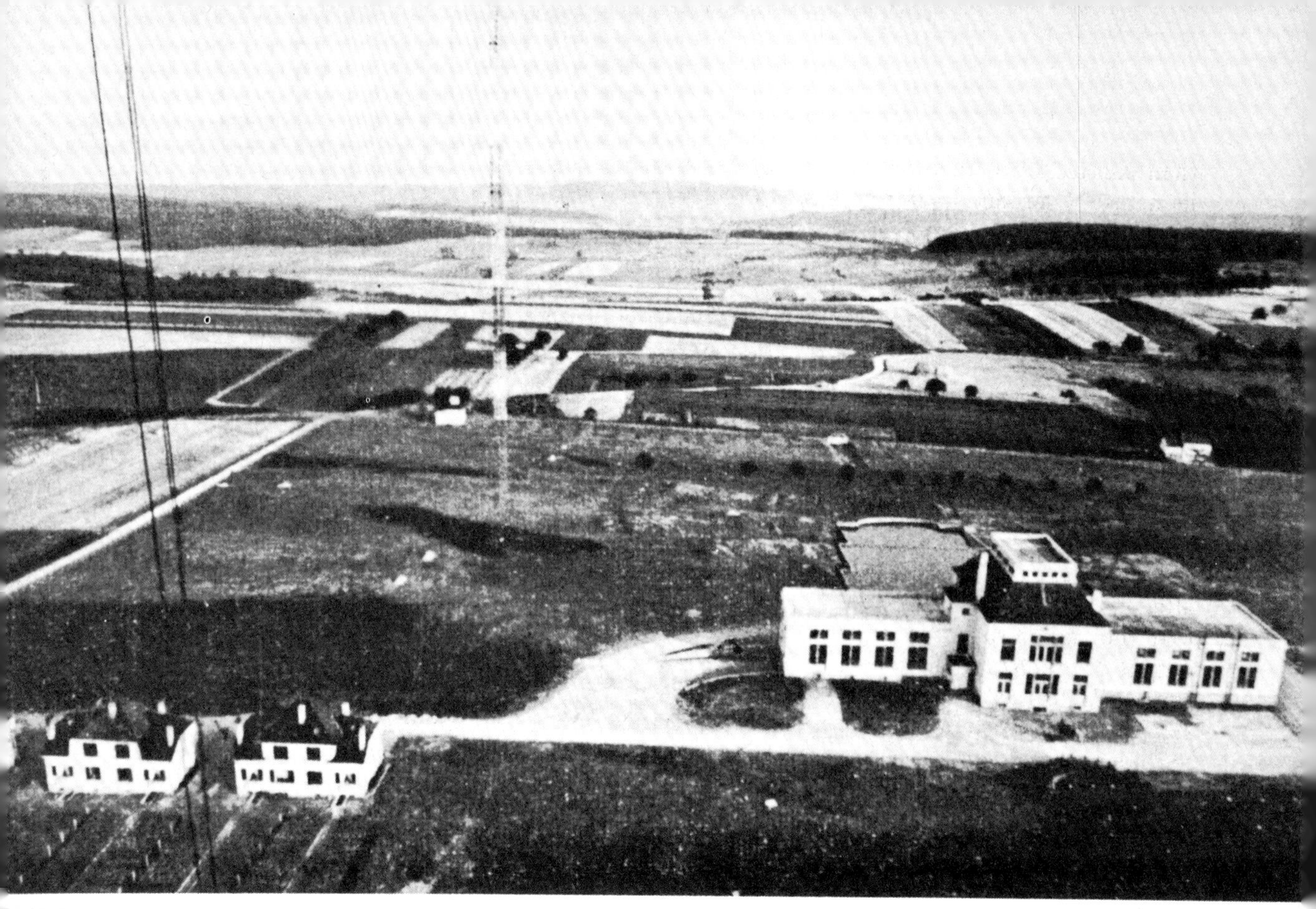

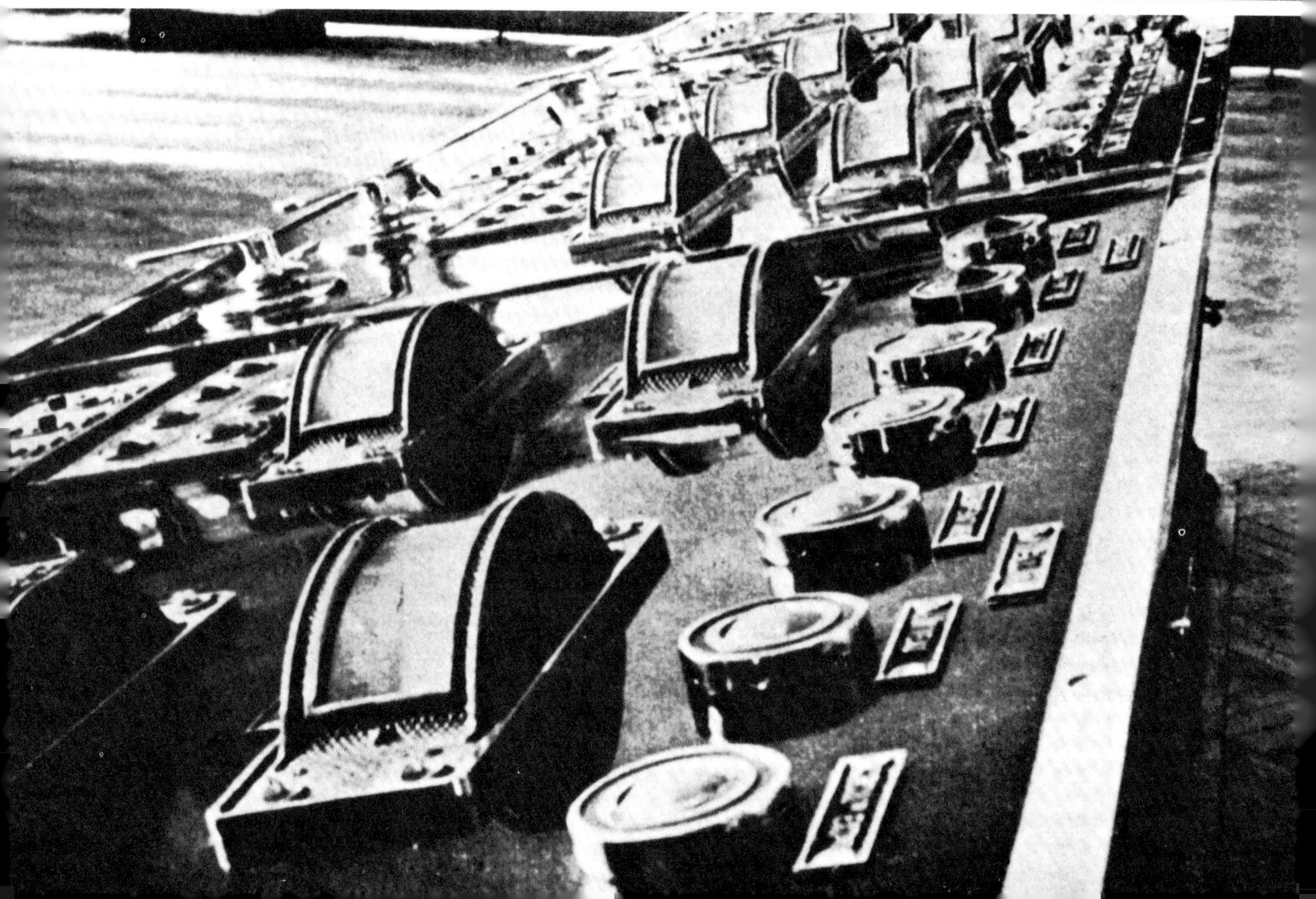

their control. Two factors conspired to produce such control and dictate its nature. One was the proliferation of commercial radio stations in the USA, which had blossomed following the initial broadcasts from KDKA in Pittsburgh, Pennsylvania on 2 November 1920, and the other was closer to home. In July 1922 there was a broadcast of a garden fete from Hampstead. In the main the programme consisted of what the Press of the day described as 'unconsidered trifles of the lightest type' – exactly the sort of thing everybody wanted to hear and precisely what the government had already determined they should not.

The immediate result came on 18 October of the same year with the formation of The British Broadcasting Company Limited, which derived its income from half of the 10 shilling licence fee and a 10 per cent royalty on all receiving sets sold. Its brief was to broadcast news, speeches, lectures, educational matter, weather reports and, almost as an afterthought, concerts and theatrical entertainment. It was at this point that the rather sombre programming which would characterise BBC output throughout the twenties and thirties, and which would lead eventually to the typical 'Reith Sunday' was established. It awarded a significant advantage to the foreign stations with their lighter approach to radio entertainment and marked the beginning of a 50-year-long struggle between the BBC and its audience which would not be resolved until 1967.

But while the Post Office and the BBC between them struggled to gain and retain control of the airwaves in Britain significant developments were taking place on the international front. Radio hadn't only caught on in Britain and America, and by 1922 there were transmitting stations in Canada and New Zealand and, more importantly, Belgium, Germany, Spain, Czechoslovakia, Poland, Finland, Norway and France. Like the British, the French had felt that radio would be best controlled by the government, and in 1923 declared a state monopoly under the auspices of their own post office, which later went on to license various independent stations. Even so it was clear that radio traversed international borders in a way which had previously not been possible, and it was equally clear that some form of international co-operation and control would be necessary.

As long ago as 1865 there had been an international conference in Paris in preparation for this event, and there had long been an international telecommunications union, but in 1925 the Union Internationale de Radiophonie (UIR) had its first meeting in Geneva. Sitting at this meeting was the newly-constituted British Broadcasting Corporation; the previous British Broadcasting Company had been dissolved at the recommendation of a Parliamentary committee and the Corporation which succeeded it was answerable only to Parliament. The day-to-day running of the Corporation was conducted by a Board of Governors and their first Director-General was the previous chief executive of the BBC Ltd – John (later Lord) Charles Walsham Reith, a somewhat dour Scottish civil engineer who was then 36 years old.

Above
The Long Wave transmitter at Junglinster which has been broadcasting for 50 years.

Below
The 'failsafe' control panel at Junglinster pictured after the war. It has been modified since its installation in 1932.

That first UIR conference produced an agreement, in 1926, between the participating countries – there were now 16 European nations with radio stations of their own – and most had to make some sacrifices in the interest of international harmony. The BBC, which had been using some 20 medium wave frequencies, was allocated only 10, with five others to be shared with other countries, and one long wave frequency. This latter was particularly useful to the BBC since, in 1925, they had built station 5XX at Daventry in response to reception difficulties on other frequencies. This transmitter pushed out 30 kilowatts on 1500 metres and could be heard all over Europe with great clarity. It was probably the most famous radio transmitter in Europe for ten years, until its closure in 1935. Beyond any doubt it remained dominant for seven or eight years, until the emergence, on 15 March 1933, of a new English-language transmitter shovelling out 200 kilowatts on 1191 metres from the tiny European Grand Duchy of Luxembourg.

Tiny is the appropriate word for this territory of slightly less than 1000 square miles which is bordered by Germany to the east, Belgium to the north and France to the south. In 1354 the county of Luxembourg had been made into a Grand Duchy by the Emperor Charles IV. Almost immediately the Grand Duchy's neighbours began to take it in turns to subjugate the people to their own rule, and it was no surprise that following on the heels of Burgundy, Spain and the Habsburg Empire the greatest bandit since Attila the Hun took it for himself – under the hand of the Emperor Napoleon Luxembourg became a *departement* of France in 1795. By 1815 – a significant enough date for Napoleon – the Grand Duchy had been placed in the safe keeping of William I of the Netherlands, where it stayed until 1867 and the Treaty of London, when it became a constitutional monarchy with a hereditary succession from the house of Nassau. Its independence was not violated again until 1914.

The town of Luxembourg stands on a sandstone plateau bisected by the deep ravine of the Alzette River. Here also stood the second-strongest fortress in Europe (dwarfed only by that of Gibraltar) which fell into disuse after the signing of the treaty of 1867. In 1914 such optimism must have seemed ill-founded, but the people of Luxembourg should have known better – they had been overrun by their neighbours more often than any other European nation. It is true to say that the Luxembourg people are the first truly pan-European nation. It is hardly a surprise, then, that frontiers play a smaller role in their lives than in the lives of the other people of Europe.

None of which can have been uppermost in the minds of the group who met in the Café Jacoby, Place de l'Etoile, Luxembourg during 1920. This was a group of wireless enthusiasts – the Amis de TSF (Télégraphie Sans Fils) as they were called – whose aim was the promotion of interest in the new science through meetings and exhibitions and the formation of other groups around the Grand Duchy. In 1924 one of the members of this group, radio electrician François Anen, installed a 100-watt transmitter in a house in Rue Beaumont, and shortly afterwards the

Luxembourg government voted the society a subsidy to exploit the station. Almost straight away the station expanded in ability and ambition, and in 1926 began outside broadcasts of military concerts from the town's central square, Place d'Armes, and various theatrical pieces in the Luxembourg dialect. The situation persisted through 1927 – the year the BBC was granted a monopoly by Royal Charter and John Reith was knighted – and by 1928 contacts made with nearby French radio enthusiasts had grown ever stronger. The French had begun broadcasting from the Eiffel Tower in 1922 and their own radio network – if it deserves such a grandiose title – was expanding. In 1928, then, a M Jaques Tremoulet contacted François Anen and told him that Radio Toulouse was replacing its 3 kilowatt transmitter with a larger item of 8 kilowatts; Anen accepted the outgoing 3 kW transmitter for use in Luxembourg in the same year that the Fédération Nationale Luxembourgeoise des Sociétées Radiophoniques was constituted to concert the efforts of the several thousand members of the various small clubs around the Grand Duchy.

Tremoulet's main concern was in Toulouse, but he was not the only person interested in the tiny Luxembourg transmitter. The next pronounced initiative came from Henri Etienne, ex-editor of a radio magazine, *L'Antenne*. He proposed a proper radio service in Luxembourg using French and Belgian capital since the Grand Duchy had little in the way of its own industry; the main employer was agriculture, and the biggest industry in terms of money was iron and steel. Aided by Luxembourg entrepreneur Raoul Fernandez, Etienne began negotiations with the appropriate government personages in the Ministry of Posts and Telegraphs. He went on to form, in 1928, the Société d'Etudes Radiophoniques SA with a capitalisation of 280,000 Belgian Francs with himself and François Anen as principals along with Parisian businessmen Boyer, Almagro, Fortin, Chamon and Le Duc. Their object was to study the construction and exploitation of a radio station in the Grand Duchy. The Society was recognised and given legal status on 19 December 1929 and in preparation for what lay ahead the 3 kW station in Rue Beaumont ceased transmission in January 1930.

In August of that year the new Society was awarded the franchise it sought in a charter running to 18 articles. This document provided that the station should broadcast programmes which were intellectual and educational as well as of general interest. Most significantly of all it allowed for advertising to be carried as well as for foreign language broadcasts. The power of the new station was to be not less than 100 kilowatts and the wavelength should be between 210 and 500 metres as allocated to Luxembourg at the Prague conference of 1929. The use of other wavelengths was to be by international agreement, and the station was scheduled to go on the air within 18 months of signature of the document. The concession would grant a monopoly, and would run for a period of 25 years.

The agreement was signed on 29 September 1930 both by the

government and by Henri Etienne and Jean Le Duc on behalf of the Société. It aroused considerable international interest from France and Germany (especially the French Minister of the Interior, Laval) and also from Britain, where the BBC opinion was one of concern and alarm; it was immediately apparent that 100 kilowatts was more than enough power to cover Luxembourg and that the station intended to broadcast to other countries.

This opinion was further confirmed when the Société d'Etudes was replaced by a new and larger organisation which took over all existing contracts with the Luxembourg government and which had a much sounder financial base – 15 million Francs this time, spread through 30,000 shares of 500 Francs. The new company, Compagnie Luxembourgeoise de Radiodiffusion (CLR) was the majority shareholder with the next largest helping going to the Banque de Paris et Pays-Bas. The rest of the shares were largely divided among various French industrial concerns, although the concession from the Luxembourg government specifically stated that the board of directors should contain a majority of Luxembourg nationals and/or residents.

The company opened its offices at 53, Avenue Monterey in Luxembourg and bought a large slice of the plateau of Junglinster for its transmitter site. The foundation stone was laid there by Prince Felix of Luxembourg on 7 October 1931. Only a few weeks later the British Post Office wrote to the Director-General of Posts and Telegraphs in Luxembourg requesting confirmation that the new transmitter would be operating within the limits prescribed by the Prague conference. A copy of that part of the station's charter which specified exactly that was all that came back in the way of reply. The BBC thought little of this and tried through the UIR to obtain the co-operation of the French broadcasting authorities in modifying the original concession – especially as far as transmitter power was concerned – with little result. Although the new station was, at least in the eyes of the BBC, under French control (since that is where the money came from) it was clear that there was no possibility of applying pressure through official French channels any more than the Luxembourg government appeared willing to offer co-operation.

Even before the transmitter had been built it was apparent that more than anywhere else the Luxembourg station would threaten the BBC monopoly over broadcasting in Great Britain and equally clear that the BBC regarded the embryonic radio station as a challenge; battle had been irrevocably joined from this moment onwards. The BBC, however, was already engaged on other fronts, most notably with an enemy situated in the unlikeliest of places – the small fishing village of Fécamp in northern France. The nature of the enemy was fairly unlikely too. Captain Plugge was one of the last great adventurers, had organised what were probably the first package tours on the continent and by the late twenties was busy touring Europe in a car equipped with the world's very first car radios manufactured by Philco. His travels brought him eventually to the

Normandy coast and into Fécamp, where the head of the Benedictine distillery there was experimenting with a small radio transmitter located in his drawing room, right behind the piano. Plugge was fascinated and thrilled, and wasted no time in becoming involved, with the express intention of beaming radio programmes to southern England.

Max Stanniforth was the first employee of Plugge's grandly-named International Broadcasting Company, whose income was derived from the sale of commercial advertising on air in the American style; probably the very first British company to advertise on radio in this way was Spink, the jewellers, closely followed by Dunlop. This was, however, something of an arbitrary choice as Max Stanniforth was sent to Fécamp in 1931 with a box of records and a box of adverts and more or less left to get on with it. Radio Normandy broadcast to England every night between midnight and 3 a.m. – the only time available after the French service had finished with the transmitter. The programmes consisted of 90 per cent popular dance music – which was precisely the sort of diet not available to the audiences of Sir John Reith's BBC.

As the IBC stations multiplied in number, embracing Toulouse, Lyons and Paris, the threat from Luxembourg, with the proposal of the most powerful transmitter in Europe, was met with maximum effort. Principals in the BBC struggle to thwart Etienne were Vice Admiral Sir Charles Carpendale for the Corporation and F W Phillips at the Post Office.

On 31 October 1931 *Wireless World* magazine had reported that the identity of the new sponsor for the vast transmitter at Junglinster in Luxembourg had been identified. Gleaned from the pages of the French newspaper, *Journal Officiel*, came the news of an award, the Legion d'Honneur, to Raoul Fernandez for obtaining the concession in Luxembourg 'entirely under French control'. Carpendale commented that 'publication of this warlike announcement shows you who's at the back of Luxembourg as we always knew', demonstrating a fine distrust and apparently more than a cordial dislike of his government's erstwhile allies. The statement by the Luxembourg government that the object of the new station would be fair propaganda and exchanges of cultural programmes between nations was greeted with considerable scepticism. The BBC was of the opinion that in such circumstances the stations should be run by the League of Nations or some similar non-profit-making organisation, but in any case definitely not by a French company. 'I cannot see,' wrote Carpendale, 'how one could ensure fair treatment on a basis of this kind, well knowing the things which have happened in the past.'

Things were still happening in the present as well, however. Etienne had been travelling abroad a great deal, calling on a wide variety of radio stations suggesting co-operation and assistance, and even asked the BBC for technical help in the construction of the Junglinster transmitter (which was unsurprisingly refused). He made no favourable impression on the BBC at all, and still less on the head of Berlin's Radio Dienst,

Rawitzki, who described him as a dreamer who failed to answer letters or keep appointments, who made pointless journeys at company expense, always accompanied by 'Madame' Etienne – usually a Luxembourg lady by the name of Josette Lefevre – and was doing the company no good at all. In fact Etienne seemed to be doing it so little good that Rawitzki made a special trip to Paris to speak to one of the company's major shareholders and tell him personally of his misgivings.

He only saw an assistant, who summed up the meeting in writing and concluded the memo with an opinion of his own – 'We must prepare ourselves for a rude awakening,' he said, 'or the affair will turn out badly.'

Worse was to come when it was discovered that the French Sûreté had been keeping Etienne under surveillance for several months; his frequent journeys around Europe by road were the object of some suspicion and there seemed a distinct possibility that Etienne was involved in drug smuggling on a substantial scale, although the Sûreté had been unable to obtain any proof. But the suspicion was enough and Etienne was removed, his responsibilities taken over by Jean Proix.

This information was greeted in England with some alarm; the Luxembourg international Long Wave proposal, observed the BBC, was no longer under the control of 'that enterprising pirate' Etienne, but Proix, Tabouis and Lacour-Gayette who were far more formidable opposition, being correctly described as men of 'position, antecedents and high cultural standing'. Nevertheless their overtures to the BBC were greeted with no more enthusiasm than Etienne's had been, even though this time they offered the Corporation the chance to subscribe some capital and nominate a member of the board or simply to pay to keep the English programmes off the air. The BBC perceived another option, however, recorded in an internal memo, which was to 'oppose it (Luxembourg) tooth and nail'. This latter sentence was heavily underlined in red with the word 'YES' written beside it in large letters by Carpendale.

And no wonder, as Captain Plugge's IBC went from strength to strength, moving eventually to the point at which it would be selling airspace to British advertisers on Radio Luxembourg as well as all the other stations. By now Max Stanniforth had been joined on Radio Normandy by Bob Danvers Walker, an Australian broadcaster of some standing and later to become one of the best-known voices in radio. His arrival at Normandy coincided with an improvement in technical facilities and the tiny carpet-lined studio gave way to a much larger room with a horseshoe of six turntables around a central microphone; a basic arrangement which has persisted until the present day in most radio studios.

At the time all recorded material came on transcription disc; not quite Edison's revolving drum, but hardly much more sophisticated. Tape recording had yet to be invented, so these large 78 rpm records – generally 16 inches or more in diameter – were standard equipment, and

The two giant 790hp diesel generators at Junglinster. Either one of them produces enough power to beam a LW signal to Britain.

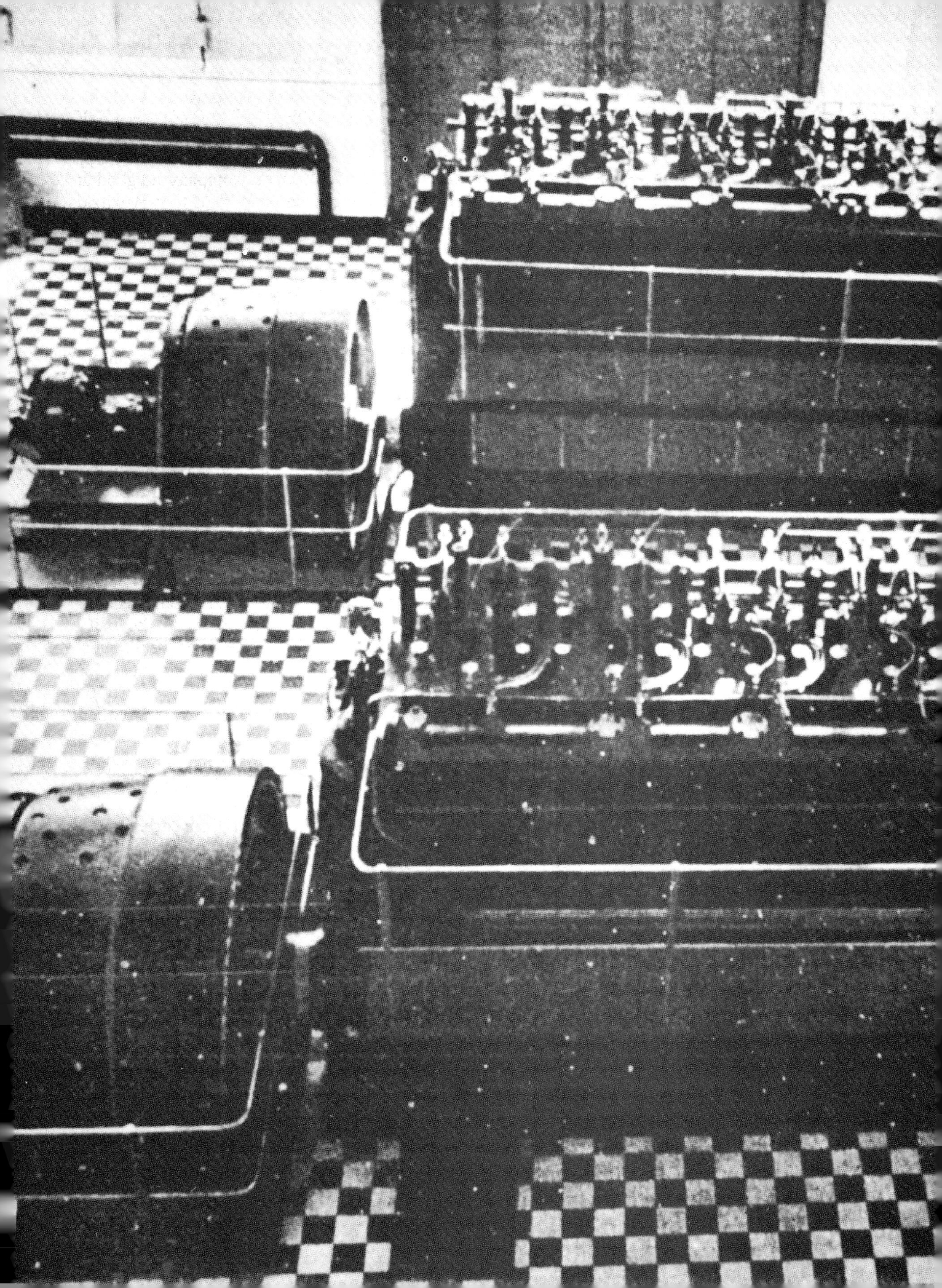

for many years the problem of hissing, crackling and scratching would characterise radio broadcasts of recorded material. Which to a large extent explains why most people – especially the BBC – preferred live broadcasts. However the newly-vacated studio at Radio Normandy was given over to film projectors; giant Western Electric units designed to show 35 mm films. But in London sponsored programmes were recorded via an optical camera on to 35 mm film – soundtrack only, of course – and the films sent out to Fécamp where they were laced up and broadcast, producing a sound quality far superior to that of the clumsy discs.

They had another advantage in that a full half-hour programme could be recorded on a single film; once it was laced up and running nothing, bar mechanical hitches, could interfere with smooth transmission. This was a situation the advertisers, who were already in the habit of sponsoring programmes rather than paying for inserts during programmes, much preferred. Travelling at 78 rpm even a 16-inch disc doesn't last for a long time, and announcers on those first commercial stations had to mix several discs to make up one half-hour programme, which is why the studio needed six turntables. Clearly there was considerable margin for error and clearly there were considerable errors. With money at stake the film was a much better way of going about things. The improvement in technical quality was a secondary benefit which would later be a source of great annoyance to the BBC.

In the meantime, all through 1932, the advent of the new Radio Luxembourg was growing ever closer. Possibly the first intimation the British public had was a report in the *Daily Mirror* on 20 January 1932, saying that the station was being built. In June of the same year the British government made diplomatic representations to the Luxembourg government claiming that the transmitter, which was expected to operate on 1250 metres Long Wave, would be in contravention of article 5 of the 1927 Washington Conference to which the Luxembourg government was a party. Luxembourg replied that they had not yet awarded the 1250 metre wavelength to IBC and were still searching for a suitable frequency which would in any case not be in contravention of the Washington agreement. In July *Wireless World* reported that the IBC had already sold airtime on the new transmitter, which would be broadcasting to Britain on Sundays only, 'for a considerable period'.

Experience on Radio Normandy had shown that advertisers preferred to sponsor whole shows rather than buy spots; most of them wanted to be associated with a particular artist or dance band, and were buying 15- or 30-minute slots on Normandy, Toulouse, Poste Parisien, Lyons and others. All of these stations were providing programmes that were 90 per cent dance music – Geraldo and so on – the kind of entertainment the BBC rationed out to its audience on a rather miserly basis.

It was this sort of music programme which had given rise to the diplomatic exchanges through the summer of 1932. In keeping with its agreement with the Luxembourg government the new radio station was obliged to commence broadcasting within 18 months of signature of their agreement, but what with the Etienne affair and other matters construction of the transmitter at Junglinster was well behind schedule. Accordingly a 10 kilowatt transmitter had been purchased from Belgium and had begun transmissions daily between 12.30 and 1.30 on 1250 metres, playing solely popular dance music from records.

Although 10 kilowatts was relatively low-powered, the BBC were clearly worried that when the large transmitter came on air it would use the same frequency and blanket England with its output. Having said that this would not be the case the Luxembourg government could hardly allow it to happen, so when in January 1933 the 200 kilowatt transmitter began testing it was not on 1250 metres.

The BBC monitoring service at Tatsfield first logged a tuning note of 600 cycles and in March recorded the first test transmissions on 1185 metres. They were apparently 'very strong' and appeared to be actual programmes rather than simple test transmissions.

They protested again, pointing out that Luxembourg had not been allocated a Long Wave frequency, but 223 metres and 230.6 metres in the Medium Waveband. Luxembourg replied that these were transmissions which 'are still of an experimental nature'. To prove the point they switched frequencies again, and on 15 March 1933 Radio Luxembourg began a series of 'test transmissions' on 1191 metres in the Long Wave which had a distinctly permanent character. Despite what the Luxembourg government may have said about experimental broadcasts the Compagnie Luxembourgeoise de Radiodiffusion was now committed in writing to 'émissions régulières' which the BBC found to be very strong, with reception as good as any national station in all the countries it reached – Britain, France, Belgium and Germany. Reception was excellent and the potential audience huge. So huge, in fact, that F W Phillips wrote again to Carpendale. 'We must,' he said on 24 March, 'use all our influence to stop this' – the memo arrived on Carpendale's desk the same moment as a memo from Tatsfield which said that Luxembourg had been monitored every evening between 7 p.m. and 11 p.m. for the past week.

The station was broadcasting to a different country each evening and the announcements were all in the relevant language. On Monday they broadcast to Italy, on Tuesday Belgium, Wednesday Luxembourg, Thursday Germany, Friday Holland, Saturday France and Sundays were the English day. As Britain went through all the agonies of a typical Reith Sunday, Radio Luxembourg's test transmissions commenced at 7 p.m. with 45 minutes of light music followed by a lengthy five-minute weather forecast. Symphony music carried on to 8.30 when there was a 10 minute talk which was brief enough by comparison to the alternative and really served primarily to establish that the programme was in English, for England. The light music continued right up to 11 p.m., broken only for the news at 9 p.m. and again at 9.45, and it was now clear that these test transmissions were nothing of the sort. In fact they were of such a permanent nature that the IBC felt sufficiently emboldened to make two approaches through official channels. In letters written from the IBC offices in Hallam Street their Mr Shanks first sought the assistance of W E Weston at the Post Office in obtaining landline concessions between England and Luxembourg and also, in an act of startling cheek, asked the BBC to publicise Radio Luxembourg broadcasting schedules. Incredibly the BBC complied with this request although it was to be for only a short while. And the Post Office at least considered the request for landlines that was put to them before deciding against it.

The frequency which Radio Luxembourg had adopted – 'pirated' was the word the BBC used – was not one which had been allocated to them at any of the international conferences which had so far taken place and to which the Luxembourg government had been a party. Their sudden appearance on Long Wave generated a considerable amount of ill-feeling, and not only in Britain. Iceland was the first country to complain, since Radio Luxembourg's transmissions were uncomfortably close to their own and strong enough to produce substantial interference. And although the Junglinster transmitter didn't technically interfere in Britain it was a major competitor to 5XX and in direct contravention of the BBC policy. Such policy was to provide the listeners with things which Sir John Reith and his fellow-governors believed were good for them. This did not mean that programmes were what people wanted to hear; in fact the opposite was frequently true, but all the time the BBC operated within the monopoly granted in its charter there was no danger that the policy could be overturned – at least not by a station broadcasting from anywhere in Britain.

BBC objections to anyone 'pirating a Long Wave frequency for a country too small to need it and forcing advertising into Great Britain' continued through the year, partly based on such evidence as they could find of interference caused by the station. In April of 1933 the monitoring services at Tatsfield reported that interference from Luxembourg was clearly audible on Munich, Beromunster, Muhlacker and Trieste, but the BBC seemed to be more concerned by this than anyone else. And since their various protests, diplomatic and otherwise, seemed totally ineffectual they started looking for other ways to combat the new station.

A flurry of memos throughout April led the BBC to the first obvious step and they swiftly decided to boycott Radio Luxembourg within their own programmes and ceased all mention of the station in *World Radio* which had up until then been giving details of the programme schedules as the IBC had asked. The logical follow-up to this was to obtain the co-operation of others in ignoring Radio Luxembourg entirely, and in this they sought the help of the British Press. However, initially there was a feeling that it would not be advisable to wait until Radio Luxembourg began to broadcast sponsored programmes unless they could get the necessary help on the basis of opposing anyone who stole a wavelength without permission.

B.B.C.
INTERNAL CIRCULATING MEMO

SUBJECT:— LUXEMBOURG.

7th April, 1933.

It is suggested that we should endeavour to prevent publicity with regard to the Luxembourg Station in every way possible. Obviously we refrain from mentioning it in "World Radio", and there is also the question as to whether we can persuade some of the leading newspapers to do likewise.

I am not quite sure whether it would be advisable to defer our action with the outside press until Luxembourg actually starts sponsored programmes, or whether we can approach the press on the basis of trying to get them to co-operate in discouraging anyone who jumps a wavelength.

Angwin is coming here tomorrow concerning the Lucerne business, and I will speak to him about any conceivable action which the Post Office might take other than normal action at the Conference.

It seems to me that a possible way of combating Luxembourg would be to allot the wavelength to somebody else, not as their only wavelength, but to get someone with a sporting spirit to take it on and try and clear the channel. However, I rather imagine this would not work out in practice, because it means that Luxembourg would move to another channel.

NA/MKO.

One of the early BBC memos about Radio Luxembourg. Later, when the station began broadcasting, the BBC turned their efforts towards performers and tried to 'persuade' them to boycott the new station.

The other possibility considered was rather more drastic; allocation of the wavelength Luxembourg were using to someone else 'with a sporting spirit' who may care to 'try to clear the channel'. In other words someone who would do their very best to jam or blot out the Luxembourg signal. In the end this idea was discarded since it would have been easy enough for Luxembourg to switch frequency and once they'd been provoked and given the idea, who could tell where they might spring up next?

But there was clearly a need for the BBC to do something if they were not to lose the battle entirely. Captain Plugge's IBC was moving from strength to strength, bombarding Britain with English language programmes from a number of radio stations spread out all over the continent. However, the transmitter power of Radio Normandy, Toulouse, Poste Parisien and others was relatively low; Normandy was the nearest geographically, but had a catchment area which really only extended across the south of England and up as far as London. The massive transmitter at Junglinster spread its signal out all over Britain and reception of Radio Luxembourg was as good in Scotland as it was in the south, sometimes better.

The arrangement which existed at the time with the IBC was that they sold airtime to companies in Britain and paid a percentage of this to the owners of the various radio stations under whose banner they operated. This was to be the same with Radio Luxembourg. IBC had obtained the concession to sell airtime on the new station and in this way both the IBC and the CLR would make a profit. This is the simple base of commercial radio. The fact that IBC had been awarded the franchise some considerable time ago had, of course, made nonsense of the Luxembourg government's denials that full-time broadcasting to Britain on an unauthorised Long Wave was not anticipated. It was the only way that the CLR could operate, a fact which should have been self-evident.

It was inevitable that the campaign to sell airtime should begin soon, and when it finally broke, the IBC made maximum use of Radio Luxembourg's huge power. 'THE MOST POWERFUL BROADCASTING STATION IN EUROPE' screamed the adverts when the campaign began in May of 1933, in *Advertiser's Weekly*. It went on to announce that the first programme for British listeners which would be available to sponsors and advertisers would be on Sunday 4 June, on 1191 metres. Interested parties were invited to contact the IBC in Hallam Street, just round the corner from the BBC, for information about prices.

The BBC were horrified, and the campaign against Radio Luxembourg accelerated to maximum effort; telegrams flew across Europe to the UIR in Geneva and diplomatic representations were made to governments as the BBC governors pulled out all the stops. They were rewarded in their efforts as, in the face of such a massive outcry, the IBC and Radio Luxembourg backed down for the moment at least. On top of protests through official channels the BBC had now also found the co-operation it had been seeking from the British Press, although only for

Huge cooling tubes inside the Junglinster transmitter building.

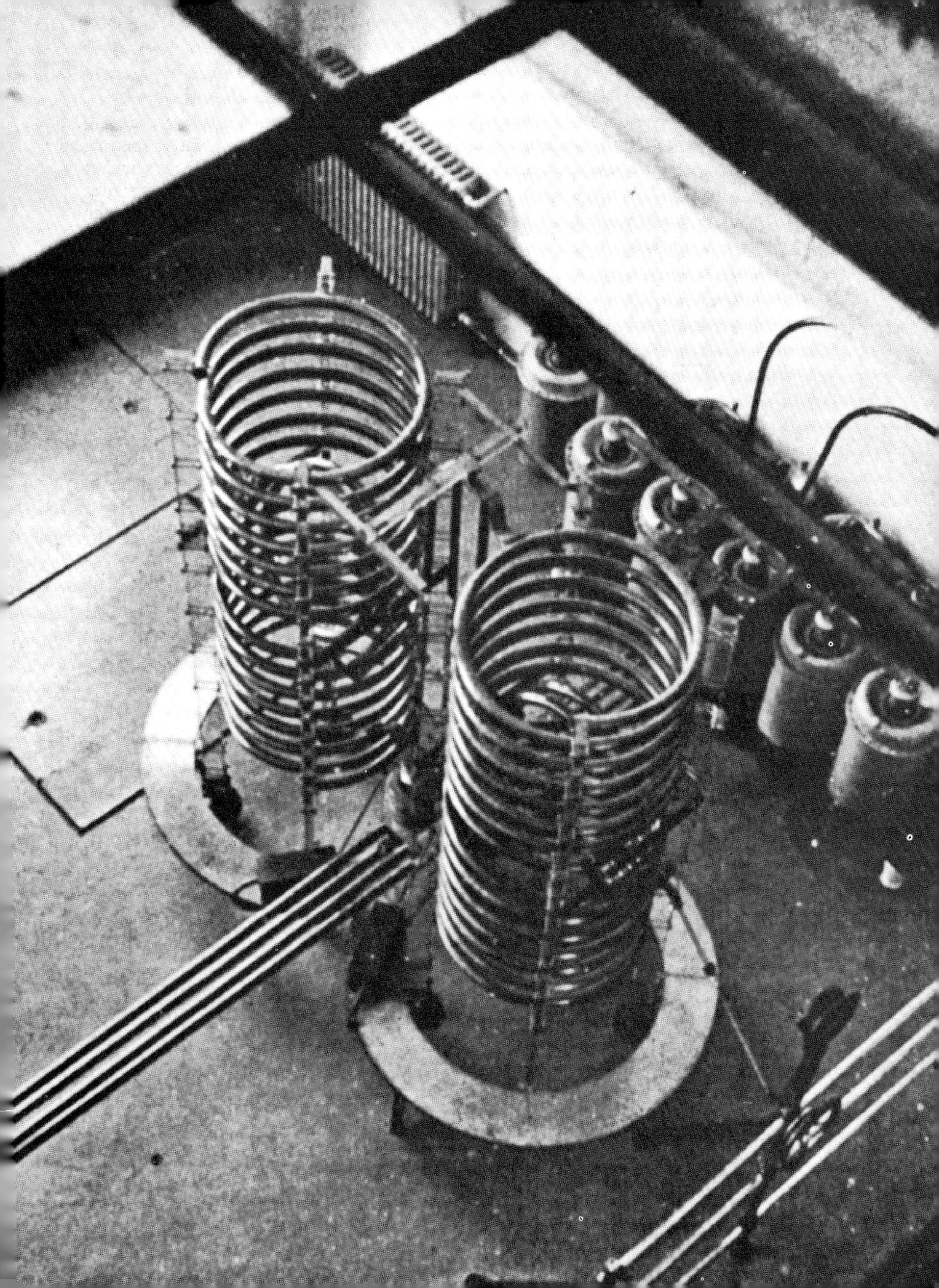

the basest of reasons – money. The newspaper publishers saw the IBC and Radio Luxembourg not only as a threat to the BBC (which possibly may not have worried them that much) but also as a threat to themselves, through the medium of their advertising revenue. The IBC presented enormously strong competition and therefore a threat, which they met head-on and began a campaign to boycott Radio Luxembourg which with only one or two exceptions was maintained for almost 50 years.

Meanwhile Radio Luxembourg and the BBC got together, in a meeting at Broadcasting House on 24 June 1933, to discuss wavelengths, piracy and possible solutions in an atmosphere which was intended to be one of warm international friendship but which was in truth exceedingly frosty. The BBC were expecting the pirate radio amateurs to visit them cap in hand and apologise, perhaps to try to make amends, before being roundly admonished and sent on their way with instructions on how to behave by an organisation which clearly believed that if God had meant people to have radio then they would have been born British.

Sadly the attitude of Radio Luxembourg was quite the reverse. They had been severely reprimanded by the UIR on several occasions already, most decisively by the resolution of June 1932 which said that the power of the Luxembourg transmitter did not correspond to the requirements of a country that size (it is in fact smaller than the county of Surrey) and so ran the risk of causing disturbance to other European countries. Further, they had said that the choice of a Long Wave frequency was contrary to the spirit of co-operation which had previously existed among European member-nations of the UIR.

At the meeting in Broadcasting House the question of the 1933 Lucerne Conference was raised; Luxembourg had not been represented at the previous conference in Prague (which was why they ignored the 223-metre Medium Wave frequency allocated to them at that conference) but they had agreed to send a delegate to Lucerne. However, when the CLR wrote to the BBC after the 24 June meeting to sum up the situation from their viewpoint, their position was, to put it mildly, unequivocal and far from what the BBC had anticipated. 'Should the international co-operation it seeks,' ran the letter, 'not be found, Radio Luxembourg, while deeply regretting it, would have to go on with the work it assigned itself and which it considers to be the logical consequence of the development of broadcasting,' proving that they could be as pompous and single-minded as anyone, even the BBC.

Throughout 1933 Radio Luxembourg continued to operate on a Long Wave frequency in the area of 1200 metres. Broadcasts in English were made on Sundays only, and the frequency varied as the engineers adjusted the transmitter and searched for a spot on the tuning dials of Europe which would provide them with maximum impact but minimum opposition.

Despite the technical benefits, this juggling of frequencies achieved little in terms of international public relations. The BBC continued to monitor Radio Luxembourg transmissions through the listening post at

Tatsfield, and the GPO continued to make frequent, if not regular, protests to anyone who was even marginally interested in the situation.

By late in the year the situation had settled down somewhat, at least from Radio Luxembourg's point of view. They had finally found a frequency which seemed to suffice, and from 28 October 1933 their broadcasts began to assume a regular character. Every Sunday from 7 p.m. to 11 p.m. Radio Luxembourg's English language transmissions were beamed to Britain, presented by Jean Bruck, Eva Siewert, Annette Cornevin and Leon Moulin and featuring record programmes as well as Radio Luxembourg's own 30-piece orchestra, conducted by Henri Pensis. As yet, even at this late stage, no advertising or sponsored material was included in their programming as the station made one last attempt to have their right to broadcast on Long Wave legitimised.

Luxembourg sent a delegate to the UIR conference at Lucerne in 1933, and listened as the Lucerne Plan, due to come into effect in January of the next year, was thrashed out. Unfortunately the 'international co-operation' which Luxembourg sought and about which they had written to the BBC was clearly not forthcoming. Once again the conference was agreed that Luxembourg was far too small to justify the allocation of a Long Wave frequency and yet again it was allocated a Medium Wave frequency which Luxembourg once more rejected. Since the outcome of the conference had been, from their point of view, totally unsatisfactory, Luxembourg refused to sign the resulting Convention. It was now quite clear that the sponsored programmes to Britain which the IBC had deferred in the summer of 1933, were soon to become a reality, despite yet another resolution passed by the UIR. This one held that the 'systematic diffusion of programmes or communications specially intended for listeners in another country and which have been the subject of a protest by the broadcasting organisation or organisations of such country constitutes an inadmissible act from the point of view of good international relations'. The UIR called upon its members to avoid any such transmissions which constituted an improper use of broadcasting, and further asked the governments controlling the broadcasting organisations not adhering to the resolution to take such steps as possible to induce such organisations to 'submit to the principles of good international understanding'.

Sadly the Luxembourg government regretted that Compagnie Luxembourgeoise de Radiodiffusion was a private concern entirely beyond their control. In fact the CLR was so far beyond their control that in January 1934, a mere 24 hours after the Lucerne plan had come into effect, Radio Luxembourg seized a frequency just vacated by Poland, and on 15 January finally began broadcasting sponsored programmes in English on 1304 metres Long Wave. This was the most decisive and momentous step yet taken by the radio station and would have far-reaching effects on the nature of all radio, commercial and otherwise, for the next 50 years.

At first Radio Luxembourg had no programmes which had been

originated specifically for its own use, but through the IBC they began to transmit sponsored musical programming which had been paid for by a variety of advertisers and which had originally been intended for Poste Parisien and Radio Toulouse. The fortunate existence of this pre-recorded material meant that there was little or no build-up period and the station was able to operate at full capacity immediately, which they could never have managed without the much-denied contract between themselves and Captain Plugge's organisation.

The BBC were completely impotent in this matter; their protests through every channel available to them had been to no avail whatever since both CLR and the Grand Duchy itself refused to be bound by what they regarded as the arbitrary decisions of the UIR at its various conferences. Although they continued to maintain as much pressure as they could, even stepping up the level of protests, it was obvious that they could not prevent Radio Luxembourg from broadcasting. If they were to have any hope of halting the affront to their monopoly then other methods would have to be used. From this moment on the BBC campaign against Radio Luxembourg entered a new and rather unwholesome phase.

2: CONSOLIDATION

By the beginning of 1934 the people of Radio Luxembourg had embarked upon their great adventure in commercial radio and were now totally committed to their English-language enterprise. In doing so, however, they had effectively alienated themselves from the European radio community and were isolated in the Grand Duchy. Although it was quite possible for them to continue broadcasting just in English they were dependent upon the revenue produced by the IBC if they were ever to make a profit. Indeed, the need to broadcast sponsored programmes to Britain had been seen right from the very start as the only economic basis on which the station could survive, which is why the provision for foreign language broadcasts and advertising material had been included in their original charter.

The GPO had not and would not grant them landline facilities between the Grand Duchy and Britain, so all of their material had to be pre-recorded and sent over by sea. And although the duplication of programming between continental IBC stations persisted right up until September 1939 it was clear that it could not form the major part of the station output. Obviously Radio Luxembourg needed an identity and character of its own, which must be provided via exclusive programmes and also from its own British announcers. Again, in the early stages, there was a considerable amount of duplication between announcers and it was quite common for people to work on both Radio Normandy and on Radio Luxembourg.

Of necessity the station output was of two kinds, that which was pre-recorded in London, and that which was originated in the Luxembourg studios – located, incidentally, away from the main office, in the corner of Luxembourg's municipal park, in a small building which looked like a typical golfing clubhouse and was originally part of the famous fortress of Luxembourg. Over the years the studios at Villa Louvigny have been expanded considerably, up to the point where they are now the headquarters of Radio Tele Luxembourg and house the studios for their radio and television broadcasts to most of Europe.

In 1934, however, the studios consisted of one room big enough to accommodate an 80-piece orchestra, another smaller studio for the continuity announcer, and a control room.

The presenter/announcer was required simply to link together the programmes supplied by the IBC in London and, unlike Radio Normandy, did not have to operate the equipment himself. The transcription discs were set up and played by an engineer working in the control room, visible to the announcer through a large glass window. This was an arrangement almost unique to Radio Luxembourg and which would persist right through to the very late sixties, despite the difficulties created by the fact that the engineers were almost all native

Luxembourgers and spoke little or no English.

Out at Junglinster a similar situation existed. Not only was the transmitter the most powerful in Europe, it was probably the most sophisticated and had been built with reliability in mind. Using a principle of duplication very similar to that now employed by NASA spacecraft, every major or vital component had an exact twin built into the circuit and which could be switched in should the primary system fail. This policy, which extended even to the two vast 800-horsepower marine diesels which powered the transmitter's generators, meant that there was need for only two engineers, either of whom could operate the entire arrangement from a control position which truthfully consisted of only two important switches.

Because of this simplicity there was really only a need for one British announcer to be present in Luxembourg and for a long time this post was held by Stephen Williams, who was actually an employee of IBC, not Radio Luxembourg. However there was a multitude of other people who appeared on Radio Luxembourg through the medium of pre-recorded discs made in London, and it was to these people that the BBC now directed its attention.

BBC hopes of a complete Press embargo on the doings of Radio Luxembourg had already met with almost total success. With the single exception of the now-defunct *Sunday Referee* the Newspaper Publishers Association had placed a total ban on information concerning Radio Luxembourg. No British newspaper would accept an advertisement mentioning a commercial broadcast and no newspaper would publish the programme schedules of either Radio Luxembourg or Radio Normandy, yet despite this the continental stations quickly built up huge audiences simply through their policy of providing the public with the kind of radio entertainment they wanted to hear. This included using as many big-name stars as they could get their hands on, and they found this relatively easy.

In the early days of Radio Normandy sponsors had been able to buy short spots of 15 minutes or upwards for only a few pounds, but as the audiences grew and the stations became more popular the advertising rates rose to quite substantial sums – to the enormous chagrin of newspaper advertising managers who found themselves unable to compete. Because of this ever-growing revenue the commercial stations were able to offer entertainers attractive sums to tempt them away from theatres and the comforting safety of the BBC.

The nature of the radio output was also changing in response to the demands of the listeners – who wrote in huge numbers to their favourite radio stations – and the advertisers. These latter had already demonstrated a preference for being associated with one artist rather than many, and often the artist in question would be a comedian or some other form of variety entertainer as well as singers or dance bands. Consequently the programmes put out by the commercial stations assumed a much wider character and contained all manner of acts, using

THE MOST POWERFUL BROADCASTING STATION in Europe for BRITISH ADVERTISERS

The International Broadcasting Co. Ltd., announce the first programme for British listeners on

SUNDAY JUNE 4th
from
RADIO LUXEMBURG
1191 metres   200 K.W.

This new station which will be the MOST POWERFUL IN EUROPE is available for British sponsored programmes

✱ *For full details and rates apply to*

INTERNATIONAL BROADCASTING Co., Ltd

11, Hallam Street, Portland Place, London, W.1.   Tel.: *Langham* 1221 (3 *lines*)

RADIO LUXEMBURG • RADIO PARIS • POSTE PARISIEN • RADIO TOULOUSE
RADIO COTE D'AZUR (Juan les Pins) • RADIO NORMANDIE (Fecamp)

The first official IBC announcement of Radio Luxembourg's opening in 1933 was aimed primarily at sponsors. In any case this opening was delayed and transmissions didn't begin until late October of the same year. Sponsored programmes and regular broadcasting began in January 1934.

the big-name stars of the period.

Many of these had begun their radio careers with the BBC and many of them began to feature on both commercial and BBC radio programmes. Probably the first, and certainly one of the best-known, was Christopher Stone, whose career as a BBC compere went back to 1927 when he became probably the first ever disc jockey to broadcast to a British audience (even though the term disc jockey had not yet been coined). Stone was already popular on BBC radio, and his appearances on Luxembourg became more and more frequent and increasingly popular. His style of presentation was already markedly more relaxed than anyone else on BBC radio and Radio Luxembourg allowed him more freedom than he (or anyone else) had been used to. This was one of the keys to the success of Radio Luxembourg. Not only was their programming in a lighter vein, but they allowed their announcers to be far less formal and far more conversational than the BBC.

Although BBC announcers had dropped their wing collars and evening dress by this stage, at about the same time as the Corporation had moved from Savoy Hill to Portland Place, they were still not permitted to descend to a personal level with the 'listeners-in'. They allowed each musical item to come to a clear finish before making brief, almost punctilious statements; the next item would only commence when they had finished speaking, usually after an interval of one second.

On Luxembourg, however, the announcers would address their audience as individuals, frequently by name if someone had written to them, and often employed the 'voice-over' technique which is a commonplace, if not actually mandatory, feature of almost all modern radio.

Unfortunately, people like Christopher Stone were not only a major part of Radio Luxembourg's character and success, they were by now one of the station's few vulnerable links.

From very early on in 1934 it was clear that the BBC was suffering as a result of Radio Luxembourg's output. The BBC saw Radio Luxembourg as 'a severe handicap' to its programming policy, 'especially on Sundays', and engaged further diplomatic assistance from the Foreign Office, most of whose protests were based around the UIR of 1933 concerning transmissions in a foreign language. Luxembourg countered by saying they believed that the resolution referred only to the dissemination of political propaganda and therefore felt that they were not in breach of it. Although the BBC held that this reply was 'evasive', there was little they could do about it. In any case they were by now almost alone in their protests; the French government was reluctant to intervene since the station was controlled by some fairly heavyweight French interests and the new government in Germany were rather keen to secure the co-operation of Radio Luxembourg for their own purposes. Goebbels even went so far as to install a direct teleprinter link between Luxembourg and Berlin, although it was withdrawn swiftly when he discovered that Radio Luxembourg preferred to broadcast the news as seen by the French agency Havas rather than the Nazi version of events. Even so his interest in the giant transmitter had been aroused, although it would be six more years before he would be able to use it as he wished.

In the face of dwindling international support for the campaign against Radio Luxembourg the BBC turned their attentions homewards. If they couldn't control the European community at least there was one group of people on whom pressure could be brought to bear, and it was Christopher Stone who provided a suitable test case for the Corporation to flex its muscle.

'His engagements with us,' ran the memo, 'need not continue.'

This was an arrangement with which the BBC seemed eminently pleased, since they at once began making arrangements to see who else they could ban. However, it soon became clear to them that this was not as sensible a plan as it had originally appeared, since they would have to ban just about every entertainer they employed, leaving themselves with programme schedules almost completely devoid of the kind of talent which they needed, while Radio Luxembourg had it all.

Christopher Stone's last engagement with the BBC was on 29 August 1934, and the employment of others was under review. If it was not practical to ban people who worked outside the BBC fold then at least the other artists could be told that acceptance of work for transmission on Radio Luxembourg 'certainly does not help things for them' at Broadcasting House. It soon became official policy to (unofficially) tell people not to work for the station. This was managed by the simple expedient of instructing the BBC Variety Exchange to 'casually disseminate' the fact that people who were working for Radio Luxembourg were not helping themselves in the eyes of the BBC.

Among the artists to whom this information probably came as something of a casual shock were Stanley Holloway, Jessie Matthews, Jeanne de Casalis, Finlay Currie and the immensely popular Flanagan and Allen, all of whom had to come to some sort of decision on the subject. To help them make their minds up there was the object lesson of poor Christopher Stone, whose many engagements for the BBC (at a standard seven guineas per hour) had now come to a complete halt following a widely circulated internal memo which stated that he was not to be offered any employment within the Corporation after 31 August 1934. Despite several puzzled letters to various people in the BBC Christopher Stone was resolutely ignored, although when listeners wrote to the BBC asking what had happened to him they were informed that 'he has chosen to sever his connection' with the BBC.

Christopher Stone was the first of several people to be banned in this way for one reason or another, and even though the existence of such bans was denied in public by the BBC, in private they wrote each other memos, adding new names to the list. Meanwhile large numbers of artists began to turn down engagements for Radio Luxembourg in response to BBC pressure; Jeanne de Casalis turned down the then-munificent offer of £135 for 12 30-minute programmes on Radio

Luxembourg because it would have jeopardised, if not prevented altogether, the possibility of future work with the BBC. Stainless Stephen followed suit, as did Clapham and Dwyer, but sadly they were not quick enough, and appeared on Luxembourg some time after the BBC had given the Variety Exchange its instructions about casual dissemination.

Accordingly their situation was examined by the BBC who found that the programme in question had been recorded for Radio Luxembourg long before they could have had any idea about the BBC attitude, which would indicate that they should be forgiven. But it was not to be. In the light of their blissful ignorance the BBC decided that 'we cannot therefore ban them', but they also concluded that there was 'no harm in engaging them a little less often than they would otherwise have been'.

These kind of stern measures could clearly be extended beyond mere artists. It was the BBC who suggested to the British Phonographic Industry, who were the forerunners of the Performing Rights Society, that Radio Luxembourg was perhaps better-heeled than other radio stations. The BPI collected money from radio stations every time they played a record; it's a sort of copyright fee and the arrangement continues today. But since Radio Luxembourg was reportedly charging £200 per hour for sponsored record programmes it was felt that it should pay more than other radio stations who were expressly forbidden the benefits of commercial operation as was the BBC. On 17 September 1934 the BPI raised Radio Luxembourg's fee substantially, so that it had to pay 10 shillings for each record it played.

However Radio Luxembourg was far from defeated. In truth it was only a little subdued by these new gambits from the BBC. In the middle of August 1934 there occurred an event which was itself of very small significance, but which gave a clue to the deeper and more important moves which were still being played in the tactical struggle between the BBC and its rival.

Just before 7 p.m. on 17 August the Radio Luxembourg transmitter suffered a breakdown and went off the air until 7 o'clock. The monitoring service at Tatsfield felt this of some interest and recorded the event in their log of the evening's transmissions from Luxembourg, a copy of which was sent to Broadcasting House the next day. What was more interesting was the fact that when the station came back on the air at a minute past seven compere Christopher Stone announced a programme of music which would be sung by Ronald Frankau. None of the announcements during this were pre-recorded, neither did they make any reference to the fact that the singing was recorded. In fact they gave quite the opposite impression, namely that this was a live broadcast of a concert which was taking place in Britain.

The technology for this sort of thing had existed for some while, and it was quite common for radio stations to be accorded landline facilities from foreign countries back to their own transmitters so that, for example, events taking place in France could be broadcast in Britain by the BBC as they happened. Radio Luxembourg had requested such a facility from the GPO several times already and, although allocation of such resources was the preserve of the Post Office, they had always deferred to the wishes of the BBC and refused to grant Radio Luxembourg's request. However the BBC lived in continual fear that at some time the Post Office would accede to such a request without reference to anyone else, and it did appear that this may have happened by August 1934.

Checking the monitoring service logs did nothing to dispel the illusion; Ronald Frankau had been received perfectly, with none of the hissing, crackling and scratching which was the hallmark of the 78 rpm discs of the period. However, closer checking revealed that Ronald Frankau had, at the time, been on stage at the Prince of Wales Theatre in London and that the GPO had not given a landline to Radio Luxembourg. 'The GPO,' said the BBC memo, 'has always refused and it is fair to assume they always will.'

The Frankau concert was eventually deduced to have been recorded on film in the same way as many of the Radio Normandy programmes had been since 1932. Drawing on that experience the IBC had installed Western Electric projectors in Luxembourg, but this is the first time the benefits had been apparent in sound quality. The films were recorded in London by Gaumont British and were of excellent quality. Sufficient quality, in fact, for Radio Luxembourg to attempt to pass them off as being live events rather than recordings – if the Post Office wouldn't give them a landline then they would just pretend they'd got one. As far as audiences were concerned the effect was the same.

And by now the audiences were substantial; advertising intake was correspondingly high and IBC operations were complemented by a new company called Radio Publicity (Universal) Ltd who opened their portfolio with the only newspaper which would countenance any mention of commercial radio, the *Sunday Referee*. This led to an immediate expansion in Radio Luxembourg's English service with an extra hour of programmes on Thursday, Friday and Saturday and, surprisingly, a continued appearance by big-name artists who were seemingly willing to risk the displeasure of the BBC.

There were so many, in fact, that the BBC were forced to realise that their policy towards artists who worked for Radio Luxembourg was fairly ineffectual. The Corporation described the list of artists who had appeared on Radio Luxembourg in the six months up to August 1934 as being 'sufficiently formidable', and found the technical level of the programmes recorded on film in London to be of 'high quality'. All this information was contained in one of the periodic reports which were compiled in Broadcasting House and circulated to just about everybody from the Director-General downwards.

For an organisation to whom advertising was forbidden territory, the BBC seemed inordinately concerned with Radio Luxembourg's list of clients. This was partly because they realised that the success of the

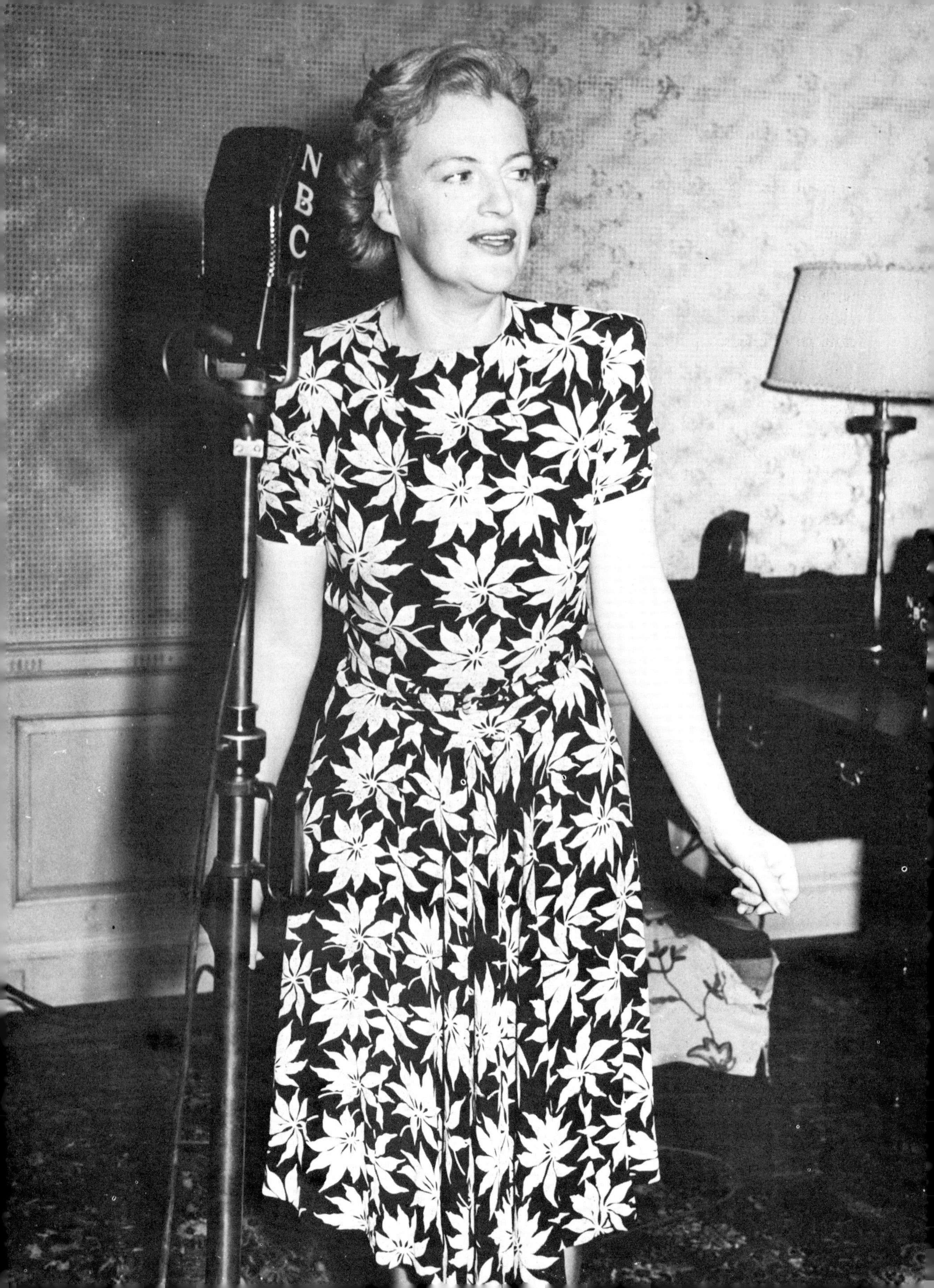
NBC

station depended entirely upon the regularity with which it could attract sponsors (and how much it was able to charge them) and also because they were still acting in conjunction with the NPA in their efforts both to prevent any newspaper giving any sort of publicity to Radio Luxembourg and to try to persuade advertisers away from the radio station's huge and growing audience.

The BBC monitoring service was continually compiling lists of companies who advertised on Radio Luxembourg and comparing them with people who advertised in newspapers as well as or instead of on radio. In November of 1934 the list ran to several pages, itemising the number of occasions on which companies had advertised on air. The list was impressive, including names like Littlewoods Pools, Palmolive, Shredded Wheat, Rothmans and Beecham's Pills. Importantly, there were some 32 firms whose adverts appeared on Luxembourg but not in the Press, including the *Sunday Referee*, Ever Ready and W D and H O Wills. Beyond any doubt Radio Luxembourg was becoming increasingly more successful despite the attempts to slow down or halt its advances.

And not only were the adverts pouring in, but the stars were still there as well. On Sunday, 6 January 1935 Jack Payne and his orchestra were on for five minutes after mid-day, performing 'Little Man you've had a busy day', followed by the Jiffy Washing Machine record programme which ran for 10 minutes this time, including records like 'Love in Bloom' and 'Cherie' by Gracie Fields. At 12.15 a really long programme started – 20 minutes of records courtesy of Soccapools and including such choice items as 'I'm on a see saw' by Jack Jackson – leading in to half an hour of records paid for by Irish Hospitals Sweepstakes and which had already been advertised in a relatively new publication – *Radio Pictorial*.

As the name suggests, this magazine concerned itself entirely with matters relating to radio and specifically to the output of the continental commercial stations like Luxembourg. In among the programme schedules – and they published a full list of all the different stations' programmes – were features about the stars, the stations themselves and the announcers. Journalists from *Radio Pictorial* would frequently visit Radio Normandy, Radio Luxembourg or one of the others and the full-length features were supplemented with photographs of the announcers and their environments. This was the kind of publicity which commercial stations had so far been denied by the British Press and was just what they needed to establish a strong following.

But back on 6 January the Irish Hospitals Sweepstakes programme was followed by programmes of records from Zam-Buk, Littlewoods Pools, and Vernons Pools, including favourite pieces like 'When My Ship Comes In' sung by Rudy Vallee, leading into the Kraft Cheese concert with Jack Jackson, Edith Day, John Tilley and the Three Aces.

By three in the afternoon things were picking up a bit more, with the Pompeian Beauty Preparations half-hour. Lady Charles Cavendish and Mary Lawson chatted about the products, Mary sang a few songs and

A war-time shot of Gracie Fields who was often heard on Radio Luxembourg in the thirties (*Pictorial Press*).

then, after Lady Cavendish had spoken for a few minutes about Helen of Troy (presumably on the basis of her legendary beauty) The Pompeian Orchestra played a selection. Although his name was not yet mentioned astute personages at the BBC deduced that it was in fact the orchestra of one Fred Hartley – so much for the BBC ban.

At 3.30 the English and Scottish Co-op sponsored 30 minutes of recorded material which included the already-troubled Clapham and Dwyer and Stanley Holloway, as well as a lady by the name of Mabel Constanduros, who was by way of being a comedienne. She did a short sketch based on a character she had already portrayed on BBC radio. Part of the BBC attitude to artists at the time was to insist that 'turns', as they were known, which had first graced the ether via a BBC transmitter were deemed to be BBC copyright and artists were forbidden to re-create such characters for other radio stations. According to a note in the margin of the BBC memo concerning this Sunday's broadcasts, Miss Constanduros was apprised of this information and promised not to do the sketch or the character for Luxembourg again.

The Horlicks Hour followed this, with the Debroy Somers band officiating. Again, according to the BBC monitoring service, the band was announced from Luxembourg as if they were actually in the studio; in all probability they were not and this was a high-quality film recording, but the monitoring service could not be sure about this at all.

More record half-hours were on the menu, and sponsors like Owbridge's Lung Tonic, Maclean's Stomach Powder, Mason's OK Sauce and Jiffy Washing Machines (again) carried the listener through to 8 p.m. and the Palmolive Concert, with a band which the monitoring service could not recognise but which they believed to be the BBC favourite Henry Hall.

It was a strange contradiction that the BBC had, in the persons of the Henry Hall Orchestra, the most popular live dance band of the period, yet they continually failed to capitalise on this popularity and use the band to combat commercial radio on Sundays. Indeed, the commercial stations took the initiative here, and frequently played records by Henry Hall and possibly even managed to get the band to record for sponsors as they *may* have done for Palmolive.

More record programmes carried Radio Luxembourg up to its midnight closedown, and sponsors were people like Bile Beans and Soccapools. In case there's any doubt, it is unlikely that Radio Luxembourg, the IBC or Wireless Publicity had any special connection with the medical or pharmaceutical industries. The vast number of medicinal preparations which were advertised on radio reflected the lack of sophistication in medicine rather than an overt concern by commercial radio with the health of its listeners or an inability to attract any other kind of advertising. Antibiotics and other drugs were unknown in the thirties, and medicine depended heavily on a huge pharmacopoeia of proprietary powders, balsams and tonics.

On the last hour of Sunday quiet records were played to relax the listeners at the end of a day in which they had been bombarded with top-name stars from first thing in the morning. It was a programme policy dictated primarily by the spending power of the sponsors rather than by any desire to produce good effective programming. It was output which the BBC saw as being of 'poor artistic quality', and it was output which was staggeringly successful.

About the only sphere in which Luxembourg could not compete with BBC output was in the area of hard news reporting. Handicapped by the lack of any on-line facilities between London and the studios in the Grand Duchy, news reporting could not be efficiently handled. And while the BBC was building up a worldwide reputation for its fast, accurate and impartial news coverage Radio Luxembourg had to take a back seat. This was highlighted again in 1936, during the month of February (the month that Radio Luxembourg changed to 1293 metres) when events of great moment were afoot in Britain.

Ramsay Macdonald had resigned as Prime Minister in 1935 and had been succeeded by Stanley Baldwin, taking his place at 10 Downing Street for the third time in his career. In January of 1936 George V died and was succeeded by Edward VIII, who was already involved with American divorcee Wallis Simpson, a union to which Baldwin was firmly opposed. The new King's accession speech, in February of 1936, was something of an international event and yet again Radio Luxembourg, through the IBC, sought permission from the GPO to set up landline facilities which would enable them to give the speech full and proper coverage. This time great consideration was given to the request by the Post Office and members of His Majesty's Government, and it is clear that the speech was viewed as being so important that HMG would have quite liked it to be as widely broadcast as possible. The GPO even wrote to the BBC and said that they were prepared to grant the facility, subject only to BBC opinion.

Radio Luxembourg was not given a landline that February.

But their policy was moving ahead at a rapid enough pace in other areas. Commercial radio has obvious advantages over the BBC as the Corporation had realised even before Luxembourg had come on the air; indeed it was the principal root of their objection that advertising revenue granted an unfair advantage. Now it began to be used to the full. In a deal with Irving Harris of Western Electric, Radio Luxembourg began to broadcast programmes recorded on film based principally on films, mainly RCA output and mainly films which had yet to go on general release including people like Wallace Beery, Jack Buchanan, Sophie Tucker and Irene Dunne. The advantages to each party were obvious enough, especially as this was happening at the time when film fans were in a state of near hysteria induced by little more than the mention of their favourite stars' names and the film companies were entering one of the most flamboyant periods of Hollywood hype. *Gone With the Wind*, one of the biggest selling films of all time, was released in 1936 and the enormous interest the making and casting of the film generated is probably unbelievable to anyone who didn't live through it. So much fuss was made over the part of Scarlett O'Hara that 30 years later MGM made another film about the making of *Gone With the Wind*. And remember that when Clark Gable started shooting the part of Scarlett had not been cast; Vivien Leigh was still in England with Laurence Olivier and Margaret Mitchell hadn't finished the book – no one knew how the film would end.

This kind of information Radio Luxembourg dished out from first thing Sunday morning till last thing at night. BBC programmes didn't begin until 10.15 on Sunday mornings and opened with church services mixed with lectures of a religious or character-building nature all through the day. Light entertainment and popular music were not allowed on the BBC until after 7 p.m. at night, by which time the radio audience had already made their programme choice. On the very rare occasions that the BBC did provide lightweight programming on a Sunday evening the effect was quite dramatic.

In October of 1936 Cadbury, who were advertisers on Radio Luxembourg, found that when the BBC programmes on a Sunday evening included light entertainment the letters from listeners to their sponsored programme on Luxembourg dropped in number from a staggering 25,000 to a paltry 10,000. Quite apart from indicating the huge audience figures and truly overwhelming response to radio programmes, those figures show quite clearly that the success of Radio Luxembourg's programming policy was due almost entirely to the BBC's reluctance to give the listeners what they wanted (as opposed to what the Corporation thought they should have).

It was in 1936 that the way in which Radio Luxembourg obtained its advertising revenue underwent a change which would have far-reaching effects on how the station developed. Up until now it had been handled by Captain Plugge's IBC (the Captain himself, by 1935, was MP for the Medway Towns) who provided all the programmes on disc or film from London and who even provided the continuity announcer out in Luxembourg. However, Radio Luxembourg had been growing rather dissatisfied with this arrangement since it was clear that the IBC, as middlemen, were performing a task which could quite easily be handled by the radio station itself, with a resulting increase in revenue. There was even a suspicion in some minds that not all of the money due to Radio Luxembourg from the IBC arrived there. As hard as the BBC had tried, they had never been able to discover exactly what the sponsors were paying for their time on air. There were rumours and guesses, of course, but there was no rate card available. This sort of business was conducted on a personal level, and the general feeling among people like the BBC and the NPA was that advertising revenue to the IBC and Radio Luxembourg should, in any case, be blocked. This in turn encouraged the various sponsors not to talk about the payments they made.

Whatever the truth of the situation, Radio Luxembourg persuaded one Charles Barker to set up a company called Wireless Publicity, based at Elektra House on the Embankment, to handle all the advertising sales for the radio station. This was done quietly, if not in total secrecy, and Wireless Publicity then engaged Ogden Smith to be continuity announcer/presenter for Radio Luxembourg's English Service, sending him to the Grand Duchy with no explanation of the background to events. Once Smith had arrived in Luxembourg Stephen Williams was summoned to a meeting on the following Saturday night.

At the time the programmes, recorded in London, were placed on a plane to Brussels, since there was no airport in Luxembourg, and then made a four-hour journey by train to Luxembourg station where they were collected by the announcer. On this Saturday night Stephen Williams was told to hand over all the pre-recorded programmes to Ogden Smith since the IBC connection with Radio Luxembourg was to be severed. Williams had received no such information from his company in London and at first refused, but he eventually had no choice. From that day forward the IBC had lost the concession to sell airtime on Radio Luxembourg and despite a high-powered breach of contract court case later in the year (which they lost), the rift was never mended. The IBC continued their arrangements with the other European commercial stations – with whom they had been a great deal more closely involved than with Luxembourg – and Radios Normandy, Toulouse, Lyons and Paris continued to flourish until the war.

Radio Luxembourg, however, had moved into a class of its own and straight away began to think of expansion. Short Wave radio was now a technical possibility, and its transmissions had a far greater range than even the 200 kilowatt monster at Junglinster. Short Wave was worldwide radio, with enormous potential, and even the BBC was aware that commercial radio broadcasts to Great Britain were possible from as far away as the United States. And although such awareness may have been the reason why both the BBC and the UIR turned down a request from the CLR to assist them in the technicalities of building a Short Wave transmitter (an act of considerable cheek, under the circumstances), it was also another reason for slowing down the campaign to close down Radio Luxembourg. There was little point if it was only to be replaced by Radio New York. And although that didn't actually happen Radio Luxembourg mastered the art of Short Wave radio fairly swiftly and their worldwide service began transmitting on 49.26 metres with 6 kilowatts on 7 June 1938. This medium is so effective that while Kid Jensen was on the station in the seventies his parents used to listen to his programme when it went on to Short Wave late at night. They live in Vancouver. And during the Vietnam war Radio Luxembourg frequently received letters from American servicemen who listened to the station from the depths of the Asian jungle. It's hardly surprising that the BBC (and others) were perturbed by the possibilities which would perhaps become a reality when Radio Luxembourg went on to Short Wave. However, despite its excellent range Short Wave has never had the same kind of appeal to mass audiences as Medium and Long Wave, and latterly FM stereo, and remains something of a specialist medium.

Meanwhile, out in the Grand Duchy, Ogden Smith wanted to go on holiday, which may not sound particularly important. But it was, because it triggered off a series of events which would characterise Radio Luxembourg's recruiting policy for the next 50 years. It is that policy which gives the radio station the individual and innovative character which allows its popularity to continue and grow.

Charles Maxwell was then a 25-year-old Scots solicitor with a desire to become an actor. In pursuit of this interest he was in London, playing in T S Eliot's *Murder in the Cathedral*, when he auditioned for Derek McCullough, the radio 'Uncle Mac'. Although Maxwell got no further with Children's Hour, Uncle Mac recommended him to friends at Radio Luxembourg and, within 24 hours, Charles Maxwell was on his way to the Grand Duchy – the first of so many who would be hired by accident and on air within hours.

For the week that Ogden Smith was away Charles Maxwell, who had been given time off from the London stage, was paid £10 a day at a time when his theatre earnings were closer to £3 a week. Better still, he was good at the job and liked the atmosphere in Luxembourg. This was something else which would play a determining role in the character of the station over the years. To work there you've got to like the place; some do, some don't. In the thirties and through the years to come the type of people who would work on Radio Luxembourg would be influenced by whether or not they could live in the Grand Duchy. Some people would never go there, and those who did were at least similar to each other in their adaptability, which has provided the station with a tiny thread of continuity between the huge variety of presenters who have worked on the station over the years.

Charles Maxwell was more than prepared to return to Radio Luxembourg as a full-time presenter very soon after his fill-in stint, and although the scale of pay was slightly less generous for permanent staff it was nevertheless excellent by comparison with the theatre and truly reflected the incredible success and popularity of the station. Five hundred pounds a year represented a sizeable advance on £3 a week, and allowed Charles Maxwell to make the most of his bachelor days in the Grand Duchy, living in a smart apartment and running an MG sports car.

In the same way as Stephen Williams had been paid by the IBC, Charles Maxwell was paid by Wireless Publicity and not by Radio Luxembourg. Because the announcers were not living in Britain their salaries attracted no British income tax and because they were paid from Britain in sterling they attracted no tax in Luxembourg either – which may seem a highly desirable state of affairs.

It was a condition of Charles Maxwell's contract with Wireless Publicity that he should at no time have any contact whatever with Stephen Williams. But since Williams was still living in Luxembourg, and since it is such a small place with a tiny English-speaking population,

RADIO LUXEMBOURG

BROADCASTING STATION

Scale of Rates
August 1st, 1936

Sole Agents for the United Kingdom
WIRELESS PUBLICITY LTD.
Electra House, Victoria Embankment, London, W.C.2
Telephone: Temple Bar 8432

The very first Radio Luxembourg rate-card, issued by Wireless Publicity.

it was impossible for Maxwell to comply, and the clause had to be scrubbed. It was replaced by a gentleman's understanding that no exchange of company information would take place.

Even though most Luxembourg people are as gregarious and welcoming as anyone else it was still a fairly lonely life for the announcers in Luxembourg. The days of the larger-staffed English Service had not yet dawned and although the announcers themselves were well-treated and much respected by the other employees of CLR, there were not many fellow-Britons with whom they could talk. Any visitors to the Grand Duchy were warmly welcomed, even tourists who were passing through were greeted in the street as friends, taken to a café and pumped for information and simple conversation.

Broadcasting for two hours a day during the week and all day Sundays, now on 1293 metres Long Wave, the life of a Luxembourg DJ was reasonably enviable. Although 7 a.m. to midnight on a Sunday was quite a long while, during the week an announcer could do his lunchtime or early evening hour and then drive off to the Moselle region for an excellent meal and an equally excellent wine without stretching his financial resources or having to dash to make it back to the station in time for the next programme.

Programmes recorded in London were still making the long haul by train from Brussels and still consisted of seven or eight 16-inch discs for each half-hour sponsored programme. However, reels of film were now more common. In conjunction with Wireless Publicity Radio Luxembourg had dropped the Western Electric system and were now using a far more sophisticated method of recording sound on to film. Developed in Holland by Philco, the Phillips-Miller system was the forerunner of magnetic tape recording although it still used optically-made markings in film gel-coat. Advertisers who sponsored such programmes bought an amount of time which allowed them a given number of words (usually 200 in each half-hour) for their advertising message. Scripts were edited by Wireless Publicity and those words were actually counted to make sure there was no cheating. By now much of the recording was being done by the J Walter Thompson advertising agency, who also operated the Phillips-Miller system and had what was possibly the most sophisticated recording studio in Europe located in the basement of their offices in London's Bush House.

One of the people then busy recording sponsored programmes in London was Neil Arden, who had come to radio as a well-known commentator on documentary films, known as 'interest pictures'. He worked, not for Radio Luxembourg, but for various sponsors, like Feen-a-Mint or Glymiel Jelly, presenting 15- or 30-minute programmes on their behalf. In 1937 he was making a series of shows called 'Music Makers', a ubiquitous title which allowed almost anything musical to fall within its compass.

As Neil Arden recalls, these programmes consisted almost entirely of recorded music, of which there was admittedly rather less than we are used to nowadays. There were only a few record labels anyway – HMV, Decca, Columbia, Parlophone, Zylophone, Rex – so a good record library was essential. Programmes were much slower-paced and relaxed than at present. In Neil Arden's own words, they were a bit like having a friend round to your house to play records with you, rather than the more aggressive presentation of modern radio.

The sponsored programmes were recorded on to large transcription discs and then made the tortuous journey out to the station via Brussels, where several of them – they lasted an average of 15 minutes each – were mixed to produce the final on-air programme. Sponsors paid for everything involved in this process, including the presenter's fee, which Neil Arden remembers as not being an awful lot, although this was compensated by the pleasure of the job. Like Charles Maxwell out in the Grand Duchy itself, the London-based presenters earned about £10 per week, which may not sound like a lot, but it was enough. Like Maxwell again, Neil Arden had a London flat and also ran a car, both paid for by his work on Radio Luxembourg.

Wireless Publicity were by now a trifle more organised than had been the IBC, and a full rate-card was available to potential sponsors, showing that by August 1936 Radio Luxembourg charged £400 for an hour's programme between 1 p.m. and 11 p.m. or £75 for a 'spot' announcement of no more than 40 words in the same period. Off-peak rates (between 8.15 and 10.15 a.m.) were considerably less – £192 for an hour or £36 for a 'spot'. As the rate-card showed, this money was only to cover the purchase of the actual airtime. Preparation of programmes (including paying the artists), clearance of copyrights and despatch to Luxembourg were all extras and all had to be paid in advance of broadcast. And to keep it all in the family, preparation of all broadcast material was to be undertaken by Wireless Publicity Ltd. For which, naturally, there was yet more to pay.

Nevertheless advertisers and artists flocked to Radio Luxembourg. Advertising was so cost-effective that sponsors could easily pay their artists a great deal more than the BBC could possibly entertain. The matter was still a subject of some interest at the BBC, despite the fact that by 1937 it was clear that their policy of banning people who appeared on Radio Luxembourg was doing more harm to the BBC itself than to anyone else. Indeed it was true that the BBC were simply refraining from employing artists who were popular with the audiences of the day and who continued to appear on Radio Luxembourg, with the obvious result that listeners simply tuned to the station where they could hear their favourites. As *Advertisers' Weekly* observed at the beginning of 1937, there were more stars appearing every Sunday on Radio Luxembourg than in a whole week of BBC programming.

In March of 1937 the BBC compiled a list of people who were appearing on Radio Luxembourg and what they were doing. Most individuals were paid somewhere between 25 and 40 guineas by the BBC and most bands were paid between 50 and 100 guineas, depending on

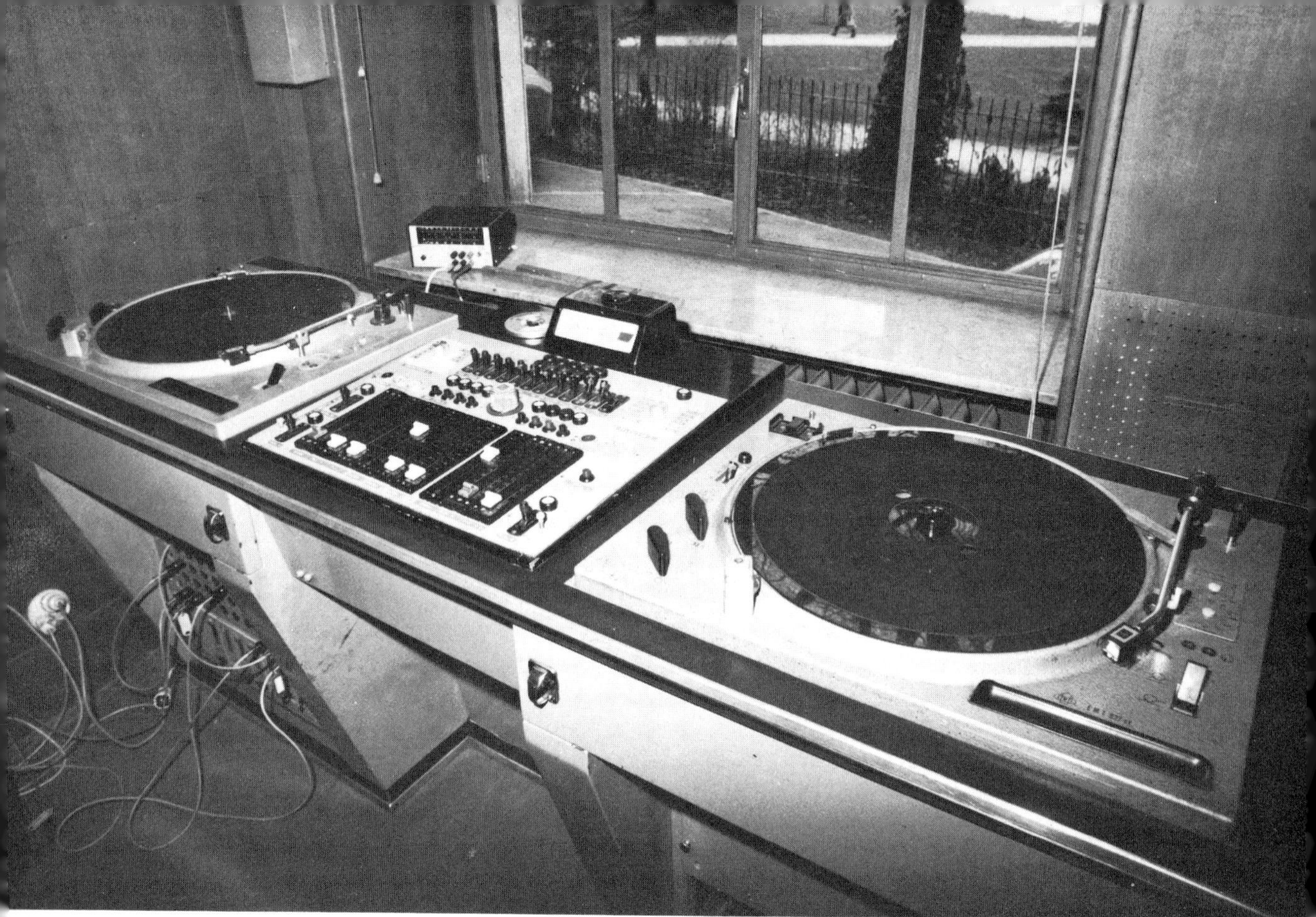

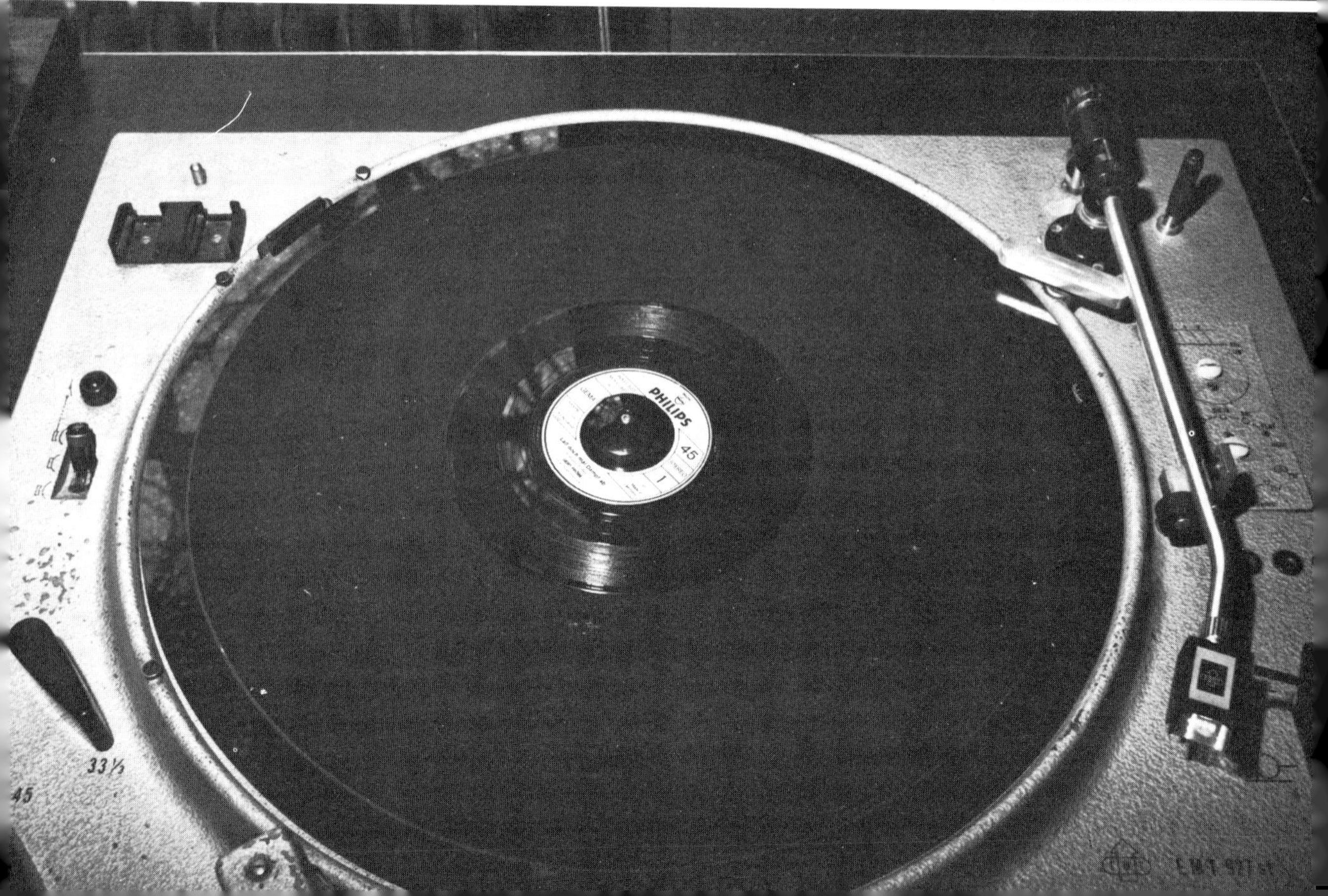
PHILIPS
45
33⅓
45

size and popularity. From the list it was at once clear to the BBC that most American artists who came to visit Britain worked primarily for Radio Luxembourg – Carson Robinson doing a series for Oxydol and Morton Downey for Drene Shampoo, for example. In addition many home-grown dance bands were doing a series of their own on Luxembourg. Jack Payne was appearing for Beecham's Pills, Billy Cotton for the Kraft Cheese programme and Debroy Somers on the only hour-long sponsored show, the Horlicks Teatime Hour. On top of that, Ambrose and his Orchestra were appearing in the Lifebuoy programmes, Marius B Winter with Rowntrees Fruit Gums and Sydney Lipton for Crosse and Blackwell.

All through 1935, 1936 and at the beginning of 1937, diplomatic representations to the Luxembourg government by Britain continued, and met with the same lack of success as always, with one minor exception. The Luxembourg government continually pointed out that since the concession to the CLR expressly sanctioned foreign-language broadcasts and advertising, little action could be taken to prevent them. However, the company itself undertook, in the summer of 1937, not to increase the amount of English-language output beyond current levels, which may have been some small crumb of comfort to the BBC. This minor concession – if it was even that – was the only reward obtained from almost six years of diplomatic protests to the Luxembourg administration, and represented such a minor achievement that in late 1937 the Ambassador in Belgium, upon whose shoulders the various attempts had devolved, concluded that no useful purpose would be served by further representations. The Foreign Office agreed with his opinion and informed the BBC. In September of 1937, Sir Charles Carpendale wound up the abortive attempts to close down Radio Luxembourg. In a memo to all BBC Governors, running to seven pages in length, Sir Charles listed the history of Radio Luxembourg so far, summing up the various attempts which had been made to prevent it broadcasting and stop it once it had started. The first half of the memo drew almost verbatim on a similar document prepared by the BBC in 1934 and indicated quite clearly that the BBC opinion about both Radio Luxembourg and radio generally had not changed in almost four years. The memo concluded with the information that the Foreign Office no longer considered diplomatic action a worthwhile course.

His seven-page summation of Radio Luxembourg was one of Sir Charles Carpendale's last acts for the BBC. He departed in the same year that Sir John Reith took over the chairmanship of the embryonic Imperial Airways (later to become BOAC) and earned himself a *Who's Who* listing as Lord Reith, first Baron of Stonehaven. Reith's influence persisted long after his departure as Director-General, and perhaps even now the BBC has not completely shaken off the dry and dusty image created during the period he was at the helm.

From the beginning of 1938 the BBC no longer tried to shut down Radio Luxembourg, though continued study was made of its

Above
Transcription turntables of the type used at Radio Luxembourg in the thirties and forties and still preserved today at Villa Louvigny.

Below
A 30-inch turntable for playing specially recorded transcription discs. The record shown is a modern 7-inch single.

programming and advertising. Exactly why this carried on is something of a mystery, since it is quite clear that despite the monumental success of Radio Luxembourg the BBC still considered them rather uncouth amateur pirates and still believed that the BBC knew how to manage a radio station best. The fact that most people ignored the BBC whenever there was an alternative available seems to have made little or no impression upon the Corporation whatever, and nothing short of a war would shake their faith in the rectitude of BBC policy. And that, as we shall see, was a special case, and they would waste no time in returning to the BBC way of doing things properly once the war was over.

The fact that the BBC failed to take very much account of the public preference for lightweight radio programmes cannot be entirely attributed to pure bloody-mindedness or complete indifference, even though the Corporation clearly demonstrated a supreme confidence in its own policy. Here was an organisation which went to great trouble to discover everything it could about a competitor, including the minutiae of its finances, came face to face with its own lack of success when compared to that competitor and yet consistently failed to do anything about it except try and have the competitor closed down. It was hardly a particularly endearing course of action, but in all fairness one of the principal reasons for it, aside from the strict programming policy imposed by Lord Reith, was the same reason the Corporation was forced to take such an interest in Radio Luxembourg itself.

Advertising in the thirties was hardly the strictly-disciplined industry it is now. Most marketing was conducted by inspiration and intuition rather than market research, largely because there wasn't a great deal of market research being done. There was no BMRB or Gallup poll for the BBC (or anyone else) to consult. Whereas nowadays audience figures are available on a daily basis almost within hours of programmes being broadcast, in the thirties the technology to do it quickly didn't exist and the impetus to have those figures had only just been provided. If the BBC wanted to know how Radio Luxembourg's listening figures compared to their own then they had to work it out for themselves; there was no one to ask.

It was only in 1938, in response to the demands of advertisers, that audience figures were made available to interested parties. Although a survey by 'Shelf Appeal' in 1935 had shown that 60 per cent of radio listeners tuned in to continental stations at a time when British advertisers were spending some £300,000 abroad in airtime payments alone, sponsors often placed their programmes on more than one of the continental radio stations. This led to the sort of situation where you could hear Carroll Levis and his radio discoveries (a sort of radio talent-spotters' half-hour, sponsored by Quaker Oats) three times each Sunday. The show was put out by Luxembourg at mid-day, Normandy at 5.15 and by Radio Lyons at 8.30 in the evening.

By 1938 the placing of programmes like this could be done with a little more accuracy than before. Advertisers were now stumping up half a million pounds a year for airtime and the survey techniques had been improved to keep pace. Erwin Wasey were producing a weekly summary showing who listened to what and when and demonstrated overall trends in listenership. The questionnaire this survey was based on was answered by more than 2000 people and was immediately valuable to advertisers. The first lesson was that weather affected radio audiences heavily indeed; when the sun was shining they all left their houses and radio sets for the great outdoors. Other lessons were there too, solicited mostly from housewives who answered a six-part questionnaire which specifically mentioned programmes by name and asked about listening times.

It became quite clear that Radio Luxembourg's peak audience was on Sunday afternoons, Radio Normandy's during early evening and Radio Lyons in the late evening. All stations except Toulouse had their peak listenership on Sundays, largely thanks to the BBC.

The surveys were equally helpful to the radio stations, especially in their pricing structures, since they at once found that in periods during which their audience may have multiplied six times over their ad rates were hardly more than doubled – something which could easily be remedied. By late 1938 Radio Luxembourg's advertising charges were said to be the highest in the world. But that wasn't particularly at odds with the surveys; Radio Luxembourg's four million listeners were almost double the number of listeners to all the other continental stations and almost double the BBC peak audience of just over two million (which they achieved on Monday evening when Luxembourg and most other continental stations were not on the air).

If you do the adding up, Radio Luxembourg's audience was only a few thousand short of being equal to the audience of all the other radio stations put together; the total audience was some eight million people and Radio Luxembourg had more than four million of them every Sunday.

Unsurprisingly advertisers flocked to be included on Radio Luxembourg, and by late 1938 Radio Luxembourg had more than 100 advertisers willing to pay the highest advertising rates in the world to reach what was quite probably the largest single audience available to an advertiser anywhere in the world. The list included not only the famous Ovaltinies, but others which have been long forgotten; Beecham's Lung Syrup, Bisurated Magnesia, Calvert's Dentifrice, Carter's Little Liver Pills, Bile Beans, Czechoslovak Travel Bureau, Feen-a-Mint, Scott's Emulsion, Vitacup and Kingscliffe Children's Treat.

Typical of all this output was the lavish J Walter Thompson studio in Bush House, which produced no less than 44 different programmes each week, occupying 78 of the 15-minute spots (which was how airtime was sold) all made in this most modern studio in Britain which had been specially built for this purpose. In addition there were weekly concerts at the Scala theatre before audiences of 1000 people, all invited by the sponsoring advertiser. The concerts were recorded live in the theatre and edited on to film using the new Phillips-Miller system, and the announcements and sponsors' messages dubbed in at the studio later on. So anxious were advertisers to keep the services of their stars that it was not unusual for people like Jack Hylton to be given six- or even 12-month contracts by their sponsor (Hylton was contracted to Rinso for their *Radio Revue*).

But it wasn't only the advertisers who were casting their covetous eyes on the three 600-foot masts at Junglinster. By 1939, as Europe echoed to the stamp of a million jackboots, the continental radio stations began to go off the air at the very peak of their popularity.

3: GAIRMANY CALLING...

'... no such undertaking has been received. This country is at war with Germany.'

It was 3 September 1939, and Neville Chamberlain had just made the announcement everyone had been dreading, although it came as no real surprise. Hitler's angry posturing had reached a fever pitch some while previously and it had long been obvious that there was only one way to halt his incessant demands. This began a period which later came to be known as 'the phoney war'. Although German troops had invaded Poland and sparked off the Second World War that was as yet the extent of the fighting, and the rash of air raid warnings which followed Chamberlain's announcement died away and a period of relative calm prevailed.

Even so the entertainment business reacted to the declaration of war dramatically and swiftly. All over Britain theatres and cinemas began closing down and the BBC collapsed their network of regional radio stations into one unit based around the previous National service and called it 'The Home Service'. This was relatively easy for them to arrange since they had been planning for the eventuality of war for at least a year, and had already been involved in a series of meetings with government on this very subject. It was quite clear that for the duration of the war the BBC would be the British government's major instrument of propaganda.

Part of the preparations for war had included the provision, at long last, of the coveted landline facility from London to Luxembourg for use by the Grand Duchy's radio station to cover the visit to England of the newly re-elected French premier, Lebrun. This was seen by the British and French governments as a fairly important exercise, demonstrative primarily of their joint resolve and solidarity in the face of Hitler's threats, and accordingly the British government let it be known that they regarded the request for landline facilities to Luxembourg in a favourable light. This attitude made it more or less impossible for the BBC to raise any objection whatever to the arrangement, especially objections based almost entirely on what could best be described as professional jealousy.

The link was used on a number of occasions after Lebrun's visit, generally in conjunction with events which government opinion felt deserved maximum European coverage. Radio Luxembourg wasn't only broadcasting to Britain, remember, so that any news coverage they gave to events in Britain received widespread dissemination throughout France, Germany and Belgium as well. This was all highly desirable PR for a government about to enter a war.

The eventual declaration of that war brought about immediate and rapid changes on the continent as well as in Britain; it was France, Belgium and Holland who faced the most immediate threat from the soldiers of the thousand-year Reich, and they too reacted swiftly. One by one the continental commercial stations started to go off the air, and on 21 September 1939, at 1.19 in the afternoon Radio Luxembourg's Junglinster transmitter closed down. On this day when History had reached a momentous crossroads, the last transmission from Luxembourg under a free government was by a local orchestra playing live in the large studio at Villa Louvigny. The piece of music they chose was written by a Luxembourg composer and was entitled 'For Liberty'.

'It was,' observed a journalist at the time, 'played with considerable feeling.'

Although the transmitter would not remain silent the voice of Radio Luxembourg would not be heard again until long after the war in Europe was over.

It seemed strange at the time that no use was ever made of any of the commercial stations by the British government. Here was a large body of professional broadcasters with all the equipment (including mobile units for outside broadcasts), the staff and the stars ready to provide a first-class news and entertainment service for the threatened European nations as well as the troops of the British Expeditionary Force and an enormous audience in Britain, which was never used. The commercial stations offered themselves to the British government on this very basis but were turned down. Plans for wartime broadcasting had already been made in conjunction with the BBC and there was no need of any outside assistance.

Radio Normandy was the exception to this, and after a two-month absence it returned to the airwaves as Radio International, with the blessing of the French government. Although the transmitter was beamed at Southern England, and although the BEF had very few radio sets between them, Radio International continued the traditions of commercial radio. Advertising was cut out, although programmes of music were provided for the troops of the BEF 'with the good wishes' of one company or another. Radio International incorporated announcers from various radio stations – Bob Danvers Walker (Normandy) and Roy Plomley (Toulouse) were joined at International by Radio Luxembourg's Charles Maxwell, and the rift between Luxembourg and the IBC was healed by response to a common enemy.

There was a fairly substantial stock of pre-recorded material and the announcers worked their way through all this, so the station remained untroubled by the problem of transporting material to Europe from London. The station changed hands at 8 p.m. every evening, when it became an Austrian 'Freedom' station, and later again when it passed over to the Czechoslovak service. The announcers for these broadcasts were nationals of the relevant countries and not necessarily professional broadcasters, which meant that the British announcers, having finished their programmes, remained on duty to control the studio for the other broadcasts.

However, the phoney war was by now coming to an end as German

Above
A Telefunken mixing panel at Villa Louvigny. This equipment was possibly installed by the Wehrmacht and used by Lord Haw-Haw.
Below
The control room as it is today at Villa Louvigny; all RTL output is monitored in this room.

F.6
F.5
F.4
F.3
F.2
F.1
S.VT2/3
F.8
F.9
SELECTEUR 1
REC.4
REC.3
REC.2
REC.1
O/P SEP.
O/P STUDIO
REC.5
LIGNE 1
LIGNE 2
LIGNE 3
LIGNE 4
LIGNE UKW
SELECTEUR 2
P.U.
EN
1 KHZ
CUE
GONG
OL
OM
OC
FM LUX
FM ALL
VU
CLE
VOL
INTERPHONE
HORS SERVICE
HORS SERVICE
HORS SERVICE
UTILISER LA CASSETTE SIGNAL STATION
SIGN. ST.
W66
W66a
TELEFUNKEN
1
5
6
7
8
9
P.U. 1
MICRO
MAGN.
MAGN 2
MAGN 3
GENERAL
GONG
P.U. 2

forces were rapidly approaching the Channel coast, and in 1940 Radio International was forced to close. It stayed open as long as possible, however, and one or two of the announcers had particularly narrow escapes, getting out of France on some of the very last boats to leave for England before the evacuation was complete.

Most of the homing announcers found that employment prospects in the wartime BBC were substantial; this was no time to 'black' artists because they had worked for a commercial rival. In any case the BBC was well aware that wartime radio would of necessity be a great deal different to the kind of programming they had been used to. It obviously needed to be lighter and more entertaining; people in air raid shelters tend to have a dim view of educational or religious talks and lectures. In any case the exigencies of war were breaking down a number of social and moral values with extraordinary rapidity and it was clear that the whole BBC style of presentation would have to adapt itself to the new situation. What was needed was a more informal and conversational approach – exactly the kind of thing commercial radio had been doing for six or seven years. Large numbers of commercial radio presenters found their way on to the BBC Home Service very quickly. With a few exceptions most of them became so firmly entrenched there that they remained at the BBC after the war and went on to become household names all over again, their period as radio 'pirates' long forgotten – Roy Plomley, Bob Danvers Walker, Stephen Williams and Charles Maxwell all did this very successfully.

Back in Europe the remains of their radio stations fell into the eager hands of the German army, providing them with ready-made instruments of propaganda with which to beam programmes all over Britain. And although the Radio Normandy transmitter at Fécamp was aimed at southern England (and especially London), although Poste Parisien, Radio Toulouse and Radio Lyons were all available, the jewel in the crown had to be the giant 200 kilowatt transmitter at Junglinster which could be heard all over Europe.

There was little point in the Luxembourg army, such as it was, resisting the might of Nazi Germany. In fact there was little point in doing very much about it at all. The people of the tiny Grand Duchy have grown used to temporary subjugation over the centuries, and in the main they settled back to await the liberation which must eventually arrive. In May 1940, though, with Britain standing alone against an enemy which occupied just about every country in Europe, it may have seemed unlikely that any such liberation would materialise for many years.

At Villa Louvigny, though, preparations for German occupation had been made, and the great bulk of Radio Luxembourg's pre-recorded programme material vanished from the studios long before the first Wehrmacht soldier arrived there. What happened to it is not entirely clear, and although stories that it was buried by radio staff in the Parc Municipal (in which the Villa Louvigny is built) abound, it seems far more likely that it simply went into warehouse storage somewhere in Luxembourg Ville, to remain hidden until the end of the war.

Hiding records from the Germans may seem a rather small way to resist them, but without all that authentic material – the discs and film recordings were of stage shows, orchestras and announcers – the German broadcasters were unable to present their output from the Grand Duchy as they would have wished. Armed with all the recordings the propaganda broadcasts could have been far more subtle and far more effective. Official German policy at the time (at least as far as Hitler himself was concerned) was that they didn't really want to go to war with Britain. They saw Britain and Germany as natural allies against most other nations and hoped to persuade Britain to join the happy brotherhood of Aryan superiority by choice rather than force. Any radio output which was offered along the lines of 'look, be sensible, we're the same under the jackboots anyway, we even like the same music and stuff' presented in an authentically British fashion, could have gone a long way to undermine the resolve of the last nation who stood against Hitler as the phoney war ended and the Battle of Britain began. Churchill, the government and therefore The Few, depended upon the wholehearted support of the people of Britain, and morale was a key factor all through the Blitz and through 1941/42.

Nobody was more aware of that than Goebbels and he swiftly began to make use of the transmitter at Junglinster to relay all sorts of programmes to Britain and the rest of Europe. Beyond any doubt the most famous (or infamous) name to be heard on Radio Luxembourg's ether was that of William Joyce, known far and wide as Lord Haw Haw.

William Joyce was born in Brooklyn, NY, in 1906, of an Irish father and British mother, and from then on confusion over his nationality continued to grow. The family moved to Britain in 1921 and Joyce received most of his exceedingly good education in this country, at the same time becoming deeply involved in politics, first with the Conservative party and then with various Fascist and National Socialist organisations.

Some time between 27 August and 3 September 1939, William Joyce slipped out of Britain and made his way to Germany, from where he began a series of propaganda broadcasts to Britain, the first one made on 18 September 1939 within three weeks of the outbreak of war, and the last shortly before the fall of Berlin in 1945.

The bulk of his audience only found time for him during the phoney war period and with the commencement of the Battle of Britain his popularity (if that's the right word for it) went into steep and continual decline. This is mostly because his prime appeal to the British was humorous; nicknamed Lord Haw Haw by Jonah Barrington of the *Daily Express*, he at once assumed a comic and ridiculous character which few people could take seriously, and was the butt of numerous jokes and several comic songs – 'Haw Haw the Humbug of Hamburg' is probably the best remembered.

The BBC, at the request of the Ministry of Information, undertook a survey of listening habits at the end of 1939 and among the questions were several aimed at discovering what effect, if any, Haw Haw's broadcasts were having on the public at home. During this survey some 34,000 people were questioned and it was found that for every six adults one listened regularly, three occasionally and two never listened at all. Fifty-eight per cent of his audience listened because he was funny, 50 per cent of them cited the fact that others listened as one of the reasons they did so themselves and only 6 per cent because they thought he was clever.

But the Germans did think he was clever and by 1942 he was appointed Head Commentator in the English editorial department of German Broadcasting Stations in Europe. Most of his broadcasts were made in Charlottenburg, Berlin, and relayed by assorted transmitters all over Europe. On 12 July 1943, his *Views on the News* followed the official German news and was announced: 'Germany calling. Here are the stations Calais one, 514 metres, Calais two, 301.6 metres, Koln, 456 metres, Breslau, 316 metres, Luxembourg, 1293 metres, and the Short Wave transmitter DXX, 41.27 metres . . .'

The BBC had found in its survey that the fairly large audience Joyce enjoyed (and which by all accounts enjoyed him) was in part a legacy from the pre-war days of continental radio; the British people had already developed a pronounced habit of listening to continental stations broadcasting in English and the Germans were fortunate enough to be able to draw on this. Clearly they were astute enough to make use of existing stations with a listening habit and equally clearly they were not silly enough to alter the frequencies. But the habit was one of listening to music and light entertainment; none of the continental stations had been able to offer a news service which could compete with the BBC, so once the novelty of Haw Haw had worn off most people reverted to their regular source of news and information – the BBC.

William Joyce was captured in Germany in May 1945 and held abroad until the Treason Act 1945 (which specifically included persons of an Irish descent) could be passed. He was brought back to London and charged with High Treason in June of 1945, on the basis that he 'being a person owing allegiance to His Majesty the King, adhered to the King's enemies elsewhere than in the King's realm, to wit, in the German realm, contrary to the Treason Act 1351'.

Evidence at the three-day trial and its subsequent appeals centred mostly around whether or not Joyce 'owed allegiance' to the King and whether he had 'adhered' to His enemies. The latter was a matter of record and not denied, although part of the prosecution submission included a payment order in favour of William Joyce (who was already contracted exclusively to Reichs-Rundfunk GmbH Berlin) and which was headed 'German European Radio Transmitter Head Broadcasting Station Luxembourg', for a sound recording fee in respect of an English-language propaganda broadcast transmitted four times on 16 October

1943 and for which Joyce was paid 200 Marks in February of the following year, the document being duly signed and receipted by William Joyce.

He was found guilty of High Treason on 19 September 1945, his appeal was dismissed in November of that year and his hearing at the House of Lords was heard over three days on 18 December 1945, almost six years to the day after his first propaganda broadcast to Britain over German radio. He was executed at Wandsworth prison on 3 January 1946. It was a verdict and sentence which aroused considerable disquiet in legal minds, mostly because it is hard to see how an Irish-American alien can be guilty of being a traitor to the Crown under British Law; at various times Joyce had held American, Irish, British and, finally, German nationality.

But despite this, and despite the rather comic nature which his broadcasts held for most people, there is no doubt that, mostly by virtue of language and accent, Joyce was commonly regarded as English by the bulk of his listeners, and was thus universally held in somewhat low esteem. And the fact that he could frequently be heard on a radio station which had spent several years establishing itself as being by the British for the British doubtless contributed to this.

Most of Haw Haw's programmes were broadcast from Radio Hamburg and simply relayed on the Junglinster transmitter, and he visited the Villa Louvigny to broadcast live on only one or two occasions. However there were other live broadcasts made from there and the typically efficient German army moved in equipment of their own to operate the studios, firstly to update the station and then continually throughout the war period to replace equipment which kept getting mysteriously lost or broken . . . Most of the new equipment was by AEG Telefunken and a great deal of it is still at Villa Louvigny. Most of it still works and some of it has only recently been taken out of service to make way for newer equipment.

But during the war years the equipment was used to push out Haw Haw, whose effect on British audiences was not exactly what Goebbels had hoped for, since he became a popular source of entertainment on an almost variety-hall level. One of the few positive effects of the broadcasts made by Germany from Luxembourg (and from Radio Normandy's old transmitter at Fécamp) was to make at least one song – 'Lilli Marlene' – a hit on both sides of the barricades. Like many other songs – by people like George Formby, Gracie Fields and, of course, the Forces' Sweetheart herself, Vera Lynn – 'Lilli Marlene' became what we would now call a 'hit' (although the 'charts' hadn't yet been thought of) entirely unaided by record sales, since the record companies were too busy on war work. Radio, already an important influence in popular music and light entertainment before the war, was doubly important during it. Through the General Overseas Service of the BBC, and through the Home Service, popular entertainers like George Formby or the irrepressible Spike Jones maintained their popularity in programmes like the new

55

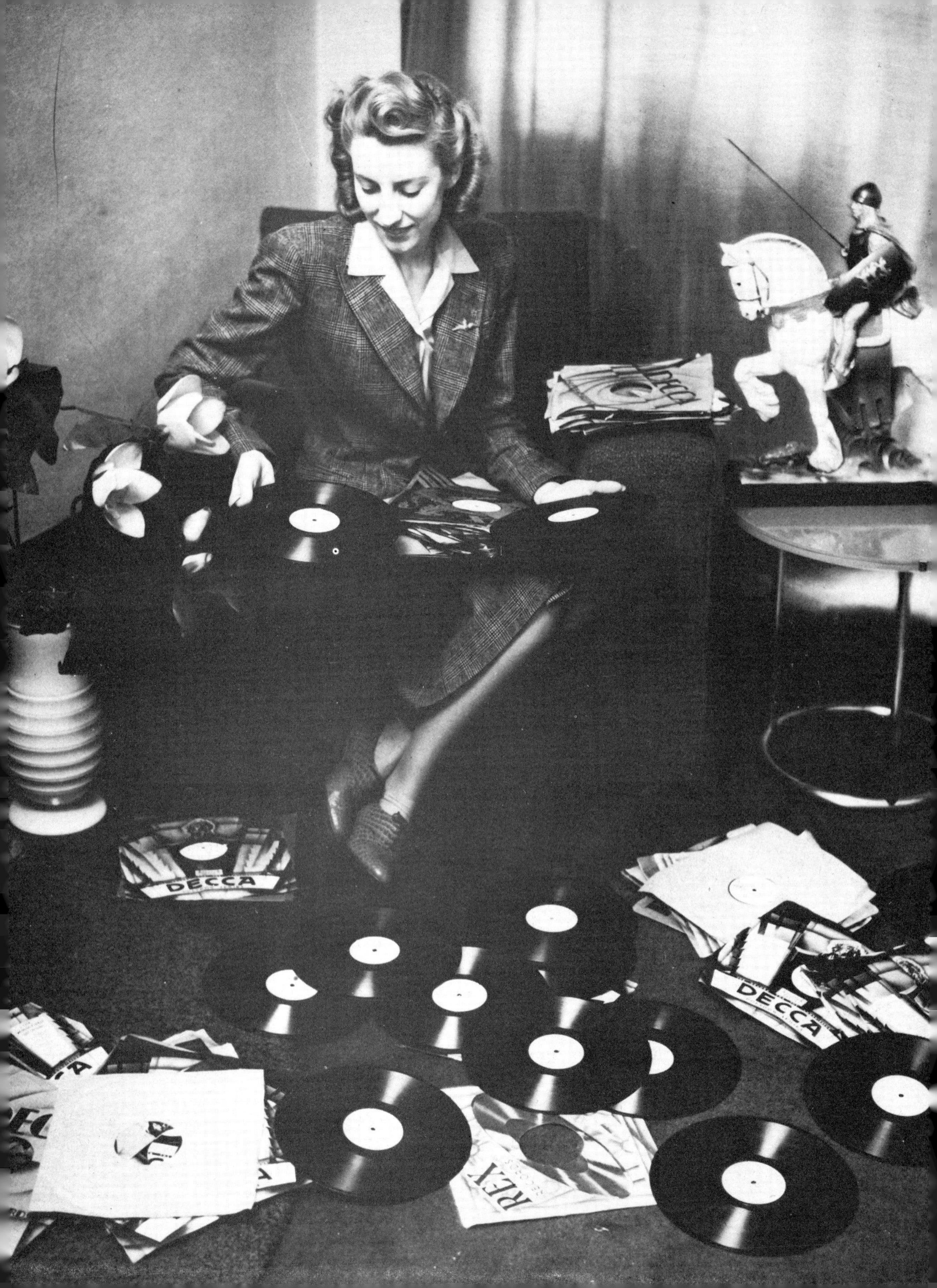
DECCA
DECCA
REX

'Workers' Playtime', aimed especially at the millions of people (particularly women) who were now working in factories all over Britain.

Despite the new wartime informality and despite the absence of Lord Reith the BBC wasn't completely ready to abandon all its principles, and some songs – particularly one which involved a great deal of flatulent raspberrying in conjunction with the mention of Hitler's name – met with extreme disapproval. Even the popular ditty 'Praise the Lord and pass the ammunition' was scrutinised very carefully to decide whether or not it offended against the moral and religious principles which the BBC under Reith had upheld for so long and for which they now presumably believed Britain was fighting.

However, the arrival of the Americans in 1942 – better late than never – began to exert an influence over broadcasting in Britain which was far from subtle. The BBC's new style of presentation, adopted with the outbreak of war and dependent upon the commercial radio announcers brought into the fold, was still fairly dry and impersonal, almost deferentially polite. The Yanks were about as polite and deferential as a heart attack, and as the corridors of Broadcasting House thronged with them their influence spread.

The BBC had already introduced a request programme for the first time ever on its Forces network, a mere six years behind commercial radio, and inaugurated a new service for the Allied troops on the continent following the D-Day landings in June 1944. On this programme BBC announcers had to work alongside American and Canadian presenters, introducing records which were sometimes far removed from the gentle Bing Crosby or Glenn Miller melodies which had been popular through the early years of the war. It was soon obvious that it was impossible for an announcer to introduce a record called 'It must be jelly 'cause jam don't shake like that' in the BBC approved fashion, and things would have to relax a bit. They did, but by that time the war was almost over and George Patton was pestering Eisenhower for permission to let his tanks push over Berlin and keep on going until they reached Moscow. Haw Haw made his final (and many people believed, drunken) broadcast from Radio Luxembourg's transmitter, insisting that if only Britain had let Hitler have Poland then war could have been avoided. Even in this final hour he was urging an Anglo-German alliance to take on what he described as 'the menace from the east', a point of view he seemed to share not only with Patton but with one or two reasonably high-placed people in the British government.

In the autumn of 1944 the radio station in Luxembourg was liberated from its German conquerors under exceptional circumstances which clearly indicate the great importance which military thinking attached to the installation. Despite the efforts of the departing Wehrmacht troops to destroy it the studio and the transmitter were captured more or less intact by a special task force of the American 12th Army Group, acting under the directions of the Psychological Warfare Division (PWD) of the Supreme Headquarters of the Allied Expeditionary Force (SHAEF).

Vera Lynn surveys her record collection *(Pictorial Press)*.

With the full co-operation of the Luxembourg government the station was immediately taken over by SHAEF and became the continental voice of a staff division of SHAEF which, according to Noel Newsome, chief of the Radio Division of SHAEF's PWD, employed it as 'a tactical and strategic weapon of the Military Government established in occupied Germany'.

Newsome claimed this as an 'outstandingly successful' experiment in internationalism involving civilian and military personnel from America, Britain, France, Belgium and Luxembourg, and the programming consisted of broadcasts produced by this mixed team as 'the voice of the United Nations on the frontiers of Germany', relaying important transmissions from the American Office of War Information in New York and the BBC in London. In addition one programme each day was presented as coming from the American 12th Army Group and another from the British 21st Army Group, with a further 40 programmes produced by the SHAEF Radio Luxembourg Detachment, which included civilians lent to SHAEF by the BBC and the OWI.

The broadcasts included SHAEF instructions and information to the armies and civilians of France, Russia, Belgium, Poland, Italy, Czechoslovakia and Holland, all in the relevant languages, mixed with classical and light music. Furthermore the station had its own team of news journalists who brought to the microphone captured enemy soldiers as well as newly-liberated citizens of countries recently released from or still partly under German occupation. A large part of this material originated by the SHAEF Radio Luxembourg Detachment was sent on for use by both the BBC and the OWI in London and New York.

In a letter to *The Times* on 20 April 1945, as the future of this enormous enterprise swung in the balance, Noel Newsome said, 'There is ample evidence that this organ of the Supreme Commander and Voice of the United Nations has, through its geographical position, great technical power and authoritative character, acquired a very large audience among all nationalities throughout the Reich. I believe . . . that a full understanding of radio in the Allied war effort and of its possible role as an agency of the United Nations after the war requires access to the facts about this most recent development at Radio Luxembourg of a completely combined Allied radio operation.'

With the end of the war in Europe the British government withdrew its participation in these joint broadcasts and left the OWI to carry on alone with its efforts in the Pacific war. But the sudden arrival of *Enola Gay* and *Little Boy* over Japan ended that struggle sooner than was expected, leaving some doubt about what should happen at Radio Luxembourg. Many of those involved – particularly Noel Newsome – felt that the station should pass into the hands of an international board of governors and become the voice of the United Nations rather than be returned to commercial ownership. Having seen the enormous propaganda power exerted by such a strong radio output many were understandably worried about what would happen if the transmitter should somehow fall into the hands of a politically motivated group of the wrong persuasion. But, for reasons of their own, Churchill's government were opposed to the idea, although the OWI was extremely keen. However, the end of the Pacific war meant that the OWI was gradually being disbanded, and control of its interests was slowly being assumed by the State Department or abandoned altogether; worldwide interests in radio were among the things which were gradually being closed down by State.

American forces had liberated the radio station in Luxembourg on 10 September 1944, and the agreement between SHAEF and the Luxembourg government concerning its wartime future had been signed some five months previous to that. In keeping with that agreement the station should have passed back into private hands on VE day in May of 1945, but it was November before the changeover was made once the State Department had decided to abstain, and the CLR took control of what was now, thanks to both the Germans and SHAEF, the best-equipped and most modern radio station in Europe.

On 12 November 1945 Radio Luxembourg resumed its transmissions to France and Belgium and for the first time in more than six years the day's broadcasting began with the words *'Bonjour le monde, ici Radio Luxembourg'*.

The English Service did not come back on the air so quickly. In part this was the responsibility of Winston Churchill, who apparently had his own plans for the radio station's giant transmitter which even to this day remain shrouded in a certain amount of mystery. Educated guessers would probably arrive at the conclusion that Churchill wanted to use Radio Luxembourg to beam his own propaganda material to countries now lying behind what he had only recently described as the Iron Curtain, possibly even to Russia herself. It is certainly well accepted that given the chance Churchill would have agreed with Patton and allowed the Allied armies to press on to Moscow, but it never happened. George Smith Patton died in an accident in Germany in 1945 and is buried in the Luxembourg military cemetery in Hamm, 10 miles outside the town of Luxembourg, along with 5000 other sons of the US. Winston Churchill was voted out of office in the General Election of 1945, a few months before William Joyce was executed at Wandsworth for High Treason.

Stephen Williams had already travelled from Broadcasting House out to the Grand Duchy at the express request, even the instructions, of the Churchill administration. He was charged with re-opening the English Service and once again building up its audiences, but this time he would have every co-operation and assistance from the BBC. Landline facilities, recording studios in London, all were now made available to him. Similar propositions were not made to Radio Normandy and the other IBC stations for two main reasons, the first of which was that the IBC offices in London had been destroyed in the Blitz and the second that the new French government did not re-license the commercial stations run by the IBC which had been operating before the war only by the permission of

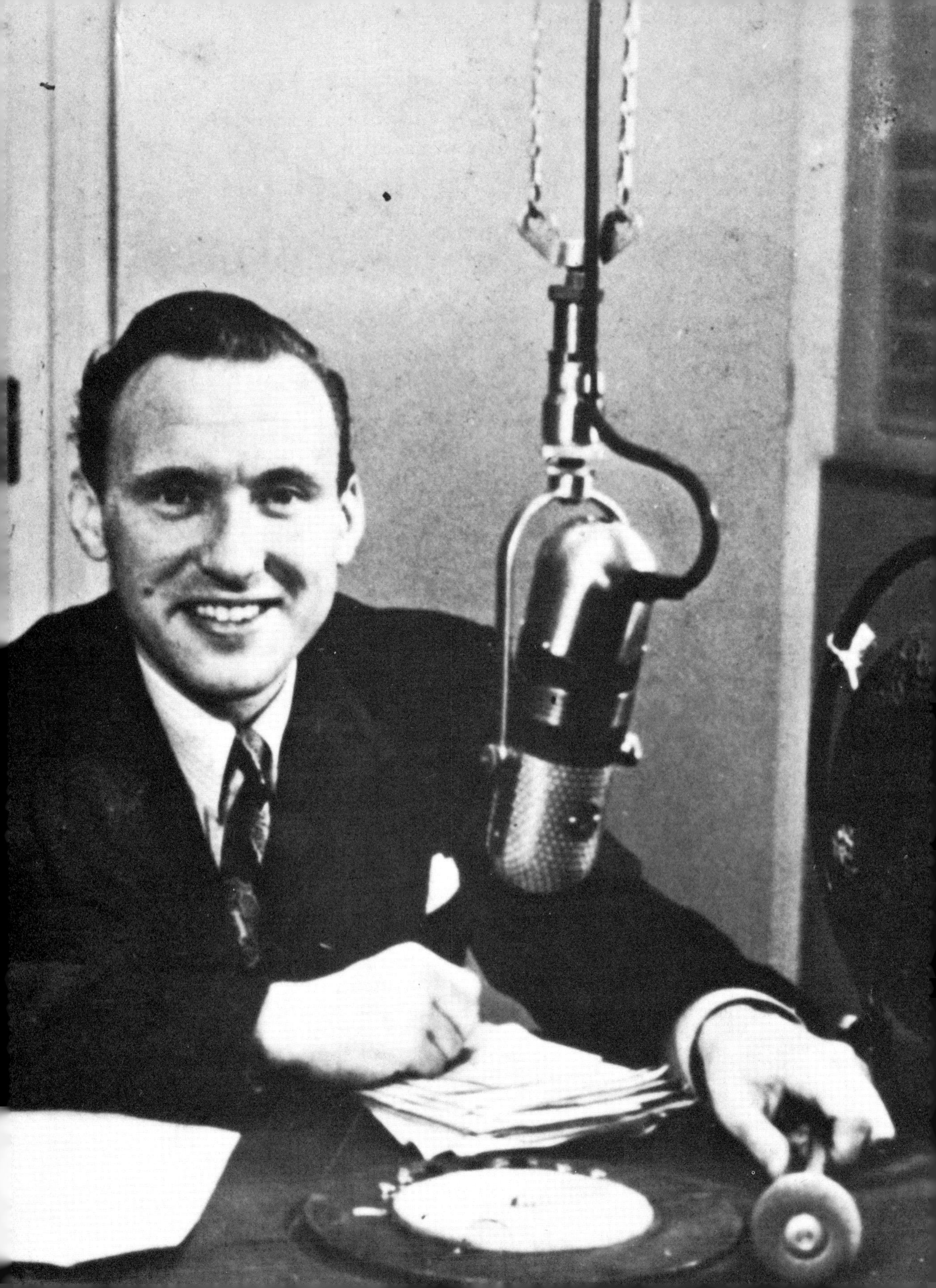

the French Ministry of Posts and Telegraphs. Worse still, the Radio Normandy transmitters had been destroyed in the D-Day landings of 1944.

But before Williams had been out in Luxembourg for more than a few months the election changed everything. Herbert Morrison told the House of Commons that negotiations in the Grand Duchy regarding the future of Radio Luxembourg had fallen through, largely due to the involvement of another country (which was not named) and that therefore the position would revert to the pre-war status quo and Radio Luxembourg would have to make its own arrangements. Fortunately it was easily capable of doing so.

The BBC postwar service had produced the Light Programme out of the old Forces Network, and as the name implied it was intended to provide the kind of light entertainment which the Corporation had adapted to quite readily during the war. However the war was now over and the BBC, while not actually regressing to its days under Lord Reith, still felt that it was time for a little normality to return to the airwaves. Yet again BBC programming assumed a rather cumbersome and plodding nature by comparison to what was coming from the Grand Duchy of Luxembourg.

All the records and film recordings which had eluded the Germans during the war began to appear from hiding and Radio Luxembourg was once again able to offer its listeners the kind of programmes they wanted to hear even if to begin with the material was noticeably dated. In the main this consisted of music from record as an alternative to the BBC variety and dance band programmes. The Americans had introduced the concept of hit records and top tens to European radio via the various Forces programmes offered either in conjunction with the BBC from Broadcasting House or, after the fall of Berlin, through the AFN – American Forces Network – from Germany. It was this transatlantic style that British radio audiences had become accustomed to over the past few years and towards which Radio Luxembourg was now leaning.

The BBC could hardly have been less receptive; certainly they were at something of a disadvantage in that almost all of their output was still coming under the censor's pen. Record programmes still had to be scripted right down to the very last comma and full stop, which meant that there was little chance whatever of their announcers and presenters getting anywhere near the relaxed and informal style being used to great advantage in the Grand Duchy. And the BBC attitude to performers was still somewhat unbending, as it had been even during the war years.

In 1944 Teddy Johnson was an aspiring and reasonably successful singer with assorted dance bands. He'd been a vocalist and drummer since the age of 14 and was working at the Streatham Locarno when Jack Payne asked him to sing with the band on three or four broadcasts he was doing with the BBC. Teddy was of course more than happy to oblige and three or four broadcasts became five or six and then more. Things didn't

Teddy Johnson in the studio at Villa Louvigny; the famous Luxembourg gong is beside him.

go wrong until broadcast number 13 or 14. There was one particular song which had a tricky bit in it which Teddy knew he would one day get wrong. In the way of these things the day he got it wrong was the day the BBC brass were all listening, and Jack Payne was told to stop using Teddy Johnson as the BBC didn't feel he was up to standard. Jack Payne was understandably upset since the BBC were questioning his right to choose individual members of his band, but he had little choice except to comply. Johnson was dropped and that was that. Except it wasn't, because Teddy Johnson wrote to the BBC asking why he had been banned. Jack Payne also wrote, in September of 1944. Meanwhile Teddy Johnson had broadcast again on the BBC, this time for Phil Green's band. The BBC wrote to Teddy Johnson insisting that he had not been banned, and he was as likely to be used on BBC programmes as anyone else. But his letter was not answered by the Chairman of the BBC, to whom it had been addressed, but by someone else, to whom it had been passed with the comment 'Please deal. I should like to know why he was not stopped from appearing in Phil Green's programme' scrawled in the margin. Same old BBC. Teddy Johnson had in fact been banned by an unbelievable (nowadays, at any rate) part of the BBC machine called The Dance Music Policy Committee, which will give some idea of just how regimented even the wartime BBC really was.

Teddy Johnson would not appear with Jack Payne again for some years, as half of the Pearl Carr and Teddy Johnson duo on a television programme presented by Jack Payne almost ten years after his band had broken up and Payne himself had 'retired'. But before then Teddy Johnson was destined for a trip out to the Grand Duchy of Luxembourg which would last several years.

TUNE IN TO LYONS RED LABEL SHOW!

Every Monday at 9.00 p.m.
KEN MACKINTOSH
His Orchestra and Singers
and **DOLORES VENTURA** at the Piano

★ ★ ★ ★ ★

BIG PRIZES EVERY WEEK!

Join in the exciting 'Spot the Tune' competition. Prizes to be won each week include a magnificent Television Set, a handsome Radio Set, and 12 exciting Food Parcels! Also a special prize in one programme only, of an AUSTIN A.40 CAR! Competition entries should be addressed to: 'Lyons Red Label Show', Radio Luxembourg, 37 Shepherd Street, London, W.1.

Presented by "Lyons of Cadby Hall" famous blenders of tea for 50 years

TWO-O-EIGHT

Radio Weekly

The Finest Needle for Your Radiogram

THE GOLDRING ACOUSTIC-FILTERED TYPE S6

- Eliminates Needle Changing
- Gives Better Reproductions
- Filters Out Surface Noise
- Increases the Life of Records

"GOLDRING Acoustic-Filtered Needles" Suits any Standard Pick-Ups

★ Look for the "GOLDRING" Display Card at your Dealers. GOLDRING Needles cost 10/9 incl. P. Tax

ERWIN SCHARF. GOLDRING PRODUCTS
49-57 DE BEAUVOIR ROAD · LONDON · N.1

GRAMOPHONE PICK-UPS ● PICK-UP HEADS ● SOUND BOXES ● NEEDLE JEWEL POINT NEEDLES ● AND GRAMOPHONE ACCESSORIES

4: 208

With the changes in government policy towards Radio Luxembourg Stephen Williams was left more or less to his own devices in the Grand Duchy and the responsibility for getting the station back on the air fell more or less on his shoulders, even though he had been sent out there by the BBC and was now working for what the Corporation would once again regard as a rival radio station. But in 1946 he was joined as an announcer on Radio Luxembourg by another Briton who had been sent out to the Grand Duchy on a government mission.

Geoffrey Everitt had left school in Royston at 14, a few years before the war began. He'd joined up at 17 and spent most of the war working for the Royal Engineers as an instructor at the Army School of Chemical Warfare; lecturing to students there for up to five hours a day provided him with a skill which would later come in useful. In 1946, though, he was sent to Luxembourg to help re-form the Luxembourg Army. In such a tiny country it was inevitable that sooner or later he would form links with other Britons who were there, and one of them was Stephen Williams. When the British Army football team arrived in Luxembourg to play their national side it was equally inevitable that Williams would invite football devotee and Arsenal fan Everitt to interview Stanley (later Sir Stanley) Rous after the match. It was Geoffrey Everitt's first ever broadcast but it passed off successfully. So successfully, in fact, that Williams offered the football fan a full-time job on the station and after his demob later that year Geoffrey Everitt had a contract with Radio Luxembourg. The station resumed its full-time independent commercial activities on 1 July 1946. There was no influx of brand-new material and they had to use those pre-war records which had been meticulously hidden from the German army.

Furthermore the advertising revenue was a problem, since most European countries, including Britain and France, still had in force wartime restrictions on the export of currency. Although advertising time could be (and was) bought on the station once again, despite a renewal of the embargo by the British Press, there was no way that the revenue could reach the station from the Wireless Publicity offices which were now in Jermyn Street, London. Still, they did the best they could, but it wasn't much. When the station began its broadcast there were five announcers – Stephen Williams, Geoffrey Everitt and three other residents of Luxembourg who all by good fortune spoke English, which made them eminently qualified for the job, never mind that they'd had no radio experience whatever.

One by one they drifted away, though, leaving just Williams and Everitt out in Luxembourg to do everything. Soon enough Stephen Williams had to return to the BBC in London and a replacement was immediately sought. He was found in Archer Street, Soho, hanging around with all the other London musicians who used to congregate there after the war. Like Geoffrey Everitt and like Charles Maxwell before him, his radio experience was zero. In fact he entertained absolutely no desire whatever to become a radio announcer.

After being forced by the BBC to part with Jack Payne Teddy Johnson had been working as a drummer at the Mayfair Hotel with the Roland Peters Orchestra. After 18 months and with about £120 in the bank he gave it up to be a freelance entertainer, having always cherished the notion of being a sort of singer/comedian. In those postwar days Archer Street, especially on a Monday, was where musicians went to meet up and get work. Having just finished a stint with an orchestra run by Stanley Andrews (father of Anthony) Teddy went down Archer Street looking for work as a musician and found himself talking to Derek Bolton, whom he had known as a bandboy with Phillip Green's band (for the BBC broadcast from Lewisham Town Hall which should never have been made). Bolton suggested that he call on Frank Lee, head of Radio Luxembourg's English Service, at their office in Davis Street, conveniently opposite the tradesmen's entrance of Claridge's Hotel. Frank Lee sent Teddy Johnson over to the IBC for a voice test at 2.30 that afternoon and by 5 p.m. was on the phone asking Teddy if he would like to visit the Grand Duchy, do a bit on air and see how the whole thing worked out. Teddy was in Luxembourg the following weekend and on air with Geoffrey Everitt that Sunday afternoon. He stayed in the Grand Duchy for a few days, enjoying the atmosphere and the spring weather, before returning to London and Frank Lee. He accepted the offer of a full-time job on the station despite the fact that the weekly wage of £10 was exactly the same as Charles Maxwell had been earning 10 years before in 1937 and was considerably less than the £80 per week he could earn as a drummer in a top-class London venue.

But there were other reasons why Teddy Johnson stayed in the Grand Duchy which money had nothing to do with. Like so many people before and after him Teddy was one of the people who fell under the spell of the place. That first visit of a week or so had been the deciding factor, long before Frank Lee had offered him a job. He'd done that first Sunday afternoon broadcast with Geoffrey Everitt, playing mostly Geraldo records, and then the two of them had wandered off to sit on the terrace of a café – Le Pôle Nord – to sit in the May sunshine and soak up the springlike atmosphere. Continental life either appeals or it doesn't and the reaction seems fairly strong; strong enough to make a lot of people refuse to live in Luxembourg but also strong enough to make even larger numbers want to settle there. Teddy Johnson was one of the latter and on that very first day his major impression was, as he puts it himself, 'this is for me'.

Teddy Johnson began his career on 20 May 1948, broadcasting to Britain every night of the week except Fridays when station boss Geoffrey Everitt took over. They shared a programme on Sunday afternoons and most of the time just played records and chatted, as well as doing live adverts. Although Christopher Stone had pioneered the disc jockey's art on the BBC in 1927, when he had been the first person to play records for his audience, and although the announcers on Luxembourg and the other commercial stations had followed suit throughout the thirties, Teddy Johnson was the first of the disc jockey breed as we understand them today. He had a regular daily programme which lasted for more than 15 or 30 minutes.

In fact Teddy Johnson's show lasted a lot longer than that and it would be more accurate to describe them as shows. The scarcity of announcers in Luxembourg meant that Teddy had to fill in a great deal of airtime without giving away the fact that there was no one there but him. Establishing a great tradition which would later be admirably followed by Pete Murray, Teddy Johnson adopted several personalities for his Luxembourg broadcasts. His first programme would be something like *Topical Half Hour*, introduced by Teddy Johnson, followed (after the ringing of the famous Radio Luxembourg 'gong') by *Music for Everyone*, introduced by E. Victor Johnson. Another blast on the gong signalled the arrival of *Irish Half Hour*, introduced by Edward V Johnson and that was the evening over with. Most of the record programmes introduced live from the Grand Duchy were request shows and elicited a substantial response – between 1000 and 1500 letters arrived in Luxembourg each week for Teddy Johnson in all his various guises, indicating quite clearly that Radio Luxembourg's personality was climbing rapidly.

In London the company was growing as well, mostly in response to the demand yet again from advertisers for sponsored shows.

In October of 1948 Frank Lee hired another young man who would use Radio Luxembourg as a first step into the world of media entertainment. Phillip Jones had listened to Radio Luxembourg all the time when he'd been stationed in Germany with the RAF and when demob time came up he'd written to the station seeking work in the hope that some smart job trotting between London and Luxembourg (or better still, Paris) would be available, based on his trilingual ability. To his surprise Radio Luxembourg wrote back saying that no such job existed but inviting him to call in and see them in Davis Street. Frank Lee's letter, dated 6 October 1948, followed that visit and offered Phillip Jones a job as Programme Assistant at the alarmingly generous rate of £5 per week, rising, if you please, to a princely £5 10s after three months if all went well.

Although it was a grand title, Programme Assistant, as Phillip Jones recalled, was a cover-up title for 'dogsbody, tea-maker and all the rest of it'. All the rest of it meant, at least in part, regular shopping expeditions. Armed with the petty cash, Phillip Jones would make trips up to the HMV shop in Oxford Street and buy the records that were needed for the following week's programmes. It was mid or late 1949 before the record companies realised it was in their interest to provide radio stations with copies of records and began the distribution of free copies to media outlets which today goes under the title of 'plugging'.

From buying and cataloguing records, Phillip Jones gradually moved upwards through the London office until he graduated to really important tasks like filling in the copyright returns. At the time the London office was responsible for producing about 75 per cent of Radio Luxembourg output. The announcers in the Grand Duchy put together some of the shows – again mostly request progammes – but the rest was either scheduled in London or pre-recorded there for sponsors, and it was into this side of the London activities that Phillip Jones gradually moved. Before long he was producing the sponsored shows which were being sent out to the Grand Duchy for Teddy Johnson and Geoffrey Everitt to play between their own slots in the evenings – items like *Tune a Minute*, broadcast under one of Teddy Johnson's many aliases.

At about the same time Radio Luxembourg began a new type of programme based on popular music. To begin with the British charts were based on the same principle as the American charts and were a record of the best-selling sheet music of the time. Geoffrey Everitt was the man who dreamed up a programme based around the top-selling sheet music. It was a weekly programme, broadcast on a Sunday evening and went in reverse order from number 20 to number one. Because the charts were based on sheet music and not on record sales it meant that there were often a number of alternative versions of the same song to choose from.

This was how the music business worked at the time and it was something which continued right through the fifties and into the early sixties. The 'cover version' was a regular feature of popular music for years. But to begin with, on the sheet music charts, it meant that the presenters could play one of several versions of any song; usually they varied it from week to week, but eventually they began to stick to the version they – or their listeners – preferred, and within a short space of time (certainly less than a year) the charts were based on record sales rather than sheet music. Sadly no records of these early chart programmes remain, and after 30 years no-one – not even the two people concerned – can recall exactly when they started. The best they can do is say that the top twenty format, still a Sunday night feature of Radio Luxembourg programming, began in late 1948 or early 1949.

What they can remember is the horror with which the chart format suggestion was greeted by almost everybody including Teddy Johnson. General opinion was that the listeners wouldn't want to hear a weekly programme which would be almost the same as the previous week's and in any case would feature all the music they listened to throughout the week; and at peak listening time, too! But, as anyone who has ever listened to the radio since 1950 will know, Geoffrey Everitt had hit on an absolutely winning formula, and it was from then on that Radio Luxembourg began once again to resume its position at the top of the European broadcasting tree.

1950 was the first year since the war that the company began to make

Top Twenty

Each week the Music Publishers' Association puts out a list of the best selling songs over the last week. Selected recordings of these melodies—broadcast on September 20 over Radio Luxembourg—can be heard again on 208 m. on Sunday, September 23, at 11.00 p.m.

Here is the "Top Twenty" list for the week ending September 8.

1. "Too Young."
2. "My Truly Truly Fair."
3. "My Resistance is Low."
4. "Too Late Now."
5. "Ivory Rag."
6. "With These Hands."
7. "Christopher Columbus."
8. "Tulips and Heather."
9. "The Loveliest Night of the Year."
10. "I Apologise."
11. "Be My Love."
12. "Sweet Violets."
13. "Unless."
14. "Jezebel."
15. "A Beggar in Love."
16. "On Top of Old Smokey."
17. "Good Luck, Good Health, God Bless You."
18. "Our Very Own."
19. "Mockin' Bird Hill."
20. "Kentucky Waltz."

Above
One of the early 'Hit Parades',
this one in the days when position was still decided by the MPA on the basis of sheet music sales.
Below
Masts of the 208 metre transmitter at Marnach which has broadcast to the UK since 1951.
Following page
Left to right, Guy Mitchell, Phillip Jones, Geoffrey Everitt.

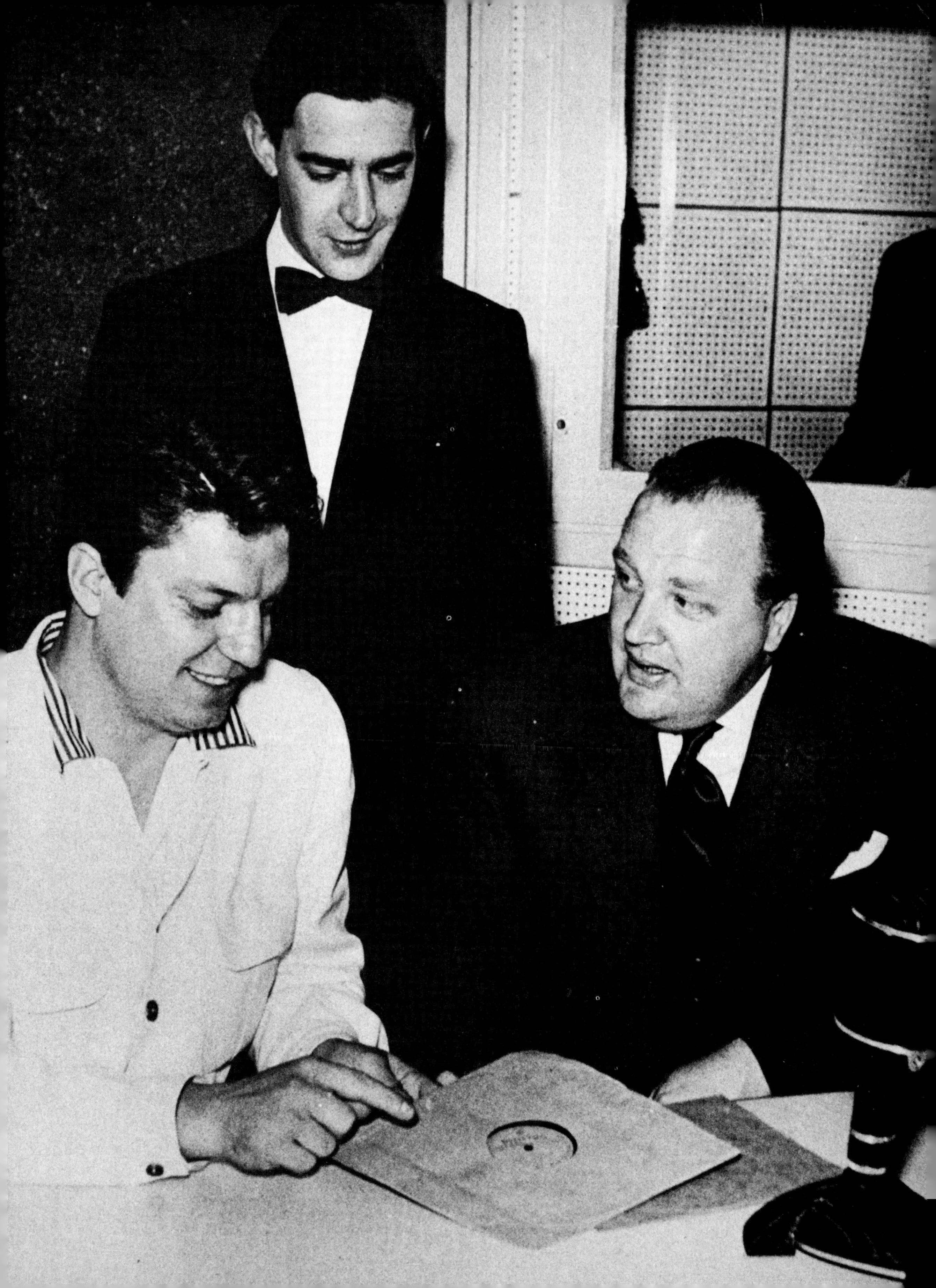

a profit; sponsored programmes, which had been trickling in up until then, began to grow in number once more. Now, unlike the pre-war days, they were made in a variety of studios and outside locations. The IBC was back in business and was making sponsored shows for advertisers who had already bought airtime on Radio Luxembourg for the programmes. This arrangement, in which the sponsor paid the station for the airtime and then paid again to performers and producers of the programme material, remained unchanged, but now the airtime was sold by Radio Luxembourg (London) who no longer insisted that they make all the programmes themselves, although they still retained the facilities to do so if required. Indeed, a large percentage of their better-known shows of the fifties and sixties were made at their own studios (they moved into their present offices in Hertford Street in 1950), but they also took programmes made by the IBC in Portland Place, Star Sound Studios in Blandford Place and others. The Luxembourg editions of *Much Binding in the Marsh* were made in a studio off Baker Street. Other concerts and variety shows were recorded before live audiences at various theatres and various town halls – Lewisham seems to have been an early fifties favourite for some reason.

Those recordings were sent out to Luxembourg and relayed from Junglinster by the two resident announcers whose lifestyle was almost totally alien to that of their listeners. Isolated in the Grand Duchy, Geoffrey Everitt and Teddy Johnson had problems of their own. Everitt had met and married a native Luxembourger and was therefore provided with a ready-made entree into Luxembourg society, but Johnson's bachelor existence revolved almost totally around his work and the Luxembourg studios in the Villa Louvigny.

In fact Teddy Johnson practically lived at the Villa Louvigny (he was not the first and he would not be the last) and when he wasn't on the air he could generally be found in the English Service's basement office scheduling out his programmes and frying up a good English mixture of egg, bacon and sausages on the camping equipment which he had installed in the office. Often the late-night aroma of cooking would attract visitors and on one occasion Teddy was surprised to find his culinary efforts being watched over by the Company's chief executive. If either of the announcers saw a car in the town bearing British registration or wearing GB plates then they would invariably seek out the owner and exchange news and views and conversation over a meal and a drink simply for the pleasure of speaking English to someone new. Communications between Britain and the continent were nowhere near as sophisticated as they are today; there was still no regular air traffic between the Grand Duchy and London, which meant that visitors were infrequent and had to make an arduous train journey from Brussels, after a somewhat uncertain flight from Croydon, Folkestone or London's embryonic new airport at Heath Row, near Staines. This meant that the announcers couldn't make the frequent trips back to Britain which are a regular feature of the current DJs' lives. In any case there were none of the live 'gigs' to attend. Presenters got their two weeks holiday each year, and while they were away from Luxembourg a relief body had to be found. On occasions Phillip Jones would fill in from London, spending two weeks at a time in Luxembourg twice a year, while Teddy Johnson or Geoffrey Everitt came home on holiday. Exciting and romantic it was not, for either party, and hardly constituted the sort of 'globetrotting' existence which Phillip Jones had hoped for when he wrote to Radio Luxembourg in 1948.

Nevertheless Phillip Jones had found himself on the ground floor of a rapidly-growing enterprise. The few sponsors, which had once again included people like Carter's Little Liver Pills, were growing, and he was now producing shows for other sponsors – Curry's (who strangely enough sold radios and bicycles, despite the apparent lack of any connection between the two), International Laboratories and others. David Jacobs was starting to record shows in London for Bournvita and Hughie Green was recording *Opportunity Knocks* before live audiences. Also coming to the fore was Jack Jackson – a bandleader for whom Teddy Johnson had worked previously – who was hosting a programme for Decca records, which was an event of some importance for everybody. It was important on two counts, the first of which was quite simply that Jack Jackson went on to become extremely popular with radio audiences and yet another of the household names which Radio Luxembourg was in the habit of establishing. Sadly, Jack Jackson died in 1977. But aside from his personal popularity the other important factor was the nature of his employer.

At the time the arrangement for sponsored shows was as simple as it had ever been; airtime was one transaction, production another and hiring of artists a third. It meant, in fact, that the nature and quality of artists who appeared on Radio Luxembourg was strictly speaking outside the control of the radio station itself. Once a sponsor had paid for the airtime he or she could theoretically leave it blank if that's what would sell the product best. Earplugs, say. Except that the station reserved for itself the role of the final arbiter of good taste, to ensure that programmes were of a sufficient standard of artistic merit. According to Geoffrey Everitt this power was used only very rarely; advertising agencies submitted programmes which were generally of excellent quality – it would not have been in anyone's interest for them to have done otherwise.

But back to Jack Jackson's programme for Decca. From a situation in the late forties in which Radio Luxembourg had been forced to send someone out to buy the records which would be played they had now arrived at a point where the record companies were not only giving away promotional copies of songs but were actually paying for airtime to ensure that their records were played. While there are very few radio stations today which would countenance programmes devoted entirely to the output of one record company (after all, the law of averages dictates that at least some of them are bound to be awful) it was less of a problem

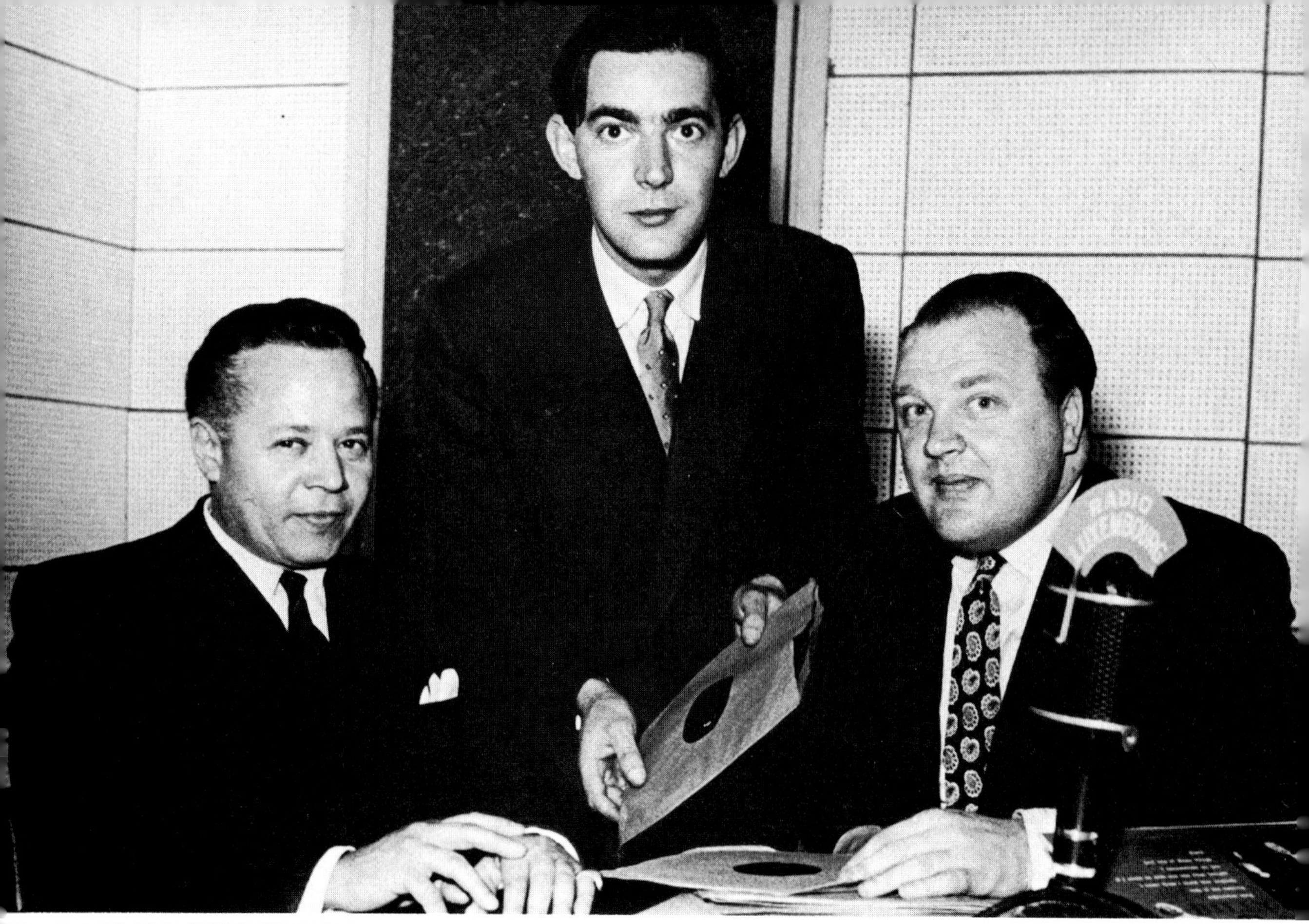
RADIO LUXEMBOURG

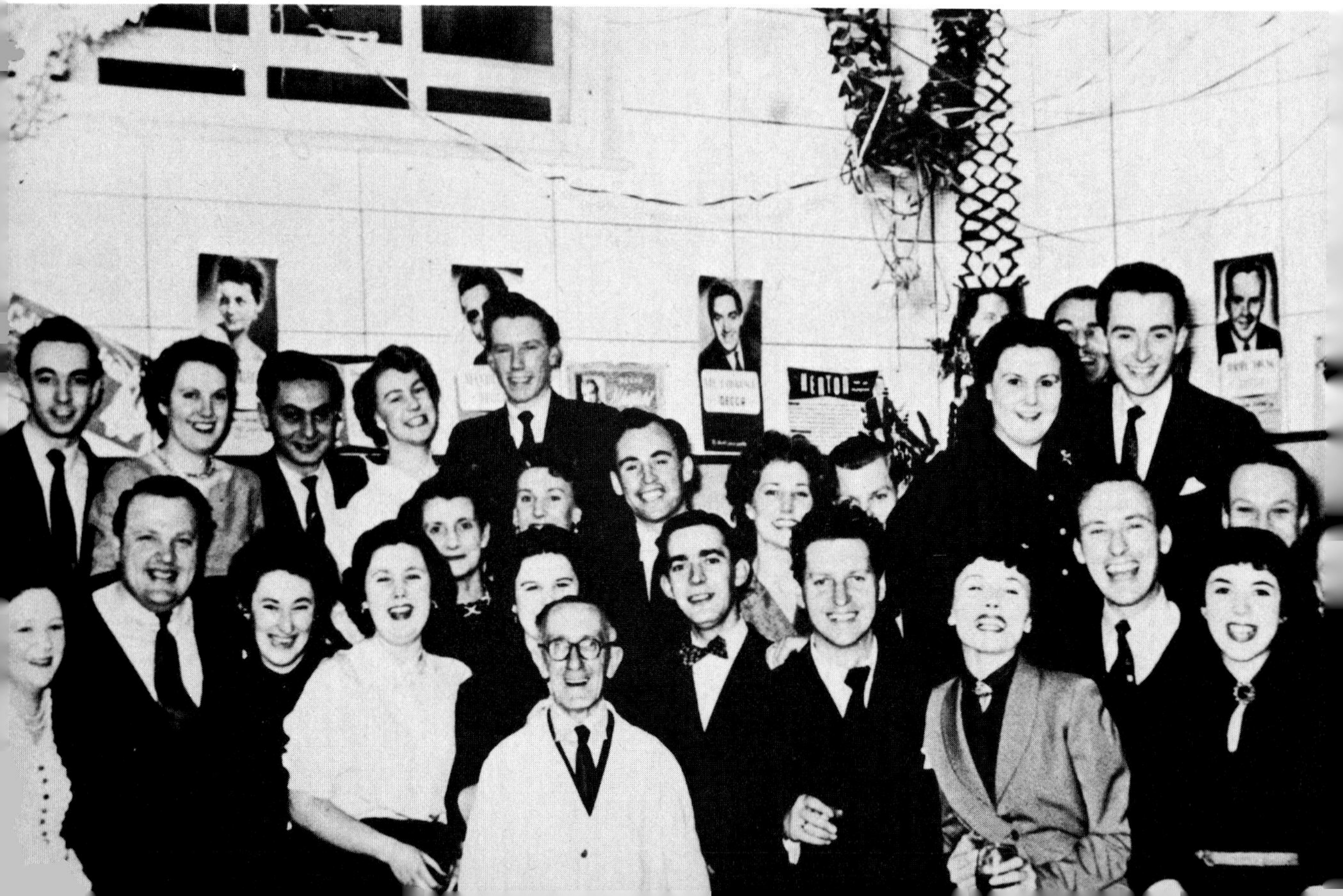
DECCA

in the early fifties although it would become more troublesome later on, as people like Harry Walters and Alan Keen would find out. In the meantime, however, it suited everyone very nicely indeed; the radio station received income and the record companies sold records. The importance of radio in this latter task had been amply demonstrated during the war years, remember, and Teddy Johnson discovered how effective radio was when he visited a music publisher on one of his infrequent visits to Britain. The publisher was baffled by the success of one of the songs in his list until he discovered that it had received extensive airplay on Luxembourg and had thus become a firm favourite.

And even when the charts were used to measure the success of record sales rather than sheet music sales the record business was operating on an entirely different level to that which we understand nowadays – something else Teddy Johnson would find out for himself. In the modern music business the production of records is an end in itself. Someone writes a song, a band or a singer records it, the record is released and hopefully enough people like the tune and buy the record to make it a hit. In the fifties the bulk of record releases were by no means new compositions. As a rule they were songs lifted from films and stage musicals; songs which everybody knew and had already heard and were therefore judged to stand a chance of success on record. Several record companies might therefore decide that a particular song from a film or musical had hit potential and all of them – three or four companies – would get their own star performers to make a recording. All the different versions would be released on different labels and it would be the song not the singer or the record which made it to the top of the charts. The very first number one hit on Radio Luxembourg's new chart was 'Galway Bay' – released by both Bing Crosby and Anne Shelton.

Thus you may hear several versions of the same song on a radio station in the course of one day. So when Teddy Johnson, who was still a singer remember, began releasing records which started to do well in the charts, he thought about pursuing his career as a singer rather than a radio presenter, especially after the success of songs like 'Beloved be faithful' and 'Tennessee Waltz'. But back in England in 1950, when he tried to interest his record company in a new song which he quite liked, nobody was interested. It had never been a hit for anyone else, it was not from a successful movie or a long-running stage show and was therefore judged to have little chance of success as a record. Only safe bets were covered. Even later, as the fifties began to wear on and the rock'n'roll era arrived, British record companies saw their primary task as getting their contracted artists to release cover versions of records which had already been hits in America. It wasn't until the early sixties that the American lead in entertainment, especially popular music, would lose the advantages which having the Hollywood film industry as part of the domestic scenery had given it, and British recording artists (as distinctly opposed to theatre or film performers) would take over and establish a lead which has still not been lost. Today American tastes in popular

Above
Left to right, Billy Daniels, Phillip Jones, Geoffrey Everitt.
Below
Christmas party time. In the front row, Geoffrey Everitt (third from left), Phillip Jones (with bow tie) and Teddy Johnson (third from right), dating the picture as probably 1951.

music lag a year or more behind European; in the fifties it was quite the opposite way round.

But hidden away in all that was another important development; Teddy Johnson departed from the Grand Duchy in 1950 and a replacement for him as resident announcer was urgently sought. Yet another in a series of highly improbable coincidences conspired to attract to the Grand Duchy of Luxembourg someone else who had no ambition whatever to be a radio presenter but who would yet again become a household name as a result of a fairly lengthy stint on Radio Luxembourg.

It was easy to see how Radio Luxembourg could turn people into household names and just why so many people were quite happy to go to work there, for Radio Luxembourg was accelerating its audience figures rapidly upwards towards an all-time high of more than eight million listeners (which would not be for a few years yet) and was beyond doubt *the* prestige radio station of the period. In fact Richard Murdoch and Kenneth Horne had just turned down offers from the BBC to accept the most lucrative radio contract so far concluded in Britain when, in 1950, they accepted £50,000 for a series of programmes on Radio Luxembourg.

Pete Murray was an actor, and had just completed a provincial tour in a play called *Larger than Life*. Back in London his agent suggested that he might care to think about working for a few months as a Continuity Announcer/Presenter on Radio Luxembourg (a vacancy which existed because of Teddy Johnson's recording contract). Pete, very frankly, confessed that he had never heard of Radio Luxembourg, but went to see Frank Lee at Hertford Street anyway, where the first question was 'What's number one in the Hit Parade?' Pete suggested it was 'Dearie' by Donald Peers, which wasn't bad at all – it was number two.

Within a couple of days Pete Murray was back at Hertford Street to do a voice test for Frank Lee, playing things like 'Come Dance With Me' by Fred Waring's Pennsylvanians – presumably one of the records Phillip Jones had bought in Oxford Street – and doing, thought Pete, not very well at all. However, he was offered the job, although he suspects that it was largely because not very many other people, if any, wanted it. Wages had escalated since the forties, and Pete was offered a whole £15 per week which, although an improvement over Teddy Johnson's £10, was somewhat less than a princely sum. But he accepted anyway, and in September 1950 he went to the Grand Duchy as a replacement for Teddy Johnson for three months.

While he was out there Pete was offered a film part back in England and Radio Luxembourg allowed him to return after only six weeks to take part in the James Stewart film 'No Highway'. When filming was complete he didn't really want to go back to Luxembourg at all, but he was honour bound to do so, and reluctantly made the trip again to complete the other six weeks of his contract. Five years later he was still there.

To begin with, Pete Murray stayed in a café called the Brasserie du

Théâtre frequented by most of the radio station's announcers, something which was possibly not totally unconnected with the fact that the owner, Herr Reisdorff, was – like Geoffrey Everitt – an Arsenal supporter. Luxembourg life – and the food, of course – had its usual effect and Pete Murray gradually became a permanent resident, stretching his £15 a week as far as a busy bachelor could do.

During the week the station broadcast from 10.30 p.m. until 1 a.m., but it was a different story on Sundays. Pete Murray worked all afternoon from 2 p.m. until 6 p.m. – hitting the by-now famous gong at frequent intervals – generally supplying the continuity announcements between pre-recorded and sponsored programmes like *Twenty Questions* or the £50,000 *Much Binding in the Marsh*. After a break of an hour – and a much-needed break at that, since two hours is a long time to be in a studio, never mind four – he would be back doing the same thing from 7 p.m. until 11 p.m. Then, just when he should have been collapsing into an armchair and/or a large drink, he went on again from 11 to midnight, not as continuity announcer but presenting the *Top Twenty Show* newly vacated by Teddy Johnson.

Following in other footsteps of Teddy Johnson Pete Murray found that his acting experience was extremely useful on radio. In the same way that Teddy Johnson had found it difficult to be on the air for nine or 10 hours at a stretch as the same person, Pete Murray also began to adopt various fictitious guises, except that he took it one stage further, and instead of switching his name and initials around Pete changed his voice to suit the programme he was presenting. Thus *Irish Half Hour*, instead of being introduced in the impeccable tones of E Victor Johnson, was now rather more colourfully presented in the lilting brogue of 'your own darlin' boy', Pete Murray. Later on, after Pete had been 'lumbered' with another ethnic half-hour the radio station received many letters from expatriate American listeners saying how nice it was to hear a programme of their kind of music introduced by 'an old-timer from back home', which was something of a surprise – and a compliment, indeed – to the presenter of *Cowboy's Lullaby*, 23-year-old Pete Murray.

Although the voice owed everything to Pete Murray and his stage training the style of presentation in a general sense stemmed more from Geoffrey Everitt than from anyone else. It was he who had told Pete that, in order to be successful in the new art of being a disc jockey, he would have to work without a script and ad-lib everything, a task which at first Pete thought he would never be able to manage, although he mastered it rather better than his first expectations had led him to believe.

Aside from the fact that actors necessarily work with a script it was still the accepted form of broadcasting on the BBC, and would be for many years to come. When Teddy Johnson, back from Luxembourg and a successful singer as well, did a two-week stint for the BBC on their morning programme, *Housewives' Choice*, in 1951 – the direct result of a hit record in November 1950 and the BBC policy of using 'name' presenters for short periods – he found that he was required to write a script and present the whole show from it. Even that wasn't good enough for the BBC, though, because although Teddy wrote a script and worked to it, he still used the same personal and conversational style which had been so much a part of his charm and attraction to Radio Luxembourg's listeners. His fortnight on the BBC began on Monday and by Thursday he was called to a script conference with his producer who told him that Higher Authority at the BBC 'didn't like' what he was doing. It was far too relaxed for the BBC and far too much like what he had been doing on Radio Luxembourg. Together they went through the rest of his scripts and painstakingly scrubbed out anything which was in any way 'personal', and took out, says Teddy, 'everything in them which was me'.

At the end of the week, on the Saturday morning, Teddy Johnson was called to the lady in charge of record programmes on the BBC (an entirely different person to whoever was in charge of Light Entertainment, and different again to the person in charge of 'live' music) and told that they hadn't liked what he had done on *Housewives' Choice*. It was eleven years before Teddy Johnson would sit in front of a microphone at Broadcasting House again.

But back in the Grand Duchy in 1951 Pete Murray, although allowed – and actively encouraged – to use his own personality with much more freedom than the BBC would permit at any time in the next 10 years, was still keeping to that gruelling Sunday schedule, which made it easy to see why not very many people relished the opportunity to work on Radio Luxembourg and easier still to see why £15 a week was not a great deal of money for the job in question. In fact if that situation had persisted for very much longer it is unlikely that Pete Murray would have stayed in the Grand Duchy beyond the early part of 1951, but several things happened which conspired to keep him there.

Perhaps least significant was the change of offices at Villa Louvigny. For years the English Service of Radio Luxembourg had occupied a basement room in the building after the extensive work which had been carried out there during the mid-thirties. This was a matter of convenience more than anything else, since the studio they used was also a basement room, yards away. This underground suite had been the location of the service right through the war years, and on his infrequent visits to Villa Louvigny Lord Haw Haw himself had made his propaganda broadcasts from the same basement studio and used the same basement offices in which Teddy Johnson conducted his culinary experiments with eggs and bacon.

However the basement was by now damp, airless and completely without windows, and after Pete Murray, with fellow presenter the late Peter Madren, had complained to the President of Radio Luxembourg they moved straight away into the spacious ground-floor office overlooking Luxembourg's Parc Municipal which is the station's home today. The old basement studio from which Lord Haw Haw and others made their broadcasts is now the record library of the English Service. Even without the shelving and the thousands of records cramming the place from floor to ceiling in every direction it is still a poky and dark little room.

And almost at the same time as the offices changed there was another, more important and far more public move. Right from the very earliest days Radio Luxembourg had earned the enmity and opposition of the BBC because it had pirated a Long Wave frequency which had not been allocated to it simply in order to beam commercially sponsored English Language programmes across the Channel to Great Britain. Now, just as audience figures were beginning to indicate the huge listenership which Radio Luxembourg would claim in the late fifties, all that was changed.

Although the English Service was large and successful the management of Radio Luxembourg could see that in the future the bulk of the advertising revenue would come from France, Germany and the Low Countries. For purely geographical reasons their signal would be far better received in these countries and there they would not meet with the same opposition which greeted their efforts in Britain. The Newspaper Publishers' Association still operated their total embargo on any mention of Radio Luxembourg, its programmes or its presenters, and still wanted all money due to the station in respect of advertising time to be blocked from leaving Britain.

Whichever way it was looked at the continental mainland seemed to be a far more lucrative source of sponsorship money than did Britain, and so it was decided that the Long Wave transmissions, with their stronger signal, should be given to the French Service. And although the English Service retained its late-night Short Wave frequency it was switched now to a Medium Wave signal which was exactly what the BBC had wanted 20 years previously, and on Monday 2nd July 1951 Radio Luxembourg began broadcasting on 208 Metres Medium Wave, which is exactly where they can be found today.

Although the change to Medium Wave affected the station's transmissions adversely – at least as far as we in Britain were concerned – it had a rather startling effect on Radio Luxembourg's audience, which began a rather amazing, if not actually meteoric climb. In part this can be attributed to the fact that Medium Wave was, and still is, the radio frequency with which the average radio listener feels most 'comfortable'. However, the main reasons for this owe more to outside influences.

The war had been over for six years by now. Rationing was still in existence (in Britain, anyway, although not in Luxembourg, which was a stroke of luck for Teddy Johnson, for his fry-ups would not have been possible had he been living in Britain) but was gradually being phased out – the Utility Goods System from the war was finally abandoned late in 1952. In almost all areas the war was fading from memory and a new atmosphere of excitement was prevalent (leading, of course, eventually to the point at which we'd 'never had it so good'). This was especially true in the world of entertainment. The BBC had resumed television broadcasts from Alexandra Palace as long ago as 1946 and now, in 1951, the cinema was beginning to operate at something like its former strength,

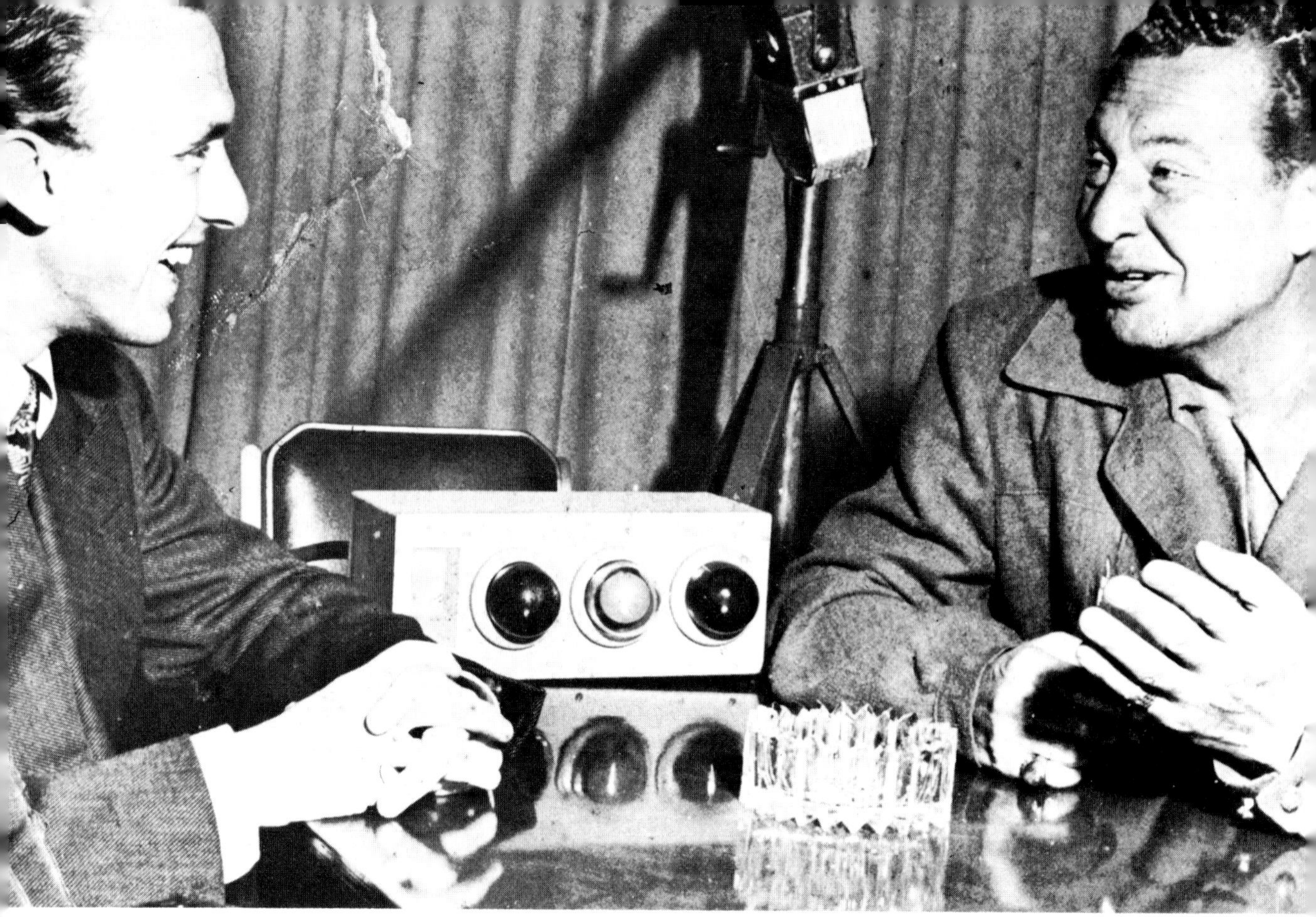

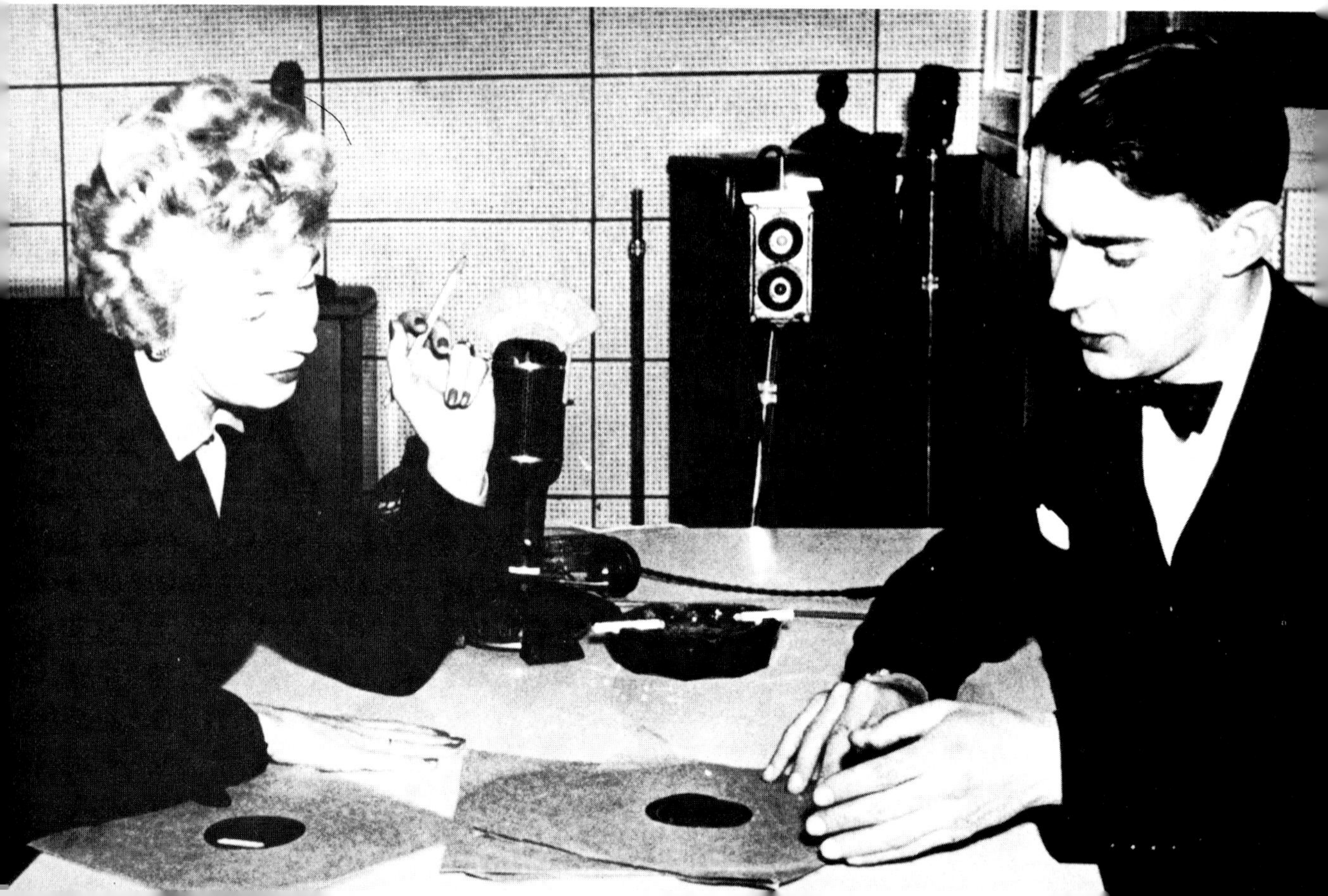

although TV would eventually ensure that it would never again rise to the dizzy ecstasies of the pre-war Hollywood dream factory. In 1951 the big films were such as *The African Queen* (Bogart and Hepburn), *An American in Paris* (Gene Kelly), *Oliver Twist* (Alec Guinness), *The Lavender Hill Mob* (Alec Guinness) and *A Streetcar Named Desire* (Vivien Leigh and Marlon Brando). On the stage Rogers and Hammerstein had just presented *South Pacific*, and the Bebop music which had emerged in about 1940 and had been perfected, like Benny Goodman's mid-thirties Swing, out of Jazz, now gave way to Cool Jazz and what was strangely termed New Music. Although singers like Eddie Fisher, Perry Como, Nat King Cole and Frank Sinatra ruled the roost another new kind of music – which American DJ Alan Freed would aptly christen rock'n'roll – was just around the corner.

In the early fifties, the time which Geoffrey Everitt, looking back on his lengthy and successful career with Radio Luxembourg, would see as the best time of all, excitement was in the air. Luxembourg's 208 schedules became even more popular. This was something which manifested itself to Pete Murray firstly by the huge increase in listeners' letters which accompanied the switch to Medium Wave, but also with the change in financial arrangements. Under the new scheme resident announcers were paid a bonus of £3 (a minimum figure, let it be said) if any advertising time was bought into their programmes. Bear in mind that the major way in which commercial messages got on to the air was still by the purchase of airtime which was then filled with pre-recorded material using the sponsor's own presenters. It was in this direction that most of the selling impetus from Radio Luxembourg was directed and it was here that they made most of their profit. The additional purchase of advertising inserts during the request programmes or the Top Twenty – which is the way in which everything is done today – was regarded as being something extra, and the amount of adverts being bought in during any programme were as a direct result of the presenter's popularity – hence the £3.

This was an arrangement with which Pete Murray at least was extremely happy, for it altered his financial status drastically. From being paid £15 he shot suddenly to the point at which he could reasonably expect an income between £100 and £150 per week which was, as he says, 'more like it', and definitely made it worth remaining in Luxembourg.

So while Pete stayed on, playing the melodies of the period with Dick Norton and Peter Madren, Geoffrey Everitt returned to London and the Hertford Street studios to share the job of producing the pre-recorded and sponsored material with Phillip Jones, who had now climbed above his 'dogsbody' status. The live, request programmes consisted largely of hits from across the Atlantic either from films or musicals, and were either the original version or – more likely on the sponsored programmes – cover versions of the same records by British artists. The pre-recorded programmes which Phillip Jones and Geoffrey Everitt were making

Above
Teddy Johnson interviews American Phil Harris (left) in the summer of 1950 when Harris was appearing at the London Palladium with Jack Benny.
Below
Phillip Jones and Anne Shelton in the London Studio.

consisted, apart from record programmes, of panel and quiz games. Some of these were made outside Hertford Street, either before live audiences or in other commercial studios like Hector Ross Radio Productions, put together by people like John Whitney and Monty Bailey-Watson. They made items like *What's My Line*, a panel game featuring people like Barbara Kelly, Lady Isobel Barnet, David Nixon and Richard Attenborough – who also appeared on the programme *Princess for a Day*, which was a sort of *Jim'll Fix It* of radio except that it was for women only.

John Whitney, who describes himself at the age of 20 as a 'spotty' youth who had left school in 'ignominy' and under the headmaster's judgement that he was completely 'unemployable', was quite determined that his future lay in radio. In fact for a short while he was engaged in the manufacture of seed-boxes and coffins, at about the same time that his application for a job at the BBC was refused; it would be twenty years before he returned – to lunch with Alastair Milne. Meanwhile the young Whitney bought himself a wire recorder and a disc cutter and set about making his own recordings. Mostly they were of church bells, but later he graduated to sound recordings of Bar Mitzvahs which he scouted from the *Jewish Chronicle* each week; copies of each event were sold for the handsome sum of one guinea each.

As experience of editing, interviewing and producing a compact and comprehensible record of such events led to better things John Whitney arrived eventually in Hertford Street, offering his independent services to Radio Luxembourg. However, they too turned him away, possibly because they viewed him as a competitor.

Eventually, with Monty Bailey-Watson and school friend Joe Sturge, Hector Ross Radio Productions was formed with offices in New Cavendish Street. The name came from a well-known actor of the period and was chosen simply because the three of them quite liked it – Hector Ross was not connected with the company.

The company did extremely well extremely quickly with shows like *Music of the Stars* and with their own large touring shows. The essence of these was the size of the audiences, and as they were, of course, sponsors the companies in question could turn each recording session (at the Royal Festival Hall or the Albert Hall or similarly-sized venues) into a major PR exhibition and trade show. It was an arrangement which suited everybody rather well, and Hector Ross Radio Productions soon had 32 shows each week on Radio Luxembourg. One of the touring shows, *People Are Funny*, was top of the 208 ratings for years. Recording for people like Pye, Curry's, Grundig and Gillette, Hector Ross Radio were also using as many big-name artists as they could. Pet Clark was recording *Music For You*, Pete Murray was doing his usual fine job for Curry's, Jonathan Routh was the man who launched *Candid Mike* and would later take it on to television as *Candid Camera*, Peter West was involved with the *Gillette Sports Parade*, and David Jacobs, Donald Sinden, Bob Danvers Walker and Larry Cross all visited the IBC studios in Portland Place which was where all the Hector Ross Radio programmes were made.

These studios were rather luxurious in comparison to the offices which Hector Ross Radio occupied at the time. Although the company went through a succession of offices before ending up in Harley Street they were all somewhat tatty, and belied the fact that the company was doing so well. In fact they had bought into TV via the Autocue system and owned their own radio station in the Caribbean – Radio Antilles – all this out of the profits made from recording half-hour shows which generally cost the sponsor around £60–70 completed and packaged, although there was still the cost of the airtime to pay; that money, though, went straight to Radio Luxembourg. In fact the offices were generally located in flats which were not intended for the purpose, and when visits from the landlord were expected all office equipment was hidden, the place was liberally sprinkled with old coffee-cups and dog-ends and occasionally the secretaries were bundled into old dressing-gowns and just hung around the place looking sluttish to add a bit of atmosphere to the deception.

In the mid-fifties the advent of television knocked the bottom straight out of the lucrative market which had grown up based on Radio Luxembourg; the station itself was having trouble filling airtime and there was little room for what, up until then, had been their largest competitor. Hector Ross Radio Productions didn't just fold up on the spot, but it began to shrink dramatically, even though the coming of TV had been long anticipated by John Whitney and others, and today it is no more. Monty Bailey-Watson died in the early seventies, but not before he'd seen his brainchild survive the coming of TV and go on to master the new medium at least as well as anybody else. John Whitney went on to be Managing Director of Capital Radio and then Director-General of the IBA – not a bad record for someone deemed 'unemployable'.

But while Hector Ross Radio Productions were busy staking out a claim to their own piece of broadcasting history, out in the grand Duchy of Luxembourg Pete Murray was busy forging a bit of his own, when he became the first person to use the most Anglo-Saxon of four-letter words on air. The Luxembourg studio was operated by the engineers, sitting in a separate control booth and separated from the presenter's studio by a sheet of glass. In front of him the announcer had three buttons. One operated the gong, one was a 'cough' button (which shuts off the microphone for precisely this purpose) and the other signalled to the engineer when records should be started. This signal lamp was a highly desirable item since most of the engineers spoke little or no English. As a rule their full-time occupation would be as engineers on the French or German Services during the daytime and they would earn extra by doing overtime by working weekday evenings and weekends on the English Service. Which means that it would not be terribly unjust to say that their concern for the technical and artistic standards of the programmes on 208 was hardly what you might describe as earnest. But they had a running order for the evening (or the day), put on and cued up the records or tapes and started them when the announcer pressed the button.

Often records would be played at the wrong speed, or on the wrong side or even the wrong record entirely would be on the turntable. Teddy Johnson used to apologise and explain that the mistake was that of the engineer who had accordingly just been shot – an announcement he says he wouldn't dream of making today since it is far too believable.

However, on this particular day Pete Murray had just introduced the latest episode of the science-fiction serial *Dan Dare* (which was a regular and popular show on Luxembourg for some time) and relaxed back to speak to music publisher Roy Berry, who was visiting the Villa Louvigny at the time. The engineer had contrived to put on a recording of Felix King at the piano rather than the latest thrilling instalment of *Dan Dare*. 'Oh God,' said the distressed Pete Murray, 'he's put on the wrong f***ing programme.' That, sadly, was not all the engineer had done wrong. He had also left the microphone fader open as an accusing red light on the studio wall indicated, and several hundred thousand people were treated to a historic moment on radio. Most of them laughed, fortunately, although Pete didn't think it would be that funny. He denied having said that particular word, claiming instead that he'd said 'wrong flipping programme', when the British Press rang up (the *Daily Mirror* were first) and felt certain that he would lose his job as a result.

He didn't though, which was lucky for him, because a DJ in the same circumstances today could easily get the sack – many have had it for less – even though it's a commonplace expression on TV, and this all took place in 1953, when there wasn't really very much television in existence for people to say much worse things on.

But it was coming. In 1953 the Americans were actually conducting their first experiments in colour television, although the first commercial TV companies wouldn't go on the air in Britain until summer of 1955. For now Marlon Brando had just expressed the feeling of the youngsters, the first generation of war babies who couldn't remember the Depression and were growing up in the never-had-it-so-good society. The film was *The Wild One*. 'What are you rebelling against?' Brando was asked. Reclining on his motorbike in jeans and leather jacket, with semi-military cap pulled over his eyes, 'What have you got?' he replied. James Dean would be next, *Rebel Without a Cause* was due out in 1955. But before then Bill Haley's 'Rock Around the Clock' released in 1954, received less acclaim than did his cover version of Joe Turner's R&B single 'Shake, Rattle and Roll'. It was not until the song was used as title music for the anti-establishment film *Blackboard Jungle* – and by early 1955 became a number one hit in both Britain and America – that it was recognised as *the* classic song which introduced the rock'n'roll era.

5: ROCK 'N' ROLL

1955 was a fairly big year for the media in Great Britain. It marked the opening of the first commercial television stations and released a flood of creative potential in the entertainment business which whirled Britain to the forefront as a source of creative excellence. It is not true to say that this happened only because of ITV or that it would never have happened without it, but it could never have happened so quickly and in the same way had it been only the BBC who were around. The BBC had, by the mid-fifties, established a fairly permanent character which still persists. They were very good – excellent – at what they did, and the quality of BBC output was (and is) generally second to none. But they only did what they were used to doing and resisted change strenuously until someone – Radio Luxembourg, ITV or the pirate radio ships – made them alter course.

It was also a year of change at Radio Luxembourg, partly occasioned by the advent of the new TV stations and partly for other reasons. The most public change was the departure of a number of people who had been associated with the station for a considerable period of time, especially behind the microphone. Pete Murray departed in 1955 to resume – although only briefly – his acting career. Changes were taking place in the financial structure. It had become apparent that Pete and his colleagues were earning a great deal of money – more, in fact, than the President of the company – and so the 'bonus' payment for advertising time was abolished in favour of an annual profit-related bonus which is still paid to every employee at about Easter each year. The immediate effect as far as Pete was concerned was to reduce his income from a possible £150 a week to a maximum of £20, so he left almost at once, returning to England to resume acting. He continued to appear on 208, though, as a presenter of pre-recorded shows sent out from London, but his choice of music was rather more limited than it had been. In fact it was limited to records produced by one company, Decca, something which he, and later presenters of programmes sponsored by various record companies, found both irksome and boring. The result was that by 1956 he had abandoned radio in favour of acting on TV, with a starring role in a highly acclaimed play, *The Last Enemy*. He waited some 10 months for another role without any luck before returning to life as a disc jockey, and the rest, as the expression goes, is history.

Also departing from Radio Luxembourg was Phillip Jones. Wireless Publicity had been replaced by Radio Luxembourg London Ltd in 1954 and it was this company that Phillip Jones forsook to pursue a career in television, starting first as a lowly trainee director (at an equally lowly salary) before progressing through the ranks of his new medium. He is currently Head of Light Entertainment at London Weekend Television. The job he had shared now devolved on to one person, and in 1955

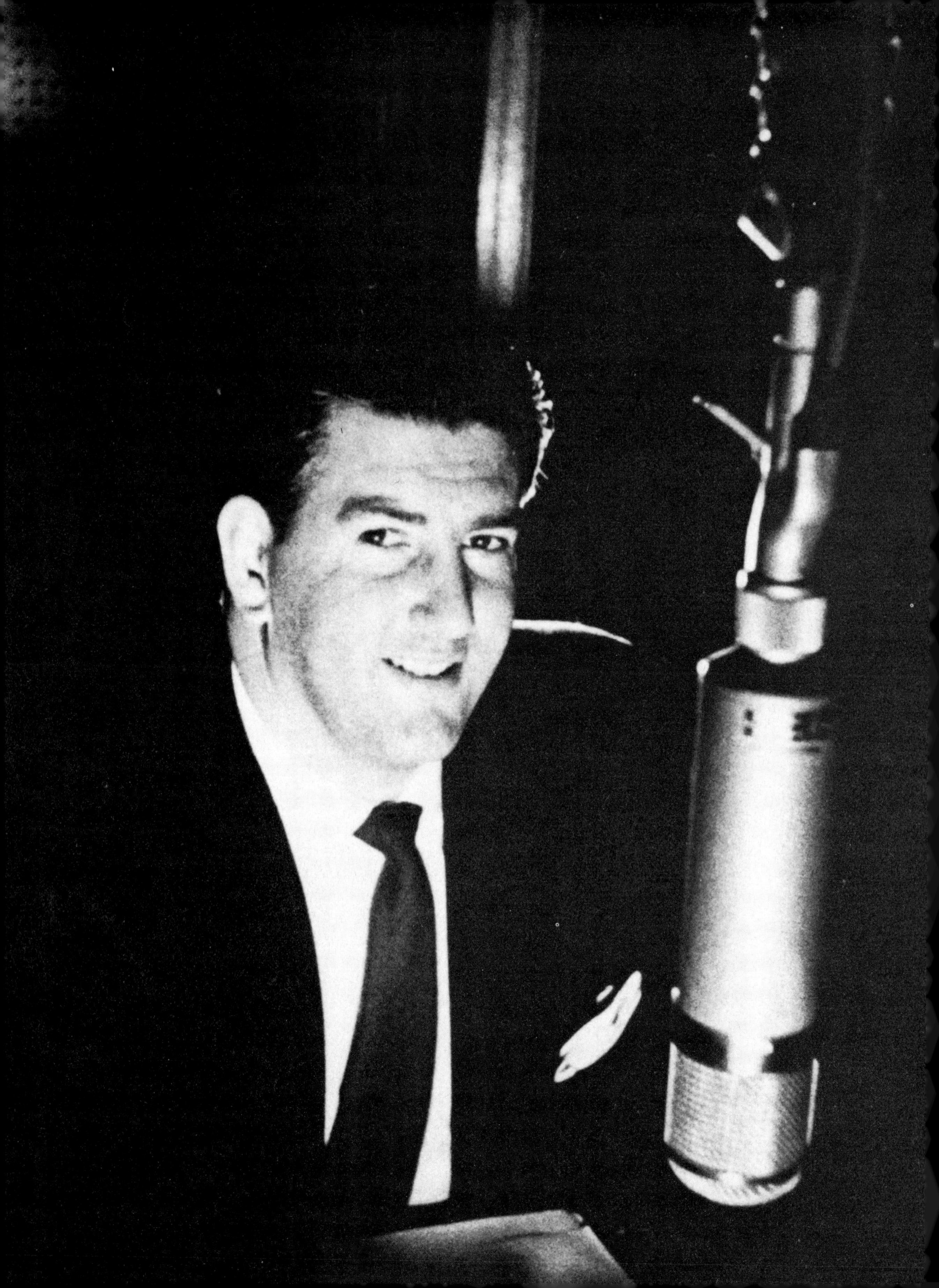

Geoffrey Everitt became Radio Luxembourg's Chief Producer, in charge of all the output from the London studios.

Out in the Grand Duchy the lineup was changing too, and getting much larger than it had been previously. Pete Murray's replacement arrived in Luxembourg on the day that the very first commercial television broadcast was made in Britain, 22 September 1955. While everyone else was forsaking radio to get into television here was someone who left a job as one of BBC TV's original sports commentators to go into radio.

Like Phillip Jones, Keith Fordyce had been in the RAF, stationed in Germany, counting, as he says, crates of baked beans for the RAF, when he wangled his way into the British Forces Network in Hamburg. After a brief spell there and another freelancing wherever he could, he had moved into BBC TV and from there on to *Housewives' Choice* in 1955. Then he heard that everyone was leaving Luxembourg to work for ITV and so went along to Hertford Street to see if there was a job going. The answer, in what was by now typical Radio Luxembourg style, was 'Yes, if you can leave within seven days'. Keith Fordyce was given an air ticket and £10 in cash and sent to Luxembourg forthwith, although he overslept on the morning of his departure and nearly didn't make it there at all.

When he arrived in the Grand Duchy his colleagues were Peter Madren, David Gell, Mel Oxley and Dick Norton (who left almost straight away) and, once again in true Luxembourg style, he was on the air the day after his arrival. This was a little slower than usual – most new recruits seemed to have got straight off a train or a plane and walked into a studio without having time to take off their coat.

But Keith Fordyce was soon doing the usual variety of programmes in short order. As had previously been the case most of the live presentation consisted largely of request programmes which were threaded in around the sponsored shows which came out from London. And since advertisers always wanted the peak listening spots it meant that, as a rule, the request programmes occupied the beginning and end of the day's scheduling, with the musical, quiz and talent shows filling in the bulk of the evening. However, sponsorship was everywhere, and since request shows also had keen audiences of their own there were often sponsors who would sponsor fifteen minutes of a show, so that an hour-long request programme would be brought to the audience by up to four different people during its 60 minutes. In addition there was sponsorship from H Samuel, so that during the hour the frequent timechecks were courtesy of them – 'and now the time by my H Samuel Everite watch is . . .' – as well as mention of the various people who had chosen to sponsor that particular 15 minutes – BMK Carpets and a plethora of football pools tipsters.

For the rest of the time there was a variety of other shows. *Dan Dare* was on for 15 minutes every night thanks to the generosity of the Horlicks Company, there was a programme sponsored by the Italian

Barry Alldis hosted many late night request programmes.

State Tourist Office called *Italy Sings* and there were other shows, which are better known than that. Eamonn Andrews was by now in charge of *Princess for a Day* but Hughie Green was presenting two shows, both recorded before an audience, *Double Your Money*, a quiz game, and a talent contest called *Opportunity Knocks*. These two highly successful programmes, together with another popular show, *Take Your Pick* presented by Michael Miles, went on to become even more successful on television than they had been on radio. *Opportunity Knocks*, in particular, ran for years, lasting into the late seventies on ITV. There were other shows as well; the forerunner of television's *Candid Camera* appeared first on Radio Luxembourg in the fifties and was generally well received, except by the gentleman whose house was flattened in the course of a joke suggested by his wife. It wasn't that bad, since it was a pre-fab of the kind which had of necessity sprung up after the war and which were now being demolished and replaced by council housing. Even so the poor chap who came home from work and found his house in ruins failed to see the funny side of it all, which is perhaps not terribly surprising.

He was, luckily, only one out of the radio station's huge audience. The listeners were attracted to Luxembourg partly by the friendly atmosphere which the station had created for itself right from the very beginning and partly thanks to the preponderance of big names which appeared regularly on 208 – more regularly than they did on the BBC. Warren Mitchell had tried being a disc jockey, working as a summer replacement for a few weeks, but he didn't like it and didn't stay. David Gell and Mel Oxley left in 1956 and were replaced by Barry Alldis and Howard Williams. He left after a year and Don Moss arrived in the Grand Duchy to complete the three-man lineup now headed by Chief Announcer Keith Fordyce. But coming from London on tape were any number of well-known stars: Beryl Reid (*Tuesday Requests*), Basil Rathbone (*Masterspy*), Richard Murdoch (*Wednesday Requests*), Sam Costa (*Record Club*), Pete Murray (*The Voice of Prophecy*), Jack Jackson (*Record Roundup*), Tommy Trinder (*You Lucky People*), Alan Freed (*Jamboree*), Winifred Atwell (*The Winifred Atwell Show*), Jack Good, Jimmy Young, Jimmy Savile, Alan Freeman, Jo Stafford, Cliff Richard, Patrick Allen, Bryan Johnson, Ronnie Aldrich, Ray Orchard, Kent Walton and David Jacobs. And they, if you please, were merely some of the people who were *presenting* shows on Radio Luxembourg in and around 1956, 1957 and 1958. The list of theatrical and musical artists who appeared in those shows or who appeared in hour-long specials, all recorded in London for Radio Luxembourg, is even longer and even more impressive.

In 1955, when it came to playing records, Radio Luxembourg was more important than the BBC. Several records banned by the BBC on religious grounds ('Answer Me' by David Whitfield and 'Hold my Hand' by Don Cornell) became best sellers simply because they were played on Luxembourg – they were not heard anywhere else. This amply demonstrated the power of Radio Luxembourg and at the same time illustrated

Above
Masters of disguise, Barry Alldis (left) and Keith Fordyce.
Below
The office of the English Service at Villa Louvigny, Alldis and Fordyce clowning as usual.

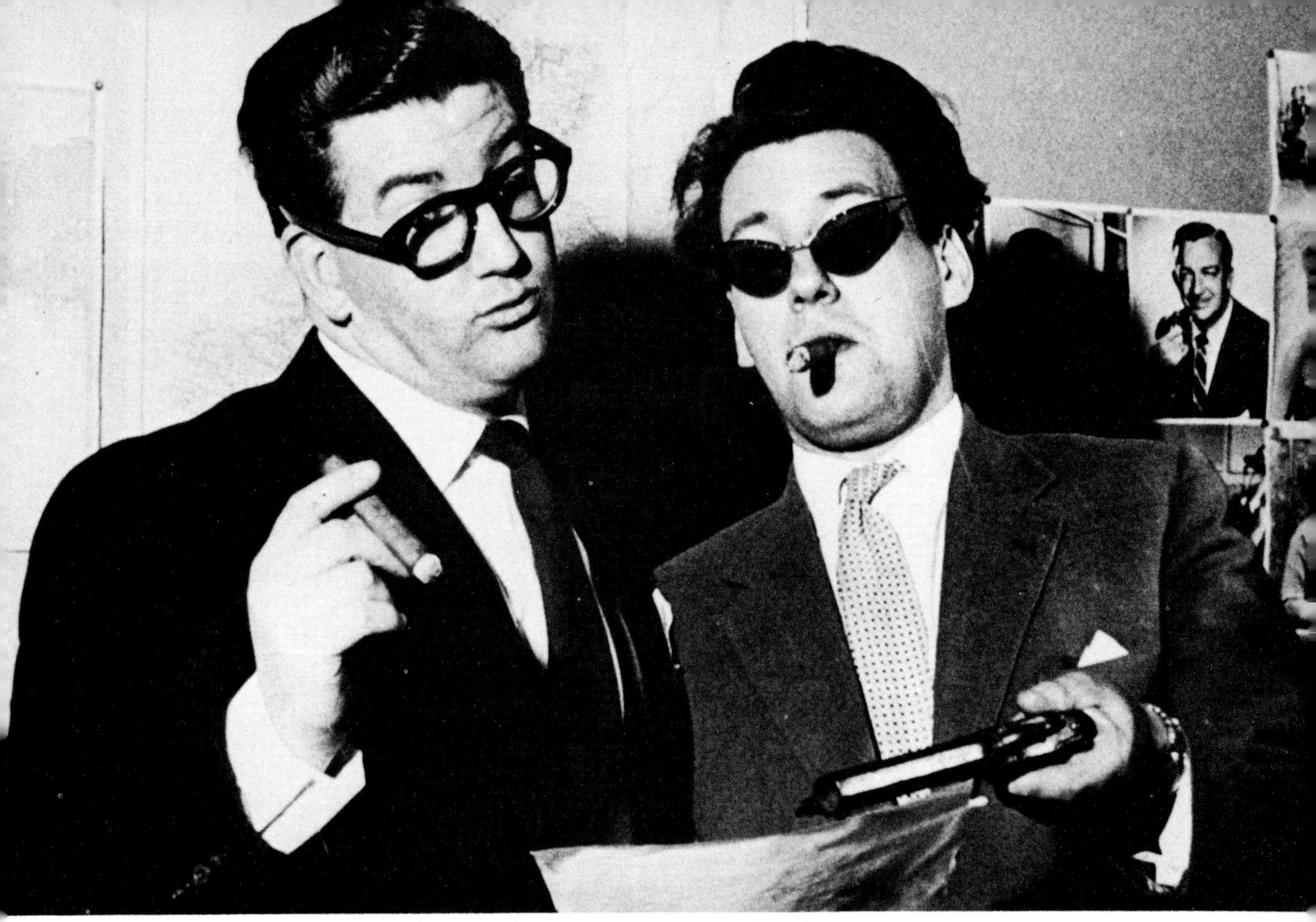

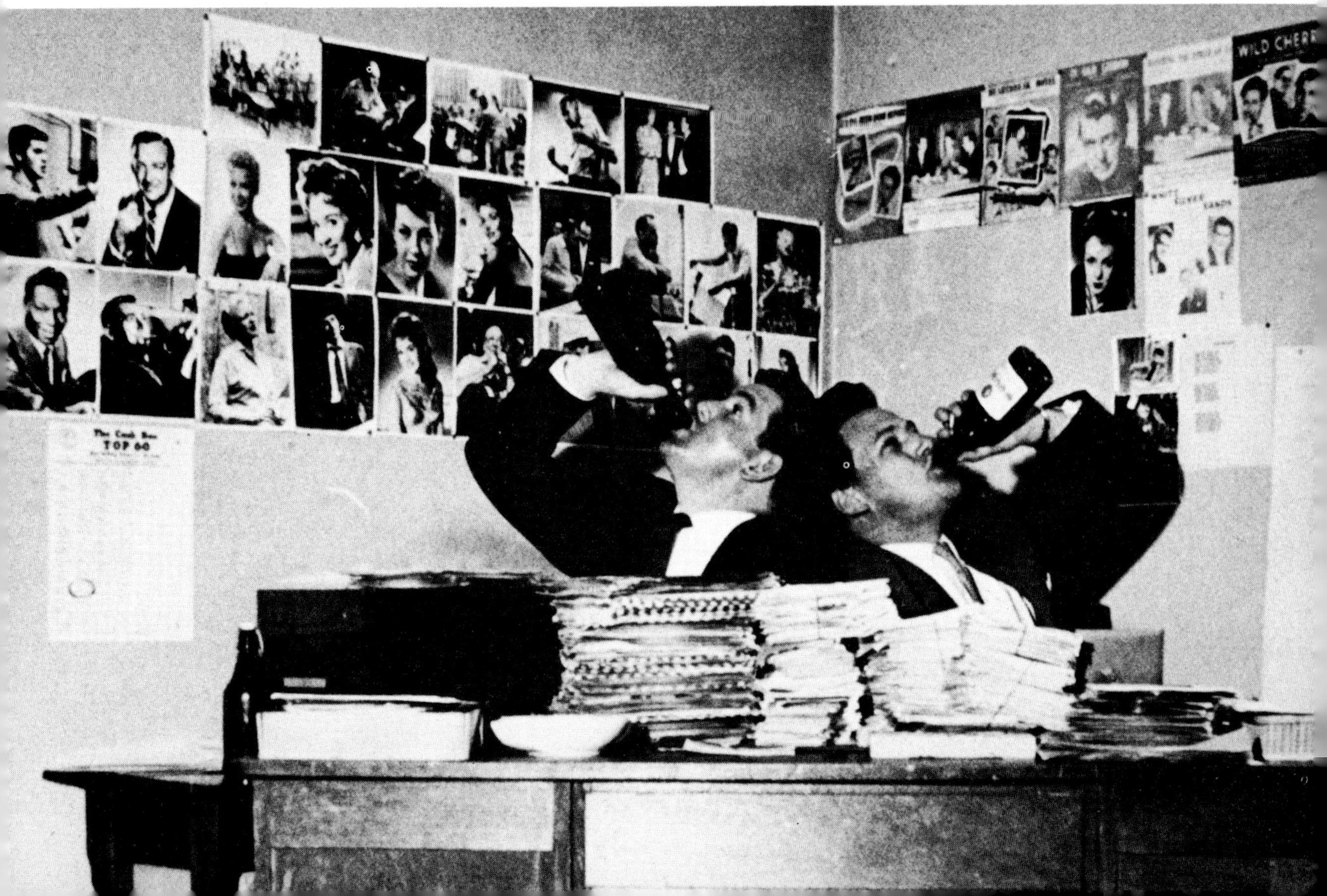
WILD CHERR
The Cash Box
TOP 60

the BBC's continuing inability or refusal to come to grips with its audience and supply what was required rather than what was deemed suitable. In consequence of this the record companies, and that included the American ones, directed their major efforts at Radio Luxembourg rather than the BBC. New records were sent to the Grand Duchy rather than to Broadcasting House, and frequently American publishers or record company bosses made lengthy transatlantic phone calls to speak with the DJ team. 'It may not have been particularly innovative by now,' says Keith Fordyce, 'but it was unique and tremendously exciting.'

He was lucky to be there, though. Within a few weeks of starting on Radio Luxembourg he and fellow-conspirator David Gell were both in big trouble. At one point during the evening David Gell handed over to Keith Fordyce and they were obliged to read an advert for the *Sunday Pictorial*. It had to be done live and it had to involve two voices, who each took it in turns to read a number of hard-sell lines in a loud and aggressive fashion more than passingly similar to early eighties TV advertising for the *Sun*. On one occasion, just before handover, these two announcers began a quick rehearsal of the night's advert for the *Sunday Pictorial*.

'Gilbert Harding is a hit,' shouted David Gell, before dissolving into hysterical mirth, which was shared by Keith Fordyce. They had several tries but laughed each time, and the eventual 'live' reading seemed doomed to certain disaster. On the hour, at the moment of handover, David Gell launched himself into the advert.

'Gilbert Harding is a hit,' he shouted, followed by thirty seconds of helpless giggling. Although both of them were strictly censured they kept their jobs. Just.

There was another, more serious side to the affair, in that it shows quite clearly that by now the newspapers in Britain recognised that Radio Luxembourg was a force to be reckoned with and one which could no longer be entirely ignored, despite what the NPA may have to say about total embargos. Although there was not – and never has been since – anything like a complete relaxation of the ban or widespread newspaper coverage of the station and its programme schedules, one or two publications began to have rather more to do with Radio Luxembourg than was previously the case. Before the war there had been *Radio Pictorial* and the *Sunday Referee*. Now, after the war, there was *TitBits*, which by 1957 was 'the official periodical for Radio Luxembourg programmes' and, increasingly, the *Daily Mirror*, who took a more than passing interest in goings-on in the Grand Duchy.

This was only right and proper too, since the British recording industry, which was largely gaining acceptance and recognition through the good offices of Radio Luxembourg rather than the BBC, was clearly something to be proud of and required coverage of its own. At the time the cover version was still the accepted way of going about things, which meant that the British Top Twenty was little more than an anglicised mirror of what was happening across the Atlantic, and British recording artists had a fairly small chance of making a big hit unless it had already

Alan Freeman taped most of his shows in Hertford Street but also did summer relief in the Grand Duchy.

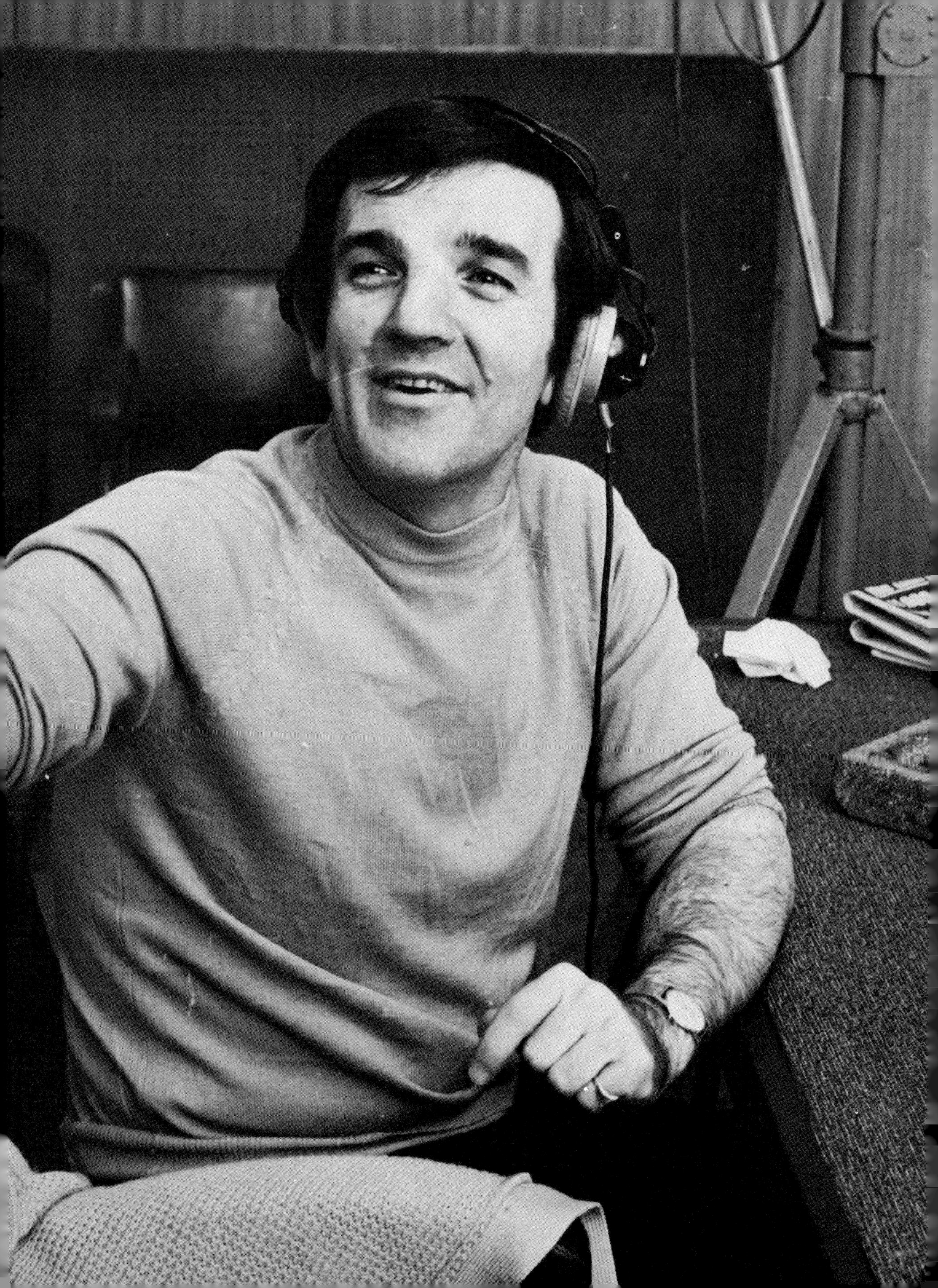

JO STAFFORD

Luxembourg's dearest friend from across the Atlantic is undoubtedly lovely Jo Stafford.

Jo has seldom been **off the air** since her remarkable rise to fame **many years ago**. Her sincerity, great warmth and tremendous ability have ensured for **her a** permanent place in the hearts of 208 listeners.

Don't forget to tune in on Monday evening at 9.15, when once again Jo and a famous guest artist will be reminding us all that it's time for a song on

THE JO STAFFORD SHOW

ALAN FREEMAN

is once again visiting the **Grand Duchy** as 208's Summer Relief Announcer, while Barry, Don and Ted take their well-earned holidays.

Alan will be heard on **several programmes** each week during the next few months, and this week he will be presenting

SPIN WITH THE STARS
Monday and Friday at 11.00 p.m.

TUESDAY'S AND THURSDAY'S REQUESTS
7.30 p.m.

SATURDAY JAZZ TIME
Saturday at 9.00 p.m.

and joining **Don Moss in** the zaniest programme of all

Pages from one of the Radio Luxembourg programme schedules which regularly featured the station's disc jockeys.

Tit-Bits
EVERY MONDAY 4½d.

The Official Publication for Radio Luxembourg

Hurry for this week's number, and place a regular order with your newsagent!

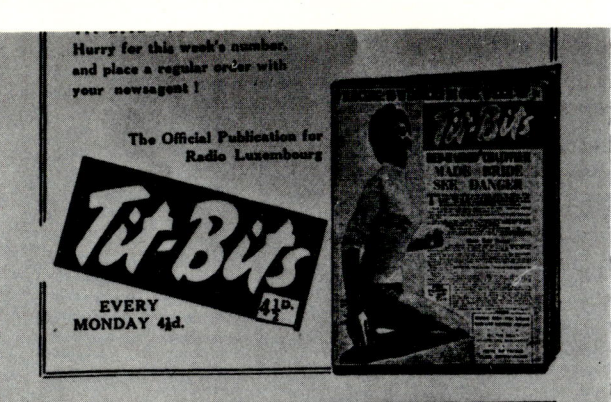

Popular Radio Personality
PETER WEST
will be spinning the discs for you in

YOUR RECORD DATE
ON MONDAYS at 11.15 p.m.

and

RECORD HOP
ON FRIDAYS at 10.30 p.m.

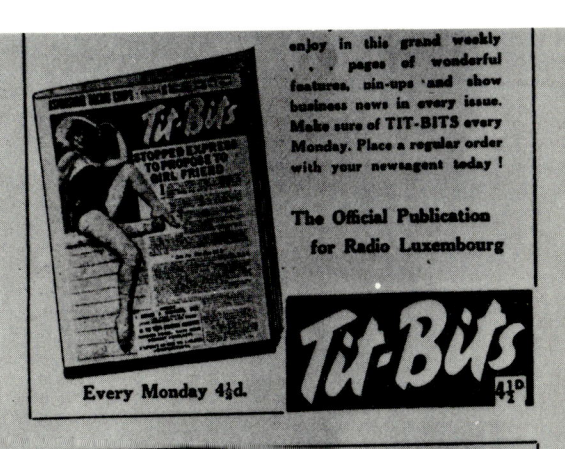

Tit-Bits
Every Monday 4½d.

The Official Publication for Radio Luxembourg

enjoy in this grand weekly pages of wonderful features, pin-ups and show business news in every issue. Make sure of TIT-BITS every Monday. Place a regular order with your newsagent today!

BARRY ALLDIS
INTRODUCES
THOSE ROCKIN' BOYS
ELVIS PRESLEY
AND
CLIFF RICHARD
ON
WEDNESDAYS
AT
9.45 p.m.

been one for somebody else.

But now, from 1955 onwards, all that was changing. Two records demonstrate the shift better than most. One of them was a song which is now a pop classic, recorded by someone who is now a pop superstar – Paul Anka. In 1957, the year that Danny and the Juniors released 'At the Hop' and the Everly Brothers had number one hits with 'Bye Bye Love' and 'Wake Up Little Susie', Paul Anka released 'Diana'. For the first time ever a record which had so far done nothing for Paul Anka in America, reached number one in Britain before it did so in the USA. This was almost solely due to its extensive airplay on Radio Luxembourg, where the presenters were in the habit of playing records which they liked rather than records which were already popular or had already been hits overseas. Almost by itself Radio Luxembourg gave Paul Anka a number one smash – nine weeks at the top in 1957 – in Britain and then, as a direct result of its British success, also in America. For the first time the British music industry had a voice of its own which was demonstrably as powerful as the Americans.

The next step was the hardest and most necessary. At least as influential, if not more so, than Radio Luxembourg, was a new television programme created by the legendary Jack Good. Filmed on stage in London before audiences of hysterically sobbing teenagers, *Oh Boy* gave the public the chance to see their idols, and the sultry, smouldering attitude which most of them affected in sincere imitation of their idol, Elvis Presley (billed on Radio Luxembourg in 1958 as 'Elvis (the Pelvis) Presley') in no small way accounted for much of their success and aided what were frequently rather second-rate covers of American rock'n'roll hits. Most of the singers and groups paraded before the cameras on *Oh Boy* were destined for instant obscurity or, at best, passing fame as one-hit-wonders. There were a number of exceptions to the rule, most notably, perhaps, Marty Wilde and Billy Fury.

But *Oh Boy*'s big success story made his debut on 15 September 1958. He'd turned professional just four weeks previously and his first record, on the EMI label, had been a cover version of a Bobby Helms song – 'Schoolboy Crush'. And as *TitBits* had faithfully reported the previous year, the way that the British recording industry survived was by making cover versions and then slapping almost anything on the B side. The payoff came if the cover version went into the charts; royalties for the A side went across the Atlantic, but royalties for the B side stayed in Britain, just as if it was the writer of the song on the B side who had penned a big hit.

In keeping with this amicable arrangement, Norrie Paramor allowed his new artist to put what he wanted on the B side of 'Schoolboy Crush' and it was this supposedly second-rate number which electrified Jack Good and prompted that very first TV appearance in late 1958. It was beyond any doubt the very first entirely home-grown rock'n'roll song with any merit whatsoever, and it went straight into the top three, the cover version of the American hit on the so-called A side completely ignored. It was the first of an endless string of hit singles for the most popular British entertainer since the war, and by 1960 he'd had three number one records and seven others in the top ten. Written by guitarist Ian Samwell, 'Move It' was a rip-roaring success, although its rendition owed slightly more to the hip wriggling of Elvis Presley than it did to the singer himself, Cliff Richard.

Along with rock'n'roll, Radio Luxembourg was riding the crest of a wave. In 1955 the listening figures had reached an all-time peak; a daily audience of 8.9 million was staggering by any standards. In 1957 the transmitter power was increased in what was seen at the time to be something of a gamble in the face of the onrushing threat of commercial television. Three hundred thousand pounds was spent to boost the transmitter power to 300 kilowatts, the project coming to completion just at the time when ITV was making serious inroads into the Radio Luxembourg advertising revenue – from 1955 onwards profits began to fall. There was a serious error in programming which allowed this to happen, because when ITV went off the air at about 11 p.m. and Radio Luxembourg alone had access to an audience susceptible to sponsors' messages their airtime was given over to a series of religious broadcasts largely consisting of indigestible chunks of Billy Graham, biblical tub-thumper extraordinaire. Unsurprisingly the Luxembourg audience fell by at least 75 per cent as soon as the programmes began and were lost for the rest of the evening – as was the revenue which accompanies big audience figures. It was 1962 before this situation could be changed, and the religious programming placed at the beginning of each evening's schedules, where it has since remained.

Apart from a vast expenditure on the new transmitter Radio Luxembourg began a big spend on personalities in the autumn of 1957, in schedule changes which were so important that they were actually announced through *TitBits*, presumably in the hope that the announcement would be enough to stem the rapid decline in audience figures as more and more people got into the television habit each evening.

The changes for autumn centred principally around a far bigger and better set of programmes devoted to listeners' requests presented by people of proven popularity – MacDonald Hobley (already well-known on television), George Elrick, Libby Morris, Beryl Reid, Richard Murdoch, Teddy Johnson and Ronnie Aldrich. The request show was destined to last for two hours each evening, using more 'live' performances from people like Joe Loss, Norrie Paramor, Ronnie Aldrich, The Big Ben Banjo Band, Rose Brennan, Tony Brent, Ken Kirkham and Don Cameron, all big names of the time.

Of course none of the 'live' performances were actually live; there was still no landline between London and Luxembourg and the cost of shipping the entire Joe Loss Orchestra (or any of the other big bands of the time) out to the Grand Duchy – where the studios at the Villa Louvigny were certainly large enough to accommodate them – was prohibitive, and that's putting it mildly. All of the bands, and most of the singers, were recorded in London and the tapes were sent out for later transmission. Covering up for this single biggest deficiency in their facilities was old hat to Radio Luxembourg, though. Right through the thirties they had developed a technique of presenting recorded material as if it was live without actually telling fibs, even pretending that they had the BBC's own Henry Hall live in their studios, and this was still a regular feature of their presentation.

Despite this handicap and the fall in audience figures Radio Luxembourg was still the major force in European radio. In 1958 it was rumoured that one or several ITV companies were trying to buy control or at least a major interest in the radio station, although this is not confirmed. Even if it were true it is far more likely that their ambition was to stifle a competitor rather than develop a potential source of income. At least it is indicative that the ITV companies believed that Luxembourg was damaging them as much as they were damaging Luxembourg.

And in 1959, when 208 was blasting out continual pop music 48 hours a week (out of a possible 56 hours on-air total), five youths in East Germany were sentenced to five years each in prison for listening to radio stations outside Germany, in particular Radio Luxembourg. 1959 was also the year that Herr Ulbricht said that Elvis Presley and Radio Luxembourg between them were diverting the attention of young people away from the Free German Youth Movement, for which doubtless the young people were grateful, even if Ulbricht was displeased.

In the late fifties, with the sole exception of 1955, Radio Luxembourg's audience figures were as good as they had ever been; the station was in a position of enormous strength. It could hardly have surprised anyone to hear that yet again the Post Office, in 1958, turned down a request from Radio Luxembourg for landline facilities between their London studios in Hertford Street and Villa Louvigny, yet they still made application. Denied all the facilities which most radio stations take for granted Radio Luxembourg continued to flourish.

Back in the Grand Duchy itself the lineup was changing again. Keith Fordyce had lived through the *Sunday Pictorial* crisis and had survived a show with David Gell in which his co-presenter had been afflicted with hiccups. He had almost always remembered to stick a piece of white paper over that one of the two studio clocks which read French time (an hour different to British time) so that he wouldn't inadvertently read the wrong one and he had got through two other serious incidents unscathed. One was a tangled reel of tape containing the voice of Royalty (which Royalty was generally believed to be physically present in the studio by the audience) which was being untangled and stuck back together by assorted technicians and presenters working all down the length of a corridor. At the end of the corridor it was going in through the studio door, into a tape machine and straight out on the air while less than 100 feet away the closing passages of the stirring address were still tied in knots. The other was faithfully recorded in the pages of the *Daily Mirror*, and concerned a jammed door into the studio. Keith Fordyce was outside the door, while trapped inside was a non-English speaking Luxembourg announcer who was just about to close down for the day and hand the 208 transmitter over to the English Service. As he made the relevant announcement the English Service was in fact legging it downstairs to another studio, clutching records, tapes, adverts, announcements and all the other paraphernalia. It was, in a word, panic.

But Keith Fordyce forsook all this in favour of a career back in England and returned to make a TV series with Pete Murray which was cancelled on the day he arrived back in England in September 1958, three years since he had departed. Later, of course, it all worked out for him with programmes like ITV's Friday evening pop show, *Ready Steady Go*, but in the meantime Keith, like so many other past residents of the Grand Duchy, began taping sponsored programmes in London.

Behind him he left a gap as Head of the English Service which was filled by expatriate Aussie Barry Alldis, who had joined the station in 1956. Born in New South Wales in 1930, when Radio Luxembourg had been little more than a gleam in the eye of various wireless enthusiasts, Barry's Public School education had led him into a music scholarship at the Sydney Conservatoire of Music and then into radio, first on station 2TM in Tamworth and later 4BH in Brisbane.

He came to London in 1955 and unsuccessfully applied for a job on Radio Luxembourg (almost certainly as Pete Murray's replacement, a post filled by Keith Fordyce) straight away. However, while playing trumpet around London clubs in 1956 he met Dick Norton, who had just returned from the Grand Duchy, and introduced himself as an out-of-work disc jockey. At Norton's suggestion he applied again and this time he was successful, arriving in Luxembourg late in 1956. In fact he arrived on 28 December, and was on air on New Year's Day, 1957, at the start of a career which would make him the station's longest-ever serving announcer. As ever it was not only important that he should be good at his job; it has always been critical that announcers should fit in well with the staff already on the station. Luxembourg is a small country and the few English-speaking people out there have always been part of a tiny, sometimes isolated community which is of necessity thrown almost continually together. Barry Alldis managed this easily and immediately, and took an active role in life on the radio station, presenting shows like *Smash Hits* with Keith Fordyce – a programme which involved on-air destruction of records which listeners particularly disliked – a sort of reverse request show.

When Keith Fordyce left, Barry became Head of the English Service on 1 October 1958, and stayed until 1966. During these early years he was Radio Luxembourg's first DJ to go on the road – perhaps even the first in Europe from any radio station – in an era when discotheques didn't exist and the concept of the roadshow-style personal appearance had not yet evolved.

Part of the characteristic of the Medium Wave signal from 208 is that

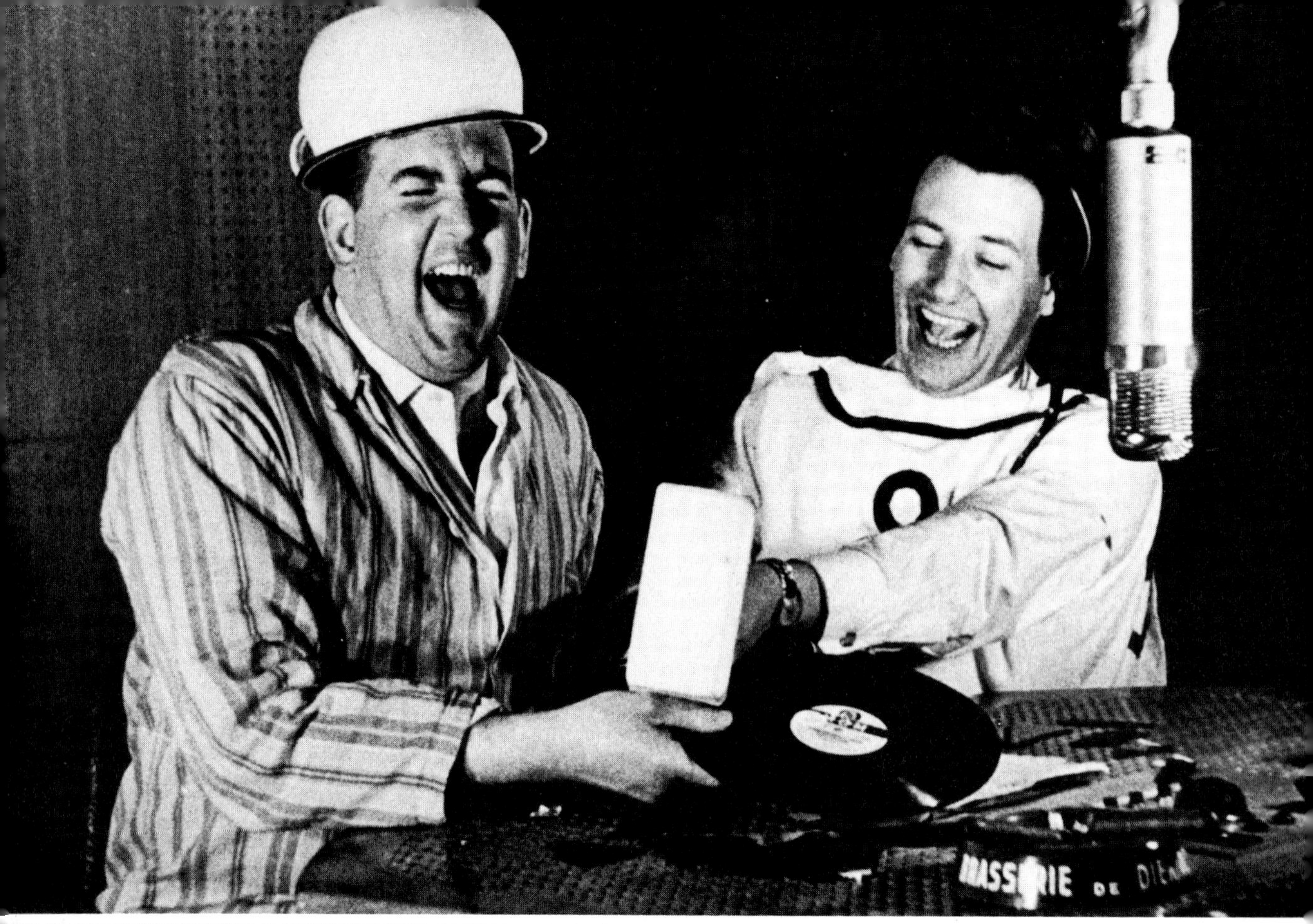

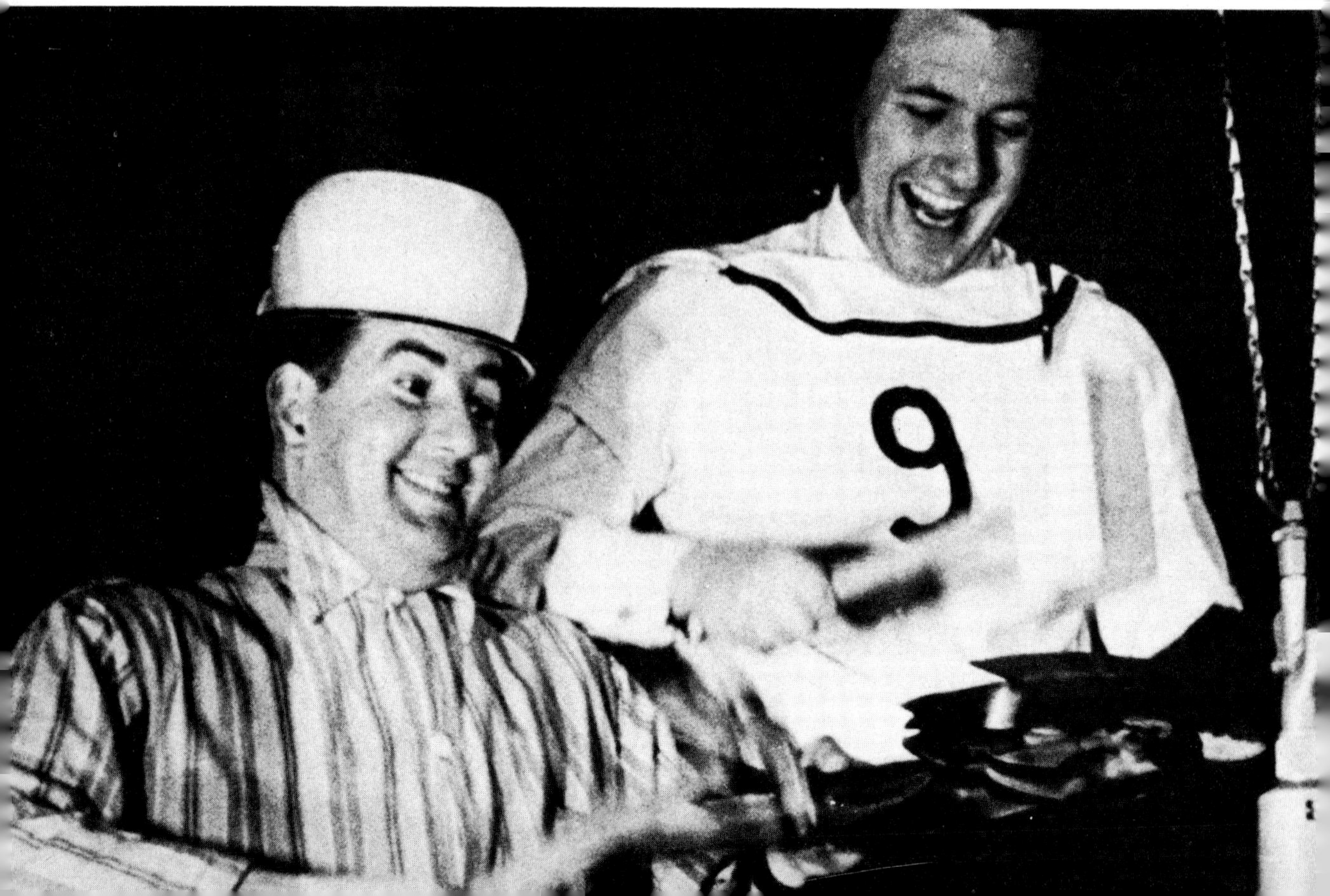

reception is patchy, and is often better at a distance than it is close to the transmitter. The signal is beamed by what is called skywave propagation, which means that it is aimed up into the sky and reflected back to earth by the ionosphere, striking terra firma hundreds of miles away from its point of origin. This method is not always terrifically reliable – weather, cloud cover and the difference between daylight and darkness all have their effects – and is the reason for the famous 208 'fade'. In practical terms it can mean that reception of 208 is better in the north of England and in Scotland than it is in the south-east, and also means that Scandinavian countries regularly enjoy good reception of Radio Luxembourg.

Because of this Barry Alldis took 208 on the road to Scandinavia, mostly doing repeats of the Top Twenty Show for live audiences, becoming a celebrity in countries like Norway, where he was regularly mobbed by young girls; the DJ personality cult was just beginning.

But it was Luxembourg – the country as well as the radio station – that Barry fell in love with, and it was almost inevitable that he should also fall in love with a Luxembourg girl – Fernande. 'I had come from Australia to London and spent a lot of time bumming around Kangaroo Valley (or Earls Court, as the English knew it). Luxembourg was so very different, so old world, that I couldn't get over it. There were fairytale castles, warm friendly people, and I was working in the medium I knew best. I was also fortunate enough to meet the girl I married, and we now have two children, so the Grand Duchy has done a great deal for me.' No wonder he stayed.

Almost at the same time as Barry Alldis went out to Luxembourg EMI took on a new Promotions Manager – Harry Walters. By now the sponsored shows which were coming out from London comprised the major part of Radio Luxembourg's daily output, using a wide variety of presenters, including ex-station DJs like Pete Murray, Keith Fordyce and Peter Madren, who mostly worked on programmes paid for by the record companies – EMI, Decca, Capitol and others. This gave the programme schedules a scrappy look which is completely alien to modern radio audiences; few programmes were longer than 30 minutes and the bulk of them were of only 15 minutes' duration. Despite the fact that Radio Luxembourg's rates had not gone up since the postwar reopening of the English Service, buying airtime on Luxembourg was still an expensive business. There was little point in buying a single spot and it was necessary to buy in at least once a week if any regular contact with the audience was to be established. Do that for a 12- or 18-week period and a great deal of money is called for, long before production costs and artists' fees are considered.

And, in Radio Luxembourg's opinion at least, not all the airtime was sold, despite the 'freeze' on prices and the monumental audience figures. As long as there were some programmes on air which were not bought and paid for by someone else there was still a chance to increase revenue.

The record companies were a good place to get it. When Harry

Barry Alldis (left) and Keith Fordyce hosting *Smash Hits* in which listeners' most hated records were played and then ceremonially smashed.

Walters took over at EMI, coming from *6.5 Special*, another much-loved TV pop programme, they were buying three or four slots on Radio Luxembourg each week, as were most other major record companies. And, like the others, they were releasing an average of 100 singles each week, plus seven-inch EPs, 10-inch LPs and the relatively new 33⅓ rpm 12-inch LPs. Forgetting all but the Hit Parade material, there were upwards of 500 single releases each week in Britain. A lot of the time they would be duplicated thanks to the cover version approach. When a song was a hit in America it almost automatically meant that it would be covered in Britain, but often every record company would get one of their own stars to record it and there could be as many as four or five versions of the same song released almost simultaneously. Only one of them would be a hit, and probably it would be the one which got the most airtime on popular radio.

And there was little enough opportunity for that. The BBC still drew a deep dividing line between recorded music and live music, preferring the live variety almost exclusively, especially for popular shows like the weekday lunchtime spot *Workers' Playtime*, still going strong after its introduction early on in the war years. Their record shows were few and far between and there were really only three places in which a small percentage of these 500 singles released each week stood a chance of getting played on the BBC. One was the Sunday show *Family Favourites*, which fortunately had a monstrous audience, the biggest on radio, only slightly short of 20 million. Then there was *Mid-day Spin*, on for an hour on Wednesdays, and *Housewives' Choice*, a daily request programme.

Under circumstances like those it is faintly surprising to find that Radio Luxembourg's entire output wasn't snapped up by various record companies pushing their product as hard as they could. Certainly Harry Walters went a long way towards it when he started in 1956. One of the reasons which led him to increase the amount of time EMI bought on Luxembourg was that a large number of their releases which went on to be hits first showed up as big sellers in the north of England and in Scotland – areas which were particularly well covered by Radio Luxembourg and in which reception was especially good. It was therefore logical enough to assume that Radio Luxembourg played no small part in the success or otherwise of new records, and so he made much greater use of it.

It was also something of a surprise to him that the sponsored shows which EMI put out on Luxembourg were having any effect whatever, at least as far as sales of EMI products were concerned. On the three or four shows each week which were being broadcast when he took over, some of the presenters were playing very few records on the EMI label and were playing rival products instead. This was apparently because they didn't always like the EMI stuff, which was hardly the point considering who was paying the bill.

Harry Walters took on some new names – Sam Costa, Alan Freeman and even popular boxer Freddie Mills – to replace the people who were

HELLO, YOUNG LOVERS!

MICHAEL HENNESSEY'S LUXEMBOURG DIARY

HELLO, Young lovers, wherever you are; Jim's coming to "208." Or, to be less oblique, Jimmy Young makes his Luxembourg début as a disc jockey next week.

He'll be taking over from Jack Good on Tuesdays at 9.30 p.m. and Thursdays at midnight. He shouldn't find it too much trouble—for he lives just a bit more than the length of his Mercedes Benz away from the Luxembourg studios.

Five years ago Jimmy Young was the top recording personality in the country. After the sensational success of "Too Young" in 1951, he rode on the crest of a popularity wave which made him the most sought-after singer in the business.

Ceded The Summit

To-day, at thirty-three, Jimmy has settled comfortably a few rungs down from the top of the ladder. Like many of the more mature performers in his field, he has ceded the summit to the clamouring exuberance of the callow, teen-adulated striplings who have only just emerged from short trousers.

With a voice that is pleasantly *sotto*, and a manner soothingly unhurried, Jimmy provides a refreshing contrast to the Americanized, high-pressure, hard-selling, phonily enthusiastic disc jockey prototype. He takes life gently, easily; but life hasn't always been easy for him.

Career Cut Short

During the war he joined the R.A.F. as a pilot, but had his flying career cut short by ill-health. He was encouraged by his doctor to take a physical training course—and he finished up as a P.T. instructor.

When he left the R.A.F. he became a trainee teacher, but to supplement his income he played the piano at a club in Hampton Court. Here he was heard, singing and playing, by BBC producer George Inns and invited for an audition.

Jimmy Young and ladder: he's a few steps down from the top

He made his first broadcast in 1949, and has since made more than three hundred. He has appeared on TV in Britain, America, Belgium, Germany and the Netherlands and he starred in the Gene Kelly film, "Invitation To The Dance."

This miner's son from the Forest of Dean can claim two "firsts" in the pop music world. He was the first British artist to have two consecutive discs—"Unchained Melody" and "The Man From Laramie"—in the No. 1 spot in the Top Twenty; and he was the first British singer to hit the top of the U.S. hit parade—with a tune he wrote himself: "My Faith, My Hope, My Love."

LP Prizes

A CHANCE for listeners to win popular LP records is provided by "Hits And Misses" which took over last Saturday from that Luxembourg perennial "Smash Hits."

A number of new releases will be played on each programme and listeners will be invited to indicate on a postcard which of them will finish in the Top Twenty.

The first two correct forecasts received will earn LPs for the senders. Ted King, junior partner in the "Smash Hits" team, is presenting the programme.

"B" Side Themselves

SOME of the richest men in the record business are the boys of the "B" side brigade. These gentlemen have devised a comfortable, foolproof and highly lucrative technique. This is how it works:

Since the American music industry largely dictates the Top Twenty, the record companies on this side of the Atlantic keep an eagle eye on songs which are leaping up the U.S. charts. They'll notice, for example, that "That Wonderful Teenage Mother Of Mine" is heading fast for the top.

They rush to record a "cover" version by one of their best-known sensations. Then comes the problem—what to put on the "B" side? Up steps one of Archer Street's ace arrangers with a special novelty instrumental which he has recently written. He just happens to have the complete score with him.

So out goes the British version of "T.W.T.M.O.M." with the natty novelty number on the reverse. The U.S. tune sells a million and, inescapably, a million copies of the ace arranger's masterpiece are sold too. It may be a diabolical piece of music, but it becomes a best-seller and leaves a shimmering golden wake of royalties.

That's why so many of the records you hear on "208" have such uninspiring "flip" sides. And why so many arranger-composers pay super tax.

THIS WEEK ON 208

(Also on 49.26m. short wave)

"TIT-BITS" IS THE OFFICIAL PERIODICAL FOR RADIO LUXEMBOURG

MONDAY (AUG. 15)
- 7.00 p.m. NON-STOP POPS
- 7.30 TED KING introduces MONDAY'S REQUESTS
- 8.30 A DATE WITH PERRY COMO introduced by DAVID GELL
- 8.45 POPS AT THE PIANO with RONNIE ALDRICH
- 9.00 RED NICHOLS AND HIS FIVE PENNIES
- 9.15 THE JO STAFFORD SHOW
- 9.45 THE LONELY MAN
- 9.30 THE SPORTING CHALLENGE BILLY WRIGHT puts the questions to LESLIE WELCH
- 9.15 CONNIE FRANCIS SINGS
- 9.30 JACK GOOD does some GOOD TURNS
- 10.00 RAY ORCHARD'S RECORD CROP
- 10.30 WARNER BROS. RECORD SHOW JIMMY SAVILE is your host
- 11.00 TIP-TOP RANK with GERRY MYERS
- 11.30 THE WORLD TO-MORROW
- 12.00 MIDNIGHT ON LUXEMBOURG with SAM COSTA

RECORD REQUESTS
If there is a record you would like to hear played for you, send your request, according to which programme you are interested in, to Monday's Requests (or Tuesday's, or Irish, etc.), Radio Luxembourg, London, W.1.

- 12.00 MIDNIGHT ON LUXEMBOURG with RAY ORCHARD

THURSDAY
- 7.00 p.m. NON-STOP POPS

FRIDAY
- 7.00 p.m. NON-STOP POPS
- 7.30 TED KING brings you FRIDAY'S REQUESTS
- 8.15 "208" ROAD SHOW Your weekly motoring half hour introduced by PATRICK ALLEN
- 8.45 JUKE BOX PARADE with BRYAN JOHNSON
- 9.00 POPS AT THE PIANO with RONNIE ALDRICH
- 9.15 DICKIE VALENTINE SHOW Fifteen minutes of song
- 9.30 PETE MURRAY'S RECORD SHOW
- 9.45 THE LONELY MAN

just leaving, and began putting out around seven or eight programmes a week of 15, 30 and occasionally 45 minutes duration, which meant that EMI alone were now spending in the region of £30 to £35,000 a year with Radio Luxembourg for airtime. On top of that the DJs were all paid £1 a minute, which added a minimum of £10,000 a year to the bill plus overall costs and, of course, the shows were all recorded in the Hertford Street studio, even though the producer and the presenter were both employed by the record company and not by Radio Luxembourg.

It was while doing all this that Harry Walters met an old friend whom he had not seen since his film extra days at Denham – Pete Murray was regularly in Hertford Street working for the Decca Record Company. Another ex-Luxembourg resident making taped shows was Teddy Johnson, whose singing career had progressed enormously and who was now regularly seen as part of a duo – the other half was, of course, Pearl Carr. In 1959, as Harry Walters was moving on from his job as EMI Promotions Manager, they had a number one smash with that year's Eurovision winner, 'Sing Little Birdie'.

Harry Walters' replacement at EMI was Arthur Muckslow, a man who would introduce a number of people to Radio Luxembourg over the years but whose first signing was one of which the outgoing Harry Walters disapproved fairly strongly. 'Why employ a passé singer?' was his reaction to the man destined to take over from Jack Good on Tuesdays at 9.30 and Thursdays at midnight. He hadn't had a hit record since 1958, although at the time his records and his track record had been something special. He was the first British singer to have two consecutive single releases go to the top of the Hit Parade ('Unchained Melody' and 'The Man From Laramie') and he was the first British singer ever to reach the top of the American charts, and this with his own composition, 'My Faith, My Hope, My Love'. But since then – nothing. So why indeed employ passé singers? asked Harry Walters, the man who is now the producer of that ex-singer's Radio Two morning programme, *The Jimmy Young Show*.

The son of a miner, Jimmy Young had become a top-class singer almost by accident, when BBC producer George Inns heard him singing in a club in Hampton Court. He hit the big time in 1951 with a song called 'Too Young' which Teddy Johnson would almost certainly have played on Radio Luxembourg shortly before departing to pursue his own, then embryonic, singing career. When the record and the chart hits 'came to a grinding halt' in about the middle of 1958 Jimmy Young remembers being 'quite hungry'. He also remembers 'starring at the Labour Exchange' for a long period. Then in 1960 he did two weeks for the BBC on *Housewives' Choice* and that was it – that was his total employment for the year until EMI snapped him up and kept him on Radio Luxembourg for five years.

Jimmy Young was one of about 30 different people whose voices appeared on Radio Luxembourg during the course of any one week during this period, only three of whom were actually resident in the

Grand Duchy itself. Barry Alldis was still the top man (and destined to remain so for quite a while longer) and a succession of other people passed before the microphone at the Villa Louvigny – Australian Brook Denning, South African Barry O'Dee, Yorkshireman Peter Carver (who came from the British Forces Network), Ted King and lots of others. Many stayed only a short while, a few stayed longer. Not all of them made a big success out of it and only some became household names in their own right. Yet looking back at this period it is hard to avoid the feeling that anyone who was anyone worked for Radio Luxembourg and that anyone who was then unknown who got a job with the station was instantly elevated to permanent star status as a result. It is certainly true that Radio Luxembourg became and remained the major proving ground for the new media cult of the disc jockey. There were only two places for anyone to work on national radio in Britain – Radio Luxembourg and the BBC. Luxembourg, as the story shows, was the innovator, the adventurer and the pioneer, and it is because of this that so many people who appeared on the station seem to have made it. And it was also true that a great number of them would probably never have sat behind a microphone at all had it not been for the huge programme output on 208 metres.

The BBC was relatively unreceptive towards new talent, preferring to use established 'names' to present their few record shows, which meant that unless you were already highly acclaimed in some other area of entertainment it was highly unlikely that you would ever get the chance of compering a BBC programme. And while the sponsors of airtime on 208 chose established star names for their programmes for obvious commercial reasons, Radio Luxembourg was the only radio station which gave untried and unknown people the chance to make themselves known and popular. Quite simply there was no other outlet, so of course all the people who became famous started on 208. They had no choice. Nowadays it is entirely possible for new talent to emerge through one of the many local radio stations, through one of the thousands of discotheques (none of which existed at that time) or through Hospital Radio – which didn't exist either. Today there are even some companies who employ resident DJs in their factories or in their shops, but in the late fifties the opportunities simply didn't exist outside Radio Luxembourg. The only serious competition which the station encountered was by now coming, not from the BBC radio service, but from television, mostly from the independent network. And it was this competition which led almost directly to the change in format which took place on 208 at about the turn of the decade, under the guiding hand of Geoffrey Everitt, who had become Station Manager in 1959 and would soon be General Manager.

In the late fifties the Luxembourg output which was, quite obviously, a mixed bag, was beginning to become something of a mongrel. The station broadcast whatever the sponsors felt was appropriate, which meant that *Billy's Banjo Show* rubbed shoulders with *The Cliff Richard*

Show, both programmes going out on a Thursday night squeezed between *The Sporting Challenge*, in which Billy Wright put listeners' questions to Memory Man Leslie Welch, and *Italy Sings* at 10.45, which was exactly what it sounded like. Ray Orchard's *Record Crop* preceded Jimmy Savile doing his thing for Warner Brothers, and on Friday night Alan Freeman's *Spin With the Stars* was followed by *Bringing Christ to the Nations* which lasted half an hour and was then succeeded by Sam Costa and *Midnight on Luxembourg* which was an EMI record programme.

Understandably, in the face of a growing television service which was at least providing entertainment on a consistent and more organised basis, the 208 audience was in the decline, falling gradually from its nine million high in 1955 towards three million in the early sixties, taking with it a number of sponsors, who naturally followed the audiences on to TV. The only way to reverse the trend was to improve the programming and attract the audiences back. The only way to do that would be to reduce the number of different 15-minute sponsored shows – but the whole object of the exercise in the first place was to attract sponsors, not send them packing.

Caught in something of a cleft stick, the answer would have permanent effects on the nature of the radio station, and represented a rather shrewd piece of observation and thought on the part of Radio Luxembourg. The station opted to go with the youth market, which at the time was hardly the major force that it is now, or even the growing force that it would become in the mid sixties. In fact the teenage revolution had just begun, and Radio Luxembourg saw it first.

Out went variety, light entertainment, drama and panel games and the like. It was gradually a fond farewell for MacDonald Hobley, Basil Rathbone, *Dan Dare* and all the rest – including the late evening religious marathons, which were drastically pared down and put on at the opening of the evening when sponsors and advertisers were much harder (if not impossible) to find.

In came non-stop pop music. From now on it was full-time record programmes devoted to people like Cliff Richard and Elvis Presley; this was total devotion to chart material at a time when the British chart-toppers in 1959 were Cliff, Elvis, Buddy Holly, Bobby Darin, Craig Douglas, The Platters and Russ Conway. By 1960 even the housewives' smiling favourite, Russ Conway, had gone, and the charts rang with the names of Cliff, Elvis, Adam Faith, Johnny Tillotson, Ricky Valance, The Everly Brothers, Roy Orbison, The Shadows, Emile Ford, The Drifters and Chubby Checker. The Twist had arrived, and so had the Beatniks, and The Beatles were on their way to Hamburg.

6: FAB GEAR

The fifties had ushered in an era of change for the whole world, not only in the entertainment business. They had brought an end to war and a feeling of hope for the future, and during the decade in which we'd reportedly never had it so good a mood of expansion had been in the air. Jet liners had gone into service, satellites had gone into space and Gagarin wouldn't be far behind. And the entertainment world, so sensitive to this kind of mood (it had collapsed entirely at the outbreak of war before gathering itself together again, remember) had responded, and the most noticeable result had been the arrival of rock'n'roll in the middle of the decade. But after a period of great excitement it seemed as if it was already on the wane, and musically the fifties passed on with the smallest of whimpers, and the growing spectre of the small screen began to threaten not only the cinema but all kinds of live entertainment, including live music. Possibly the first sign that music hadn't given up was the Twist, and Chubby Checker's song of the same name, together with Sam Cooke's far superior 'Twisting the Night Away', gave some hope for the future. Mostly, though, the early sixties was a period of stagnation more than anything else.

On 208 the Memory Man, Leslie Welch, returned in 1960 for a new series of the quiz programme *Sporting Challenge*, religious broadcasting still started the evening schedule and all kinds of music was played as Luxembourg, perhaps more so than anyone else, groped around for the formula for the sixties. They were still way ahead of the BBC radio output, with 50-odd hours of chart records being played every week while the BBC was limited by agreement with the Musicians' Union to 24 hours a week spread over their Light, Home and Third programmes. But TV was a major enemy and various voices raised in support of nationally available and local commercial radio would soon have part of their demands satisfied, and the Pilkington Committee would shortly begin its deliberations on the possibility of local commercial radio being allowed in Britain. This was a big decision; the BBC monopoly in sound broadcasting was more than 30 years old and was protected by Charter, but the sudden arrival of commercial television had naturally begged the question 'Now can we have commercial radio as well?'

Radio Luxembourg was examined closely by many different people and organisations at this stage, not least the British Press, being an actual living example of commercial broadcasting in action. However the establishment feeling was still decidedly against this sort of thing despite 208's evident popularity. It was still not quite the sort of thing a chap could let a chap's constituents listen to, lest it give them the wrong ideas – all of them doubtless above their station. No doubt, if the means could have been found, there were plenty of influential people who would have liked to preside over the close-down of Radio Luxembourg. Since this was impossible it seemed likely that the very least they could do would be to prevent any kind of proliferation, and the appearance of local commercial radio stations seemed unlikely to be a feature of the sixties.

Which was fortunate for RTL. The Compagnie Luxembourgeoise de Radiodiffusion had, in 1954, seen the possibilities of television and taken steps towards it as quickly as they could. On the continent this sort of thing was, as usual, a great deal easier than it has ever been in Britain. Although the French government did not allow commercial radio stations to be established in their country they had no objection whatever to commercial radio stations in other countries having landline facilities out of France, even if the material carried on it was destined for immediate transmission back to France. Radio Luxembourg thus had substantial studio facilities in Paris which were connected with Villa Louvigny, and thus the transmitter at Junglinster, by direct landline. The British were not even prepared to grant that small facility, so it is not surprising to find that when the CLR decided that television was something they wanted to be involved in they chose to do it in France, becoming, along the way, Radio Tele Luxembourg.

Doubtless it must have been a source of some relief to RTL to know that the appearance of commercial radio all over Britain was about as likely as the Post Office giving Radio Luxembourg a landline. Nevertheless it was being looked at, and consequently 208 was looked at as well. In general it came out of its many examinations rather well, although some of the newspapers were somewhat scathing about the very direct and simple approach adopted by Radio Luxembourg disc jockeys, which was to play popular music, concentrating on chart material and whatever got the most requests. Informed opinion, no doubt moulded by the BBC, still tended to the feeling that a radio station had a moral duty to educate and improve its audience by playing things which were good for them.

In 1962, in a newspaper interview inspired by the forthcoming Pilkington Committee report on commercial radio, 208's resident announcers Barry Alldis, Brook Denning, Barry O'Dee and Paul Hollingdale were questioned closely about the nature of Radio Luxembourg. The station was visited by record company pluggers more frequently than the BBC, and after the question of payola had been dealt with (the reporter seemed to be under the impression that the only thing which would induce a disc jockey to play some of the records on release was money) they went on to discuss the question of taste good, bad or indifferent in popular music. Paul Hollingdale was quoted as saying that he was frequently asked why he and his fellow disc jockeys didn't try to improve public taste, presumably by only playing records which were of some substantial 'quality', perhaps as perceived by luminaries at the BBC. 'We'd like to play better stuff,' he said, 'but you've got to recognise that these kids are the market. That is what they ask for.'

Of course at the time the future and well-being of the nation's by now somewhat rebellious youth was a subject of major concern, as the 1962

Be a Rebel

writes Billy Fury

IF I was advising youngsters how to "get ahead" or "become a success", I could put it in just three words—"Be a rebel!"

A rebel—to my way of thinking—is someone who has the courage to voice his convictions and ideas, even though they go against the so-called accepted ideas of others.

There's a word in our vocabulary which seems to surround us, and darn near strangle us, and that word is "Conformity".

Conformity puts over the line that making a success of almost anything can best be achieved by sticking slavishly to the rules, not stepping out of line, and doing as others do.

Well I did as others did when I first stepped into show business, and I didn't do too well. As far as most of the public was concerned, I was just another pop singer. It was my manager, Larry Parnes, and my recording adviser, Dick Rowe, of Decca, who came up with the right answer, the same one I've just given you—"Be a rebel!"

My rebellion was to switch my vocal style, switch my style of song and musical backing, and switch my appearance—including my haircut and clothes.

Well, as you know, it worked, so, as far as I'm concerned, it's—"Up the rebels!" Only when you have reached your goal, can you afford to become a little more "respectable", a little more in accordance with "Conformity".

Lots of books have been written about conformity, in the past few years, and quite a few films have used it as their theme, but, while the books and films may have become commercial successes, I'm for our younger generation, if they are persuaded to toe the line too much, and so lose the spirit of adventure.

When they keep hearing that completely following in the footsteps of their elders is proof of their "loyalty", they are in danger of believing it so much that they are likely to destroy their individuality and creativeness.

Maybe a lot of people have got to the top by patiently plodding the well-worn pathways, but take a backward look at history and you'll find that those who really distinguished themselves did so by daring to be individualists and rebels.

Mind you, when I say "rebel" I'm not talking about slovenly dressed beatniks who think that long beards, exhibitionism, walking about barefoot and just plain defiance and vulgarity, is all that's needed to be "Different". That kind of "difference" they can keep.

There are, of course, the wrong kind of rebels—I was one of these myself once upon a time, and I'm not proud of the fact. That kind of rebellion can turn a boy into a juvenile delinquent or a criminal. That brand of rebellion is for fools who end up destroying themselves and bringing heartbreak to their families.

BUT "rebel" doesn't have to be a dirty word. In the world of pop music and records, the artist who "goes against the grain" is more often the one who succeeds.

Glenn Miller was just another orchestra leader struggling to make the grade until, dissatisfied with the run-of-the-mill sounds of other orchestras, he struggled until he achieved the fabulous Miller sound that brought his name and his kind of music, immortality.

George Shearing was a pianist playing with Cyril Stapleton's Orchestra in London's West End, until he went to America and created the Shearing musical trademark by synchronising a vibraphone with his piano, and adding rhythm.

Bill Haley and his Comets kicked off the whole

Billy signs an autograph for an admirer during location filming for "Play it Cool"

YOU'RE NEVER TOO YOUNG FOR SUCCESS

☆ Says Paul Anka ☆

PEOPLE say I'm too young to have done so much. Well, what's wrong with managing to get security for yourself even in your teens?

Everybody needs security. I'm not a slow person, but I'm still the unaffected type. Like if you went through my pockets right now, the odds are that you wouldn't find a cent.

I know I have got myself the reputation of being a teenage tycoon. But I know I owe my success to all the kids who like what I write, sing, and record. The wonderful thing is that I know there are many other youngsters around who have the talent to achieve the same kind of success, despite their age, if the right opportunities come along.

Everything I earn goes into a trust fund, and I only get a fifty dollars a week allowance.

I work hard because I enjoy it. Enjoying your work is much more important than just making money.

★ ☆ ★ ☆ ★

MY parents, who ran a little restaurant in Ottawa, were frightened, at first, of what show business might do to me, because it's not like any other job.

Because I was so young, they didn't like me going away from home on tour without their being able to look after me. But, fortunately, I had some wonderful people helping me, so they didn't have to worry so much.

My father never tried to stop me trying anything in my career. He said I had proved I was sensible enough to go my own way in spite of my youth, so that's just what he wanted me to do.

This could be the start of something big — Paul Anka, aged one-and-a-half, is in his grandmother's good hands.

100

Dear Pat,

Pat Boone writes you a letter about the letters he gets...

I DON'T think I'm a crazy mixed-up adult. I hope I show that you can have a teenage following without being a wild-living, eccentric rebel, by being just an average normal person.

I'm not prudish, but I would never do anything in front of teenagers which their parents couldn't watch. Whatever I do on or off the screen, the fans may copy. Therefore, I must set them a good example. People like myself have a great deal of influence and it should be used for good.

I think that everyone has had enough of the glamorisation of the hoodlum, the motor-scooter gangs, and blackboard jungle kids. Those types may be true of a section of teenagers, but not the majority. The majority are decent, upstanding boys and girls.

Sure they have their problems, but that doesn't send them off the rails, drinking and beating up people. I don't want to be thought of as a saint—I'm not. I'm a singer. I can't think of myself as an expert in the advice department. But I can remember how confused a teenager can get! I was lucky I guess. A lot of people helped me. If anything I can say now will help any teenager, I'd like to try.

Simple, complicated, poignant, sometimes even funny, letters with their problems and questions flood into my office in Hollywood.

"DEAR PAT,
MY NAME IS BILL. I'M SEVENTEEN AND I WANT TO BE A SINGER. I'M SERIOUS ABOUT IT. I WANT TO MAKE SINGING MY CAREER AND NEED TO GET EXPERIENCE. CAN YOU TELL ME HOW TO DO IT?"

I understand dreams like this, and sympathise. A few years ago, all I had were hopes and dreams. I know how hard it is to get started in a career and I wish I could send you a formula on how to do it. I can give you a few pointers. Most important is some downright hard work to go with your talent.

You can get the experience you need if you volunteer to sing at as many community affairs as possible. It's really valuable towards the self-confidence you will need. The best of luck.

"Why can't parents understand?" turns up as the first line of a lot of the letters I get. Second lines are generally more specific, like: "What colour lipstick should I wear?"—as if I knew the girl as she feels she knows me through my records, films vision set.

I reply—"Being young is too wonderful day worrying about the colour of your lipst enjoy today. Don't try to rush the business up to that "Someday when I can do what You'll get there. But the chances are it won't fun you think it's going to be unless you've get the most out of the days in between. Yo yearning for something still further ahead.

"DEAR PAT,
MY PARENTS WON'T ALLOW ME STEADY. THEY SAY THAT I'M TOO AND DON'T KNOW MY OWN MIND

Well, lots of things about going steady you figure out in advance when you're young. I w twice before I met Shirley, my wife. Both un and I began to get a sort of trapped feeling aft

When you meet a girl you like, naturally yo sew her up for yourself, get a claim on all her You don't realise this is going to conflict activities you've always enjoyed—going bow your buddies, for instance. You've got an ob take your girl out instance. You can't leave her date. You both get tired of that. What's rea when one of you tires before the other.

Once going steady, you can't just drift apart up is hard to do. It isn't like kids saying: "I c to play with you any more!" Feelings can get h

Personally, I think for younger teenagers, th a mutual agreement to date as often as you lik cluding other dates, is better than going stea

"DEAR PAT,
MY PARENTS CAN'T UNDERSTAND WANT TO DRESS AND TALK AND A WAY MY FRIENDS DO. HOW CAN I CO THEM THAT TEENAGE FADS AREN'T FUL

Teenagers have a great capacity for instanta and excitement. It might help to point out generation has its fads. They're part of gr Whatever fads turn up ten years from now, wi look weird to us too

The girl that I Marry

WHAT kind of girls do today's boys want to marry? Well, I can't answer for all the other boys, but I know the kind of girl I would like as my wife.

The smart Alecs can make all the cracks they like, but the girl for me would be just the sort my mother has said all along would be the right sort.

Too many teen-agers think their parents' advice on marriages and morals are "old fashioned"—until they become parents themselves and find out that those parental words of wisdom they had considered to be so "square" were in fact right on the ball because they were based on long, and true and tried experience of life.

As far as I'm concerned, the so-called wise ones can

BY CLIFF RICHARD

edition of the *Radio Luxembourg Book of Stars* demonstrated all too clearly. For a large part this was simply an excuse to publish hundreds of photographs of people whose faces were already incredibly well-known but for whom there was an apparently insatiable demand. Twined in and around all this were messages of hope, expressions of confusion and pleas for help which pinpoint exactly the worries about the future of the young people of the time which were shared by their parents and by the youngsters themselves. Even more importantly was the almost religious reliance which the teenagers seemed to place in their idols. If Cliff Richard could make hit records then apparently he could also make the right decision about moral issues. As the people at the forefront of a cultural revolution which was sweeping the country, the pop stars of the moment were landed with an awesome and probably unwanted responsibility. Theirs was the ability to influence not only musical tastes, but all kinds of attitudes which really should have been nothing to do with them. Nevertheless they readily took on the responsibility. In the 1962 *Book of Stars* Cliff wrote about the girl he would marry; avid fans snapped up the information that he would marry just the sort of girl his mother would approve of. Next they digested the fact that Cliff thought that established values were not as 'square' as many youngsters believed; many of them, observed the youthful Harry Webb, a 22-year-old from Cheshunt in Hertfordshire, thought of their parents' advice as old-fashioned, but this was apparently not true.

A few pages on, Frankie Avalon, under the title 'The Most Important People in My Life', covered three whole pages telling his fans exactly why there were 'no greater people in the world than my Mama and Papa'.

And yet a short distance on came a lengthy piece by singing idol Pat Boone, in which he offered advice to that section of his following which could be regarded as 'mixed up kids'. He even answering their problem letters – 'Dear Pat, my parents won't allow me to go steady . . . My parents can't understand why I want to dress and talk and act the way my friends do . . . I can't understand all the "don'ts" my Mother and Father give me . . .' – all sent to the 28-year-old singer in the 'all-American boy' mould who had, throughout the latter part of the fifties, been the complete antithesis of Presley and scored huge recording success with songs like 'Love Letters in the Sand' and 'I'll be home'.

All of which may seem to be irrelevant to a radio station, but Luxembourg had chosen the young people as its target market, had chosen to be involved not only with their music but with everything else which concerned them. It had to understand them, and show it understood, to attract them away from TV and keep them.

Luxembourg pushed ahead with its youth-oriented formula, and found its best-remembered expression in the personality of a young dancehall manager from the Mecca ballroom in Leeds. Once again it is necessary to recall that the modern concept of a discotheque is just that – modern. In the early sixties the dancehall – the local palais, Lyceum or

Mecca – was the thing. These were, of course, much larger and less intimate than discos and had really been built to accommodate a brightly-lit roomful of young things revolving gracefully to music supplied by a live dance band. It was only with the advent of the rock'n'roll era and the concept of chart hits by a singer (rather than the popularity of a song which could be reproduced ad hoc by any half-decent ensemble) that the idea of dancing to records really caught on. No provincial five-piece could adequately represent the hysteria induced by 'Rock Around the Clock' or 'Move It' as created by the original artists; to quote, it was now 'the singer, not the song' which was of primary importance.

Up in Leeds an ex-miner, injured in a pit accident and now seeking alternative employment, had become manager of the local Mecca (which has since burnt down) and was in the habit of playing records through the evening for his youthful clientele. He was becoming successful and well-known in his own right as a result. Pat Campbell, who was at the time taping shows for Radio Luxembourg, suggested that he call at Hertford Street to introduce himself. At the time Jimmy Savile had no ambition or intention to work on radio at all, but he eventually went to Hertford Street anyway to see how radio shows were made, and was 'amazed' that it all took place in such a small and spartan room, with just a table, a chair and a microphone. He signed for Warner Brothers and began doing their shows; taped on a Thursday, there were four or five a week, of 30 minutes duration, and beyond doubt the most famous of them was the *Teen and Twenty Disc Club*.

Jimmy Savile's unscripted, unrehearsed, almost uncertain manner behind the microphone won almost instant popularity as he settled quickly and easily into the relaxed and informal manner which has become the hallmark of the disc jockey today. All the material was of Warner Brothers origin, and Jimmy Savile had no real choice about the kind of music he played – he just worked through the catalogue. But fortune must have been smiling his way, because the very first record he played, which was also Warner Brothers' first ever single release, the Everly Brothers' 'Cathy's Clown', went straight to number one. He stayed with Decca and 208 for nine consecutive years, winning the top DJ award for eight of them. It was hardly surprising, really, since his ratings were the top of Radio Luxembourg's substantial tree. It was also just reward for anyone who worked at his job as hard as Jimmy Savile. When Elvis Presley's 'It's Now or Never' went straight into the charts at number one and almost immediately went Gold as well (Presley had approximately 30 Gold discs by 1960) Jimmy Savile took the presentation disc out to Los Angeles and delivered it to Elvis Presley on a Hollywood film set. He was photographed with Presley and returned to Britain with the first-ever picture of a British DJ with the man who was indisputably 'The King' of rock'n'roll.

But this was the early sixties, and although the Americans didn't realise it – and neither did anyone else, come to that – the days of their dominance in popular music were coming to an end. The cover version

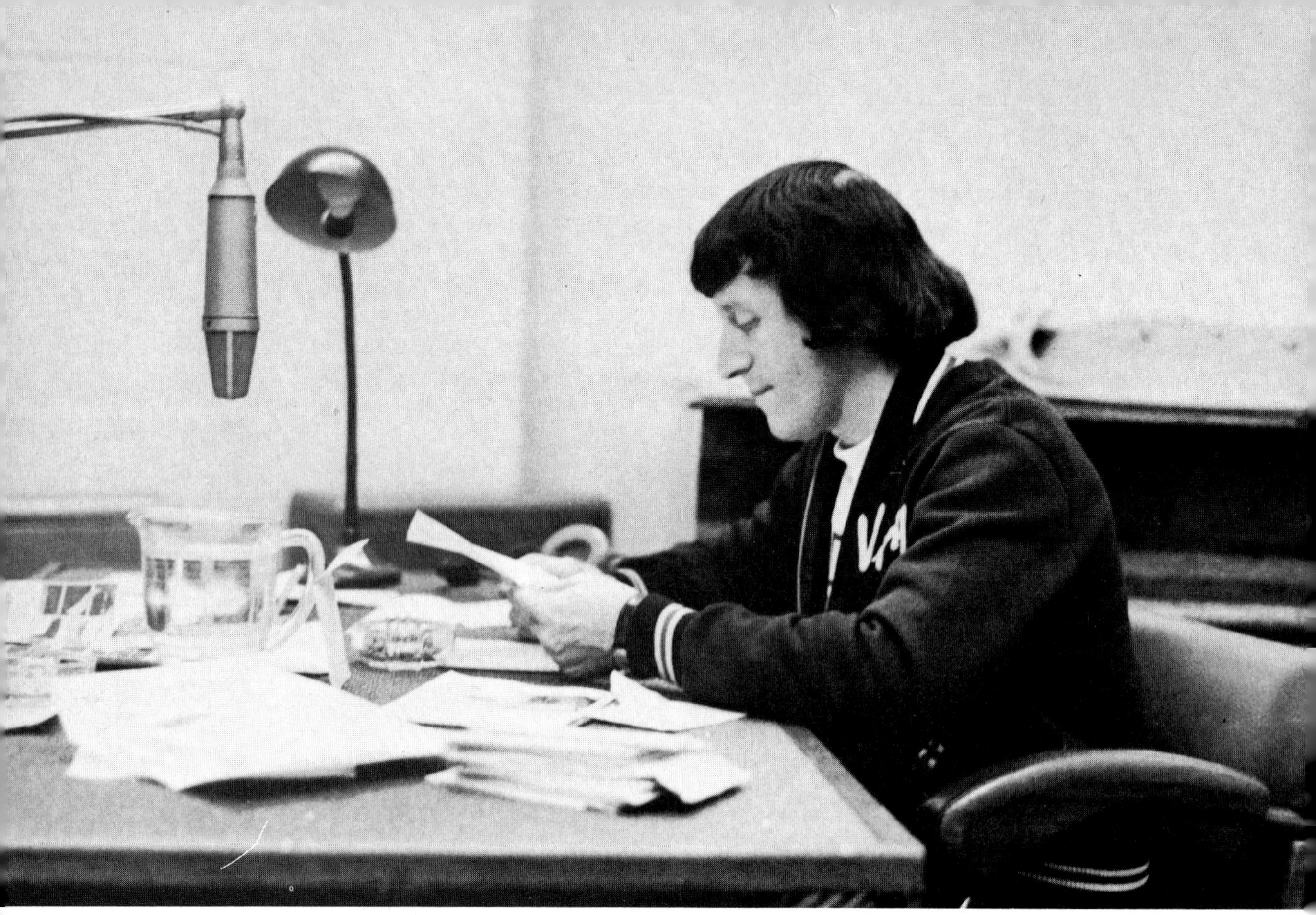

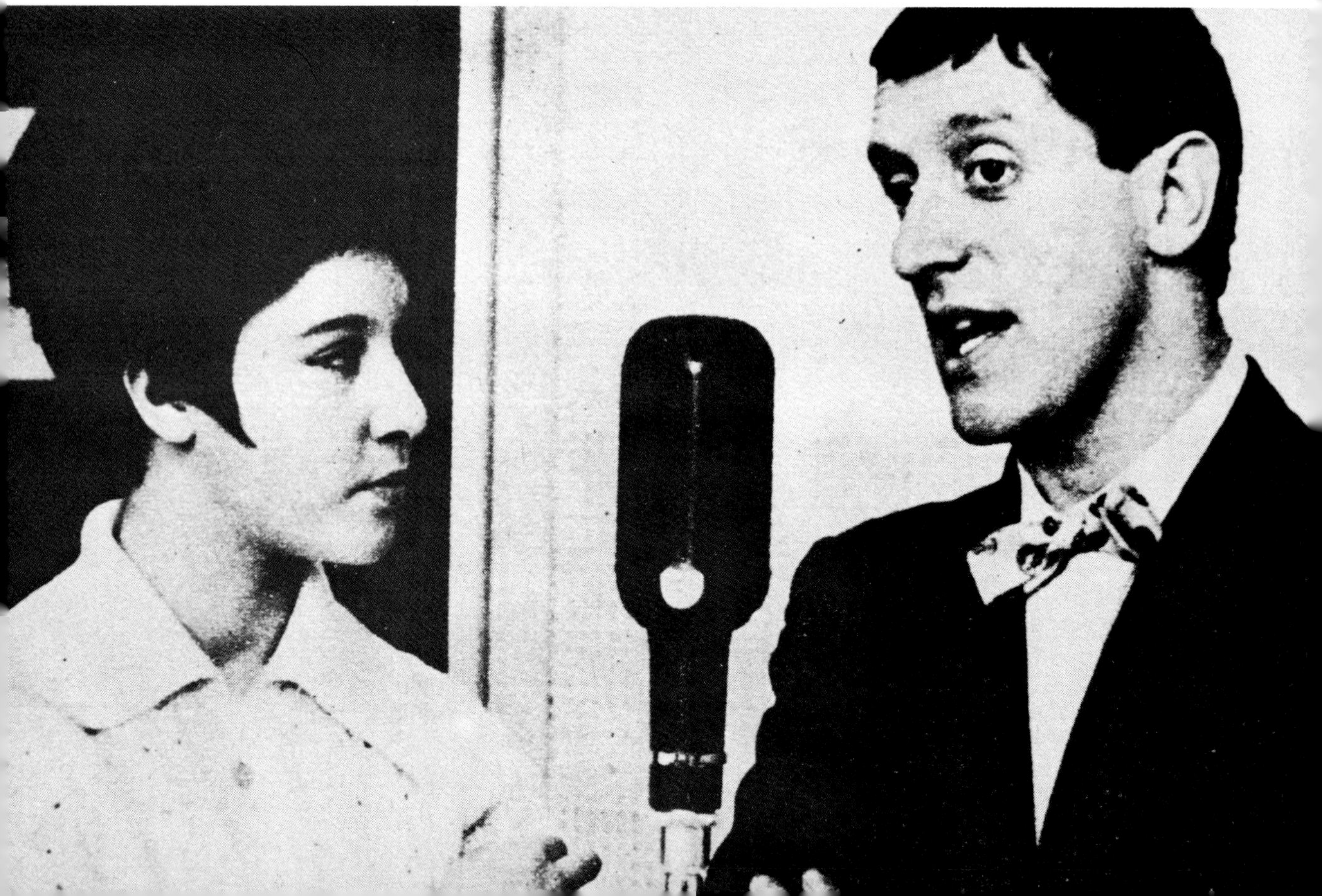

ploy which had supported the record industry in this country was about to wither and die as a result of the rapid discovery of a succession of home-grown talents who were to change the nature of pop music so completely that it would never be the same again. It was a type of music, a total sound, which to begin with at least emanated from just one tiny corner of England. Soon to be internationally recognised and hailed as 'the Mersey Sound', it was first heard on Radio Luxembourg.

Muriel Young was the very first woman to appear as an announcer on commercial television when Granada began in 1955; the second company to go on air was ATV and their front man was Shaw Taylor. And in just the same way that so many radio personalities had deserted en masse to get into TV as soon as it opened, now the picture was being reversed. In the face of ratings which had fallen by 60 per cent – down from nine to three million – Radio Luxembourg had set about recapturing its audience. The easiest slice to get back was the youngsters, so the all-pop formula was developing, and at the same time there were more and more voices appearing on 208 to which the public could already put faces. Commercial TV stations did not, seemingly, have the same objections to Radio Luxembourg as had the BBC, and a large number of TV faces began to make their way into Hertford Street to tape shows for various sponsors.

It was Arthur Muckslow at EMI who invited Muriel Young to do shows for the record company, mostly because the items she had been doing on Granada were pop-oriented; things like *Five O'Clock Club*, for example. Later on her experience in pop radio would take her back on to TV to do more pop programmes to camera – shows like *Discotheque*, which was really the forerunner of *Lift-Off*.

Muriel Young began in 1961 with an audience show called *Monday Spectacular* which was taped at EMI's Manchester Square studio with an audience of about 100 people. The idea behind it was to try to recreate the mood and atmosphere of the BBC blockbuster, *Family Favourites*, an end it achieved so well that Muriel Young later went on to do the BBC original. But to begin with the EMI show was a family affair, the audiences were aged from 20 upwards and the stars were established singers of the semi-crooner variety – Bobby Vinton, for example.

Another EMI show was *Dance Party*, again taped in front of a live audience, and with the intention of teaching the listeners the steps to the latest dance craze. Incredibly, this worked well on radio, and Marie Cartmel taught thousands of youngsters how to dance over the 208 airwaves as her instructions to the audience at Manchester Square were transmitted from Luxembourg. Muriel Young and Shaw Taylor occupied the stage at the front, Marie Cartmel and two exhibition dancers (originally the same Patrick and Teresa who later went on to do the same thing on ITV's *Ready Steady Go* for choreographer Leo Karibian and compere Keith Fordyce) taught the audience the moves. Behind the scenes the chief engineer was ex-Luxembourg DJ Ray Orchard. In this way the youngsters of Britain learned the Twist, learned jiving and

Above
Jimmy Savile in Hertford Street before *Top of the Pops*, cigars and green hair.
Below
Jimmy Savile shares a studio microphone with Helen Shapiro.

Meet the Disc Jockey — 24
MURIEL YOUNG

IN the world of disc jockeys predominated by men it is a great triumph for the fair sex when one of its members does manage to make a name for herself in this way, especially when it is one so attractive as Muriel Young. It is difficult to pinpoint the reason why there are so few women DJ's, but as the situation stands a girl has to be really good to even get herself a programme on the air.

Muriel explains her success modestly. "I've made a 'Charlie' of myself so often in public," she says, "that I think people are on my side and this may be the reason for their feeling of ease."

Born 1931 in Co. Durham, she moved as a child to Yorkshire and cycled 2½ miles to school each day. After leaving school Muriel studied to be a librarian but the winter of 1947 was so cold she came South to Watford, where she attended art school.

Later she joined a theatrical company at Henley on Thames as a scenic designer, but before long she was asked to take an acting part in the productions. However, Muriel felt that acting in a rep. company was too exacting. Only Sunday was free to spend with the family, and even that was occupied by learning scripts. As she didn't like the rôles she was getting either, she moved to London.

When *Dancing Party* takes the air it's everybody Twist— and that includes ace comperes Ray Orchard, Muriel Young and Alan Dell, star guest Joe Loss and 208's queen of steps Marie Cartmell

DANCING— the easy way

vere. Later Marie's going to teach the Charleston (yes, it's coming back), the Loco-motion—and maybe even the Twist!

A Dainty disc

LAST week that brightly-twittering, chuckling comic Billy Dainty was compering a TV *Saturday Show*. Next week he's doing another. All summer long he was pulling in the crowds at Blackpool.

But Luxembourg listeners now know him in another guise—he's been persuaded to cut a disc, and it's certainly been spinning.

"Sing what you like," he was told.

THEY Twist to trad, they Twist ... promotion, to the ... try to ...

T 'n' T Club reached 10,000,000 late night listeners, he figured—and that must be near saturation point on 208. So along came Ray Orchard to ... out the *Dancing Party* boat ... trad man Alan Dell ... Young to ...

LUXEMBOURG DIARY

And out came an unashamedly sentimental number, *Cry Upon My Shoulder*—well known as a French ballad a few years ago.

Billy, typically, is a bit doubtful about its success.

"I hope the youngsters will dig my style of singing," he chuckled. "I'm completely in the dark about the disc business."

I'd say this plaintive Dainty disc will be a hit. But Billy's unlikely to turn into another Newley.

"I like to think of myself as a funny man," he told me, hesitantly.

Thousands of his fans will be as delighted as I was to know that, after twelve years of marriage, Billy and Sandra have recently had a baby. Sandra, formerly an actress, his wife has named the boy Laurence—with Sir Larry in mind.

Rolling in it

IT was sure to happen. That long, likable East Ender, Joseph Roger Brown, has hit the really big money. The fabulous success of *A Picture of You* has taken him into the £800-plus bracket.

At this money, his manager explained to me, he just can't afford to let Joe take up the theatrical offers that have come his way recently.

They might net him £100 a week but after all, a guy's got to live.

R.H.

EARLY START

probably failed to learn the complicated and short-lived Madison. Doubtless they already knew how to do the Stroll and the Pony.

Along the way *Dance Party* also fulfilled its prime function, which was to promote the sales of EMI records. This was achieved by playing them as the dance instruction music and also by inviting recording stars along to Manchester Square to perform their latest release for the audience. Increasingly these performances were of the kind which audiences have slowly come to accept as normal. As the level of technical and engineering expertise in studio recording progressed so the record releases became more and more complex and harder and harder to reproduce live faithfully, even though the modern multi-track synthesised studio was a long way off. But the balance and mixing which could already be achieved on four-track, coupled with the growing quality and popularity of the new stereo LPs, meant that a great many of these live artists at Manchester Square were simply miming to their records. Fortunately this does not seem to have diminished the pleasure gained by the audiences either in the studio at the time or later on the 208 airwaves.

One of the groups (who according to Decca were not very good and were in any case 'on their way out' along with all other guitar-based groups) signed to EMI was a foursome from Liverpool who were sent along to play their second single release for the audience early in 1963. The first one, despite Luxembourg airplay on the EMI shows, had been only a minor success, but in among the 500-plus single releases available each week it had done well enough to encourage EMI into bringing out a second fairly swiftly.

Unlike 'Love Me Do', 'Please Please Me' was a massive hit – it went straight to number two and was followed by three more singles that year, all of which shot straight to number one – 'From Me to You', 'She Loves You' and 'I Want to Hold Your Hand'. Their first LP came out very quickly and *Please Please Me* topped the album charts for 30 weeks of 1963. In December it was dislodged by their second LP, *With the Beatles*.

When it happened, Beatlemania, as it was swiftly dubbed by the Press, was sudden and overwhelming, and within weeks the record industry was dominated by the Fab Four. Every record company talent scout in Britain took off at once for Liverpool where a succession of guitar-strumming groups were dusted off and thrust into the nearest recording studio in an attempt to generalise the Beatles' appeal into something less specific – the Mersey sound. Occasionally this was done with success, even more occasionally the success lasted beyond the initial hysteria, and produced lasting talents like Gerry and the Pacemakers, The Searchers and, later on, Cilla Black.

First heard on Radio Luxembourg, the Beatles had sparked off a surging tidal wave of change which was soon to sweep every corner of Britain, not just Liverpool, and unearth hordes of talented recording artists who had previously been undreamt of or, more likely, unheard.

But for now, in 1963, the stage belonged to the Beatles alone. 'The Beatles,' said Muriel Young, 'changed everything. Before them I used to do all my announcing in cocktail frocks and things, but after the Beatles you could wear any casual outfit you wanted. They got rid of all that stuffiness and many, many years of dressing up. And of course after them groups like the Hollies and the Animals arrived, and you looked absolutely potty in these formal clothes, completely wrong.'

Within a few weeks the nature of the audience changed completely, and *Dance Party* became host to the teenagers as the age of the would-be-dancers dropped drastically – and of course the younger people weren't really there to dance, they had come to catch glimpses of their idols. Which they did in short order. The Beatles made their second appearance at Manchester Square within three or four weeks of the first. Their presence there hadn't been announced in advance, and it certainly hadn't been advertised anywhere. But as Muriel Young faced the youthful and exuberant audience, she had only time to announce 'And now a return visit from those four young men . . .' and the rest was drowned in applause and screams. The Beatles *had* changed everything, and their appearance on shows like *Dance Party* opened the door to the flood of new bands, and to a flood of new personalities working in radio.

By the middle of 1963 Jimmy Savile, whose career in radio was now firmly established, and who was still busy being Luxembourg's top-rated DJ, had found it essential to be in London. His dancehall activities had by now transferred to the Lyceum Ballroom in the Strand, which was packed out every moment that he was there. In between his stints on stage he used the successful resident DJ from the *Disc Dance* show at Fulham Town Hall (a regular sell-out occasion) to fill in for him, and the obvious next step was to pass his stand-in along the line to Hertford Street and Radio Luxembourg, where he was instantly accepted. Not only was he acceptable to Radio Luxembourg and the sponsored shows, he was good enough to take up residency in the Grand Duchy, and when Brook Denning left 208 in May of 1963 to go to the British Forces Network in Cologne, Don Wardell made the tortuous journey to Brussels and then went on by Lux Air to the Grand Duchy. Even now Don Wardell can remember those first days in Luxembourg; he was the late-night presenter between midnight and 3.00 a.m. on *Late Night Luxembourg* and the very first record he ever played on 208 was by Buddy Holly: 'Brown-eyed Handsome Man'.

Born in Birmingham, he was 24 when he arrived in Luxembourg, and the then Head of Production Bob Brown changed his name to Don for him for the simple reason that 'we can't have a disc jockey called Dominic', which was his real name. But he was better known by another name before very much longer, as he adopted a Beatles song for his theme tune, and became widely known as 'This Boy' Don Wardell.

Don Wardell stayed only a short time in Luxembourg, returning to Britain in 1964 in response to the lure of television. Despite the fact that he, like so many others, loved the country and the people at least as well as the radio station, he returned to present Southern Television's pop programme *Countdown* with Muriel Young. Like Muriel and so many

Ex-Luxembourg DJ, now an ex-patriate, Don Wardell.

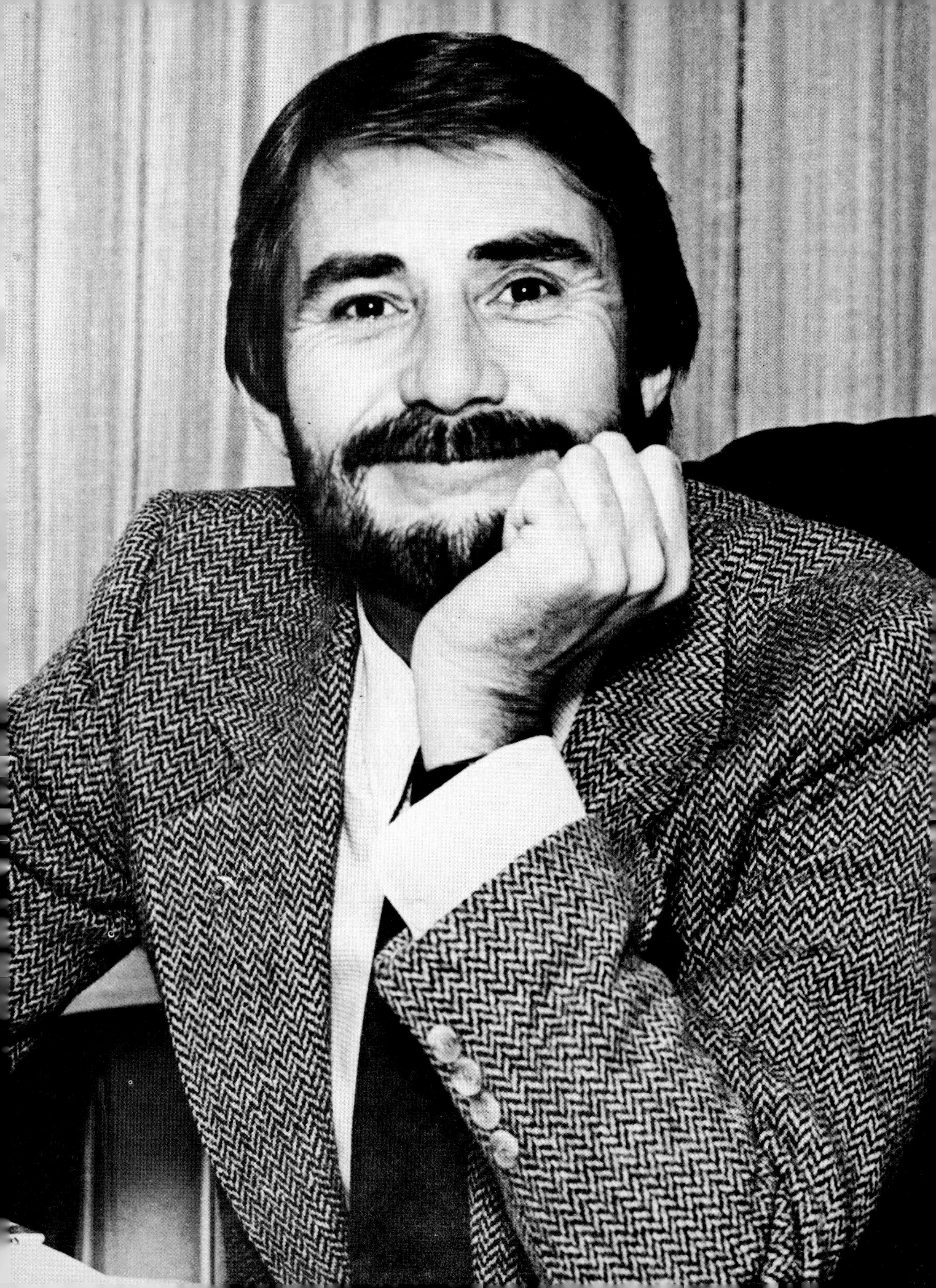

other homing disc jockeys from Luxembourg, he also found himself a spot on 208 after his return, presenting taped shows for the Pye record company twice each week, so his contact with the station never completely faded away – something which would be important for him and for Radio Luxembourg in the not-too-distant future.

In the same year that Don Wardell returned to England the Beatles, whose success had so far been confined to the UK, crossed the Atlantic and appeared on TV on the *Ed Sullivan Show*. This opened up the entire continent of the United States to the Mersey sound, and to almost anything else which emanated from Britain, which was rapidly being seen as the international centre of the youth movement, and would soon lead the world in fashion, Pop Art, and music.

When the Beatles finally hit the charts in America they did it in typically American fashion – BIG. The 1963 chart-toppers had been Bobby Vinton, The Rooftop Singers, The Four Seasons, Lesley Gore, Jan and Dean, The Chiffons and Ruby and the Romantics. When the Merseybeat sound had broken in Britain the American music industry had almost completely ignored it, possibly in the hope that it would very soon go away. But in 1964 the Beatles were there, in America, and immediately started to make up for lost time. In 1963 only one of America's 50 best-selling singles had been British (the instrumental 'Telstar'). In 1964 the proportion had grown to include 12 records, including the top two – 'I Want to Hold Your Hand' and 'She Loves You'. When the Beatles arrived in early 1964 and made that first TV appearance the resulting wave of Beatlemania was bigger than it had been in Britain, and by April that year all of the top five records were by the Beatles, and the Fab Four managed a total of 15 Top Twenty entries during the course of the year. Other British groups were close behind – The Dave Clark Five had seven records in the American Top Twenty during 1964, and they were closely followed by Billy J Kramer and The Dakotas, The Searchers, Gerry and the Pacemakers and Manfred Mann. Only two of those groups (Manfred Mann and The Dave Clark Five) were not from Liverpool.

But while the Merseybeat was out conquering the States the British music business was at home discovering the rest of its native talent, and it was during this year that The Rolling Stones and The Who, two of the most enduring supergroups, emerged from the streets and clubs of London to take their place in the charts.

Suddenly, in the middle of the sixties, the music business in Britain was transformed from its former self, and had become a vibrant and demanding animal with its own power and direction, urgently in need of more and more ways to express itself. Radio Luxembourg had obliged by being receptive to all this new music. Unlike the BBC, Radio Luxembourg was in on the ground floor, largely through the medium of the taped shows sponsored by the record companies but again through their own request programmes and their own DJ shows, which were the product of the personal preferences of the station announcers. These latter invariably included a more than fair representation of latest releases since the record company pluggers went to great lengths to ensure that Radio Luxembourg had a first-class selection of records to choose from, all of them up-to-the-minute as the still-laborious communications between the Grand Duchy and London would allow. And while transport was difficult, even patchy, telephones were even worse; International Direct Dialling was a thing of the future, and getting a telephone connection between two European countries separated by national borders and the English Channel was a major production which could occupy half an hour or longer.

Even so Radio Luxembourg's English Service was the station to listen to if you wanted to know what was going on in the music business and in the recording world. It was the only station in Europe supplying a constant stream of the latest British releases, which by now were dominating the international charts as well. This meant that 208 was at the forefront of the music trade throughout the world; by now they may not have been the biggest and they were by no means the loudest, but in street-wise terms they were beyond doubt the best.

In 1965 Barry Alldis, still Head of the English Service, was presented with his own Gold Disc, in Norway of all places. Barry had never lost touch with his first love, which was the music itself, and although his trumpet-playing had taken second place to his career as a disc jockey he continued an active involvement with music. Over the years he would compose in excess of 100 tunes which were good enough to be published, but for now his expertise in the field had made him one of the most informed and knowledgeable disc jockeys working in radio. The fact was recognised by the Norwegian youth magazine *Det Nye*, who presented him with a Gold Disc. The inscription, in English, read: 'This billion disc has been given to Mr Barry Alldis, Head of the British Department of Radio Luxembourg, by Norway's greatest youth magazine *Det Nye* for his unique efforts over a period of ten years for the world's recording artists. Sandefjord, 11/9/65.'

It was a fitting tribute to what had been a 'unique effort', and on something of a very high note Barry Alldis left 208, returning to London in 1966 where he began a series of different programmes for the BBC. Inevitably this would include *Housewives' Choice*, to which Teddy Johnson had been re-admitted some four years previously, and later would include *Swingalong, Newly Pressed, Monday Monday* and the TV series, *Juke Box Jury*. This half-hour spot on Saturday evening, which shared early-evening peak time with the still-running *Dr Who* science fiction thriller, was hosted by ex-Luxembourg person David Jacobs, and coined several catch-phrases of the time like 'Hit or miss?' and 'I like the beat'. However it would never be Barry's big chance; he made more impact on the radio show *Late Night Extra* and his own early morning show each Sunday on the as yet unborn Radio One, but all that was in the future.

His place on 208 as Head of the English Service was taken up by Don

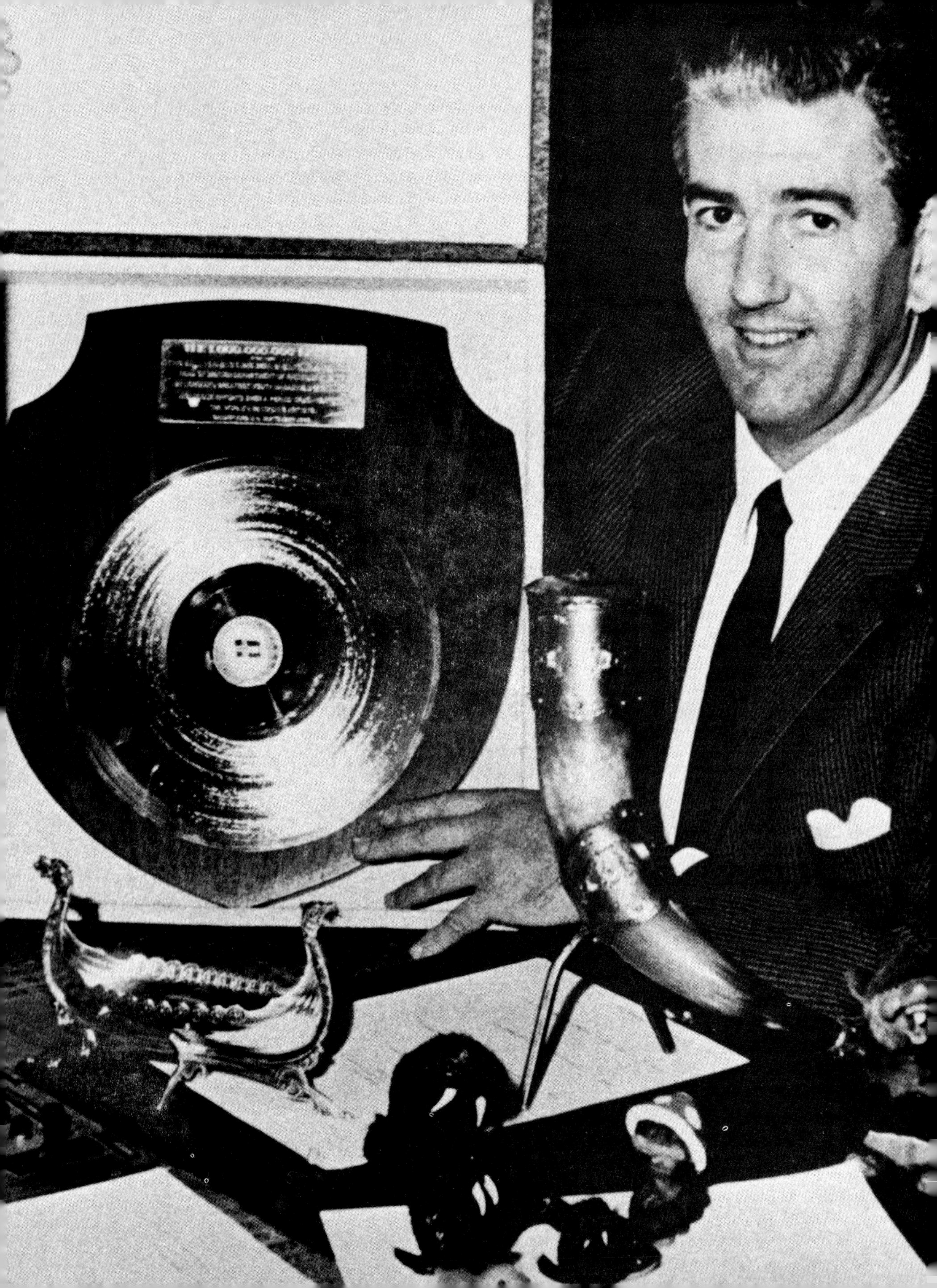

Wardell, who returned to Luxembourg in 1966. Don Wardell immediately took over the Sunday night *Top Twenty Show* (which was then jointly sponsored by Fry's Chocolate and Elida Shampoo) and also managed an unbelievable 23 other shows each week under his 'This Boy' Don Wardell persona. On top of that he returned regularly to Britain every Monday evening, flying direct now from Luxembourg to Heathrow on British Eagle's only BAC 111 jet, driving to Southampton, recording *Countdown* for Southern and then returning to the Grand Duchy in time for Tuesday evening's broadcasting. With him in Luxembourg were the team that Barry Alldis had left behind – Chris Denning, Johnny Moran and Big Bill Hearne, a 6ft 3in Canadian.

This team were almost the last to present the 'traditional' type of programme from Luxembourg, and the late sixties saw the end of a period and style of programming which had been a constant since 1946 but which in reality stretched right back into 1933. During this 30-year period Radio Luxembourg had pioneered their way through the development of radio and led everybody else, including the BBC, as the formats which had grabbed the public ear and held it for so long were thrashed out. By now 208 had become synonymous with the very best radio available and had been astoundingly popular all the while. All through this time they had been completely hamstrung by their separation from London, which at first had perhaps not been terribly important.

The lack of studio facilities in London which were linked directly to their transmitter had put Luxembourg at a distinct disadvantage compared to the BBC. However they had overcome this with enormous success, and had tempted all the stars they had ever needed on to their programmes. The cost of taping programmes in Britain and transporting the results out to Luxembourg had been huge, but it had been the sponsors who had borne the cost of all this more than willingly. Luxembourg had thrived during the whole time and doubtless could have done better had they enjoyed the same facilities as the BBC. About the only area in which Luxembourg had lagged behind the BBC had been in the area of news coverage, but at no time had this been a major drawback. Only in the ensuing years would this become more important, and Radio Luxembourg soon found that it was not too difficult an operation to manage, especially as communications began to improve. Indeed, the advent of International Direct Dialling, teleprinters and regular jet services between London and Luxembourg arrived just in time to help the radio station combat a new and hitherto unseen threat.

One of the new dangers just beginning to appear over their horizon was the very thing which had stood them in such good stead for the past few years – the emergence of an especially strong British music industry. Throughout the pre-war period and right up until the late fifties the distance between Luxembourg and London had hardly been a great inconvenience to Radio Luxembourg. The heart of the music industry had been in America all that time and Luxembourg was no further away from it than the BBC were. And their greater spending power, resulting

Barry Alldis and the gold disc presented to him by *Det Nye* magazine.

from the commercial nature of their operation, had meant that they could quite easily arrive at the point where visiting American artists went first or only to Radio Luxembourg; the BBC got second choice or even no choice at all, and Radio Luxembourg had been able to maintain a superiority in this field.

Even in the 10 years or so after the war this situation had continued, and when British artists had hit records they were almost always cover versions of American originals – which originals were more accessible to Radio Luxembourg than they were to the BBC, even had that austere organisation decided to opt for popular radio instead of educational radio. But, as Muriel Young observed, the Beatles changed everything, and the music industry suddenly blossomed. Now, as far as Radio Luxembourg was concerned, it might just as well still have been in America, but for the BBC it was right in their backyard. Luckily the BBC did very little, if anything, about it, and *Housewives' Choice* continued to be followed by *Morning Story* and so on; as far as the output from Broadcasting House was concerned daytime audiences in Britain were living on an unexpurgated diet of crooners, Victor Sylvester and *The Archers*.

Radio Luxembourg couldn't do much about it either, but it was clear that someone somewhere would have to step into the breach and do something. That something wasn't very long in coming, but when it arrived it was in an even more unlikely spot than Radio Luxembourg. In the early thirties the possibility that continental Europe would become the development hotbed for British radio was remote; that it would attract some of the largest radio audiences to an apparently insignificant country squeezed between France and Germany seemed impossible, yet it happened.

The thought, in the early sixties, that the face of broadcasting in Britain would be changed yet again by an outside influence seemed unlikely. That this said outside influence should be located in the North Sea was ridiculous.

Radio Luxembourg

PROGRAMMES FOR THE WEEK 18th FEBRUARY to 24th FEBRUARY 1962

RADIO LUXEMBOURG ★ The Station of the Stars ★

208 metres Medium Wave
(And on 49.26 metres short wave)

DAILY FROM 6.00 p.m. till 2.00 a.m.

SUNDAY, FEB. 18th

p.m.
6.00 Butlin's BEAVER CLUB with "Uncle" Eric Winstone (Butlin's Holiday Camps Ltd.)

6.15 FILM TIME Introduced by Anthony Marriott and Hector Stewart

6.30 TUNE A MINUTE A non-stop parade of all-time hits sung by June Marlowe, Joan Baxter, Kenny Bardell and Ray Burns with the Ronnie Aldrich Quintet Produced by Barclay's ("Honey Barclay's" "Infra-Draw" Method)

7.00 Jack Jackson's JUKE BOX Presenting all the latest, up-to-date, up-to-the-minute pops and (The Decca Record Co. Ltd.)

7.30 SWOON CLUB A weekly meeting of the teenagers' original Club of the Air. Swoon to your favourite recording stars. Prize for the best letters answered. Club Secretary: Patrick Allen Advice Bureau: Helen Baxter (Cussons Laboratories Ltd.) (Hillborn Hair Lacquer)

7.45 SUNDAY'S REQUESTS introduced by Bruce Denning

8.15 SPIN BEAT introduced by Barry Alldis

8.30 YESTERDAY'S HIT PARADE A reminder of the big songs of the past brought to you by

9.00 TRANS-ATLANTIC TOPS Up to the minute hits from both sides of the Atlantic presented by Pat Campbell (Nescafé Instant Coffee)

9.30 THE 208 RHYTHM CLUB Presents the best in British trad jazz. This week's star: Mr. Acker Bilk and his Paramount Jazz Band, introduced by George Melly

9.45 MATT MONRO SINGS to the accompaniment of the Johnny Spence Quartet (Peter Stuyvesant Cigarettes)

10.00 THE SAM COSTA SHOW (Carreras Guards Cigarettes)

10.30 MacDonald Hobley invites you to MAKE A TAPE in which you can hear yourself on the air, and win a four day trip to Paris, complete with a personal cabaret appearance, plus a personal audition with each city record company. Listen to leading record company. Other big prizes given weekly. Competition details of this exciting competition. (Currys Radio and Cycle Stores)

11.00 TOP TWENTY A review of the week's best selling records in accordance with the charts of the New Musical Express introduced by Barry Alldis (Stoddard and Bruntons Shampoos)

12.00 Kent Walton introduces TOP OF THE SHOP the latest and greatest in pops

Tit-Bits 4½d
The Official Publication for Radio Luxembourg
EVERY MONDAY 4½d

It's All Happening on . . .

WARNER BROS. RECORD SHOW

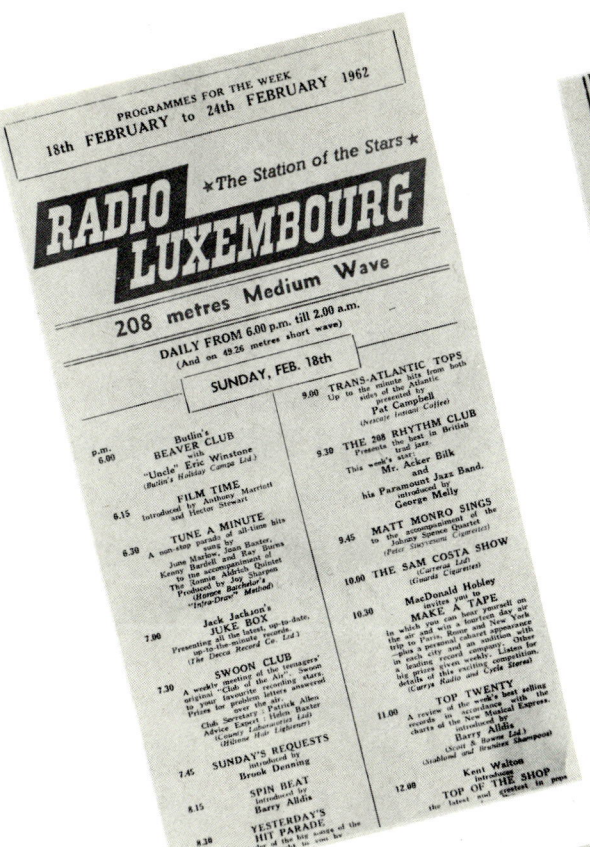

introduced by

JIMMY SAVILE

ON

TUESDAYS

AT

10.30 p.m.

RADIO LUXEMBOURG ★ The Station of the Stars ★

208 metres Medium Wave
and 49.26 metres SHORT WAVE

DAILY FROM 6.00 p.m. till 12.30 a.m.

SUNDAY, MAR. 6th

p.m.
6.00 Butlin's BEAVER CLUB with "Uncle" Eric Winstone (Butlin's Holiday Camps Ltd.)

6.15 TUNE A MINUTE A non-stop parade of all-time hits sung by June Marlowe, Joan Small, Kenny Bardell and Ray Burns with the accompaniment of The Ronnie Aldrich Quartet ("Horace Barclay's" "Infra-Draw" Method)

6.45 ROSEMARY CLOONEY Presents America's versatile singing star in her Hollywood programme (Exquisite Form)

7.00 Jack Jackson's JUKE BOX Presenting all the latest, up-to-date, up-to-the-minute pops and (The Decca Record Co. Ltd.)

7.30 SWOON CLUB A weekly meeting of all teenagers. Swoon and dance to the top stars and hear your problems answered by the Club's Advice Bureau. Prizes awarded for the air. Club Secretary: Patrick Allen Advice Bureau: Helen Baxter (Hilltone)

7.45 THE WINIFRED ATWELL SHOW starring the Queen of the Keyboard in Trinidad's Luxembourg Production (Currys Radio and Cycle Stores)

8.00 Don Mason introduces THE MAGIC OF SINATRA Take a beautiful melody, add the incomparable mystery of Frank Sinatra and that scintillating magic is in this show (Exquisite Form)

8.30 Michael Miles invites you to TAKE YOUR PICK Bringing you the mystery of "Box Thirteen" and details of how to play "Air Partner" and who "Aludox powders" on (Beecham's Cough Mixture) Vena's

9.00 Desmond Carrington introduces CALLING THE STARS Featuring sound tracks from the latest films with the stars and film personalities offering prizes of best competition for one of the leading record playing Brecknam's groups Lac-ounde

9.30 THE IRISH HOSPITALS GOODWILL PROGRAMME featuring an exciting new "Tune Titles" prize competition (Irish Hospitals)

10.00 Philips presents RECORD RENDEZVOUS introduced by Dave Gell (Philips Records) The Stargazers

10.30 WOODBINE QUIZ TIME Compered by Gerry Wilmot (W. D. & H. O. Wills) (Woodbines)

11.00 TOP TWENTY A review of the week's best selling records in the accordance with the charts of the New Musical Express introduced by Barry Alldis (Stan's Emulsion and Hand Cream, Stabling and Walkers Lemon Shampoo and Brushes) Shavex

12.00 TOP RANK TIME Top Rank features the top recordings of the Programme introduced by Kent Walton with Record Gossip by Peter Noble (Top Rank Records)

12.30 — Close Down
49.26 m. — SHORT WAVE
7.30 — 8.00 p.m. Classical Music

RADIO LUXEMBOURG (LONDON) LIMITED
38 Hertford Street, London, W.1.
TELEPHONE HYDe Park 5061 (10 lines)
(All information available for reproduction)

1	I WANT TO HOLD YOUR HAND	The Beatles
2	GLAD ALL OVER	The Dave Clark Five
3	SHE LOVES YOU	The Beatles
4	YOU WERE MADE FOR ME	Freddie & The Dreamers
5	I ONLY WANT TO BE WITH YOU	Dusty Springfield
6	24 HOURS FROM TULSA	Gene Pitney
7	DOMINIQUE	The Singing Nun
8	SECRET LOVE	Kathy Kirby
9	SWINGIN' ON A STAR	Big Dee Irwin
10	HIPPY HIPPY SHAKE	Swinging Blue Jeans
11	MARIA ELENA	Los Indios Tabajaras
12	DON'T TALK TO HIM	Cliff Richard
13	I WANNA BE YOUR MAN	The Rolling Stones
14	THE BEATLES (L.P.)	The Beatles
15		The Shadows
16	(E.P.)	The Beatles
17		Elvis Presley
18	...LK ALONE	Ger...
19		Chris Sandf...
20	(E.P.)	The...

7: JOLLY ROGER

1964 was a vintage year for pop music in Britain. Riding high on the crest of the wave of Beatlemania which was by now deluging America, practically every young British lad with aspirations to the big time was being given a chance before the microphone. Most of them faded away into obscurity – if they ever rose out of it – but a few remained. In order to give voice to this homegrown talent there arose, out of nowhere, a corresponding wealth of homegrown radio stations, festooning the North Sea with their transmitter masts and bombarding the nation with non-stop pop.

From the pirate radio stations emerged the face of daytime radio in this country as it is today, and the pirates did more to change the broadcasting position in this country than all the reports of all the Pilkington Committees ever could. If local commercial radio was not to be made legal and accessible then there were a few people who believed in it strongly enough to do it illegally. Eventually their pressure would force a radical change in the whole situation and would also introduce another previously undiscovered wealth of talent to the microphone, this time as practitioners of the increasingly-admired disc jockey's art. From the pirate ships would come the voices of Tony Blackburn, John Peel, Johnnie Walker, Dave Lee Travis, Kenny Everett and loads more.

The first pirate ship to go on the air was Caroline, and she would also be the last one to go off the air. She was followed very swiftly by Radio London, probably the most successful of them all, and then by swarms of others: Radio 270, Caroline North, Scotland, 370 and many more. Some didn't last very long, others went the full four-year term, but it seemed that every time one of them went off the air there were at least two more coming on to take its place. And when they finally did all close down their DJs, almost without exception, moved on to either the BBC or to the Grand Duchy of Luxembourg. In this way 208 collected Tony Prince, Tommy Vance, Tony Blackburn, Mark Wesley and others. And come 1968 it wasn't only people from in front of the microphone who were looking for a new job – Radio Luxembourg inherited producer Ken Evans and then Alan Keen who would become General Manager of Radio Luxembourg (London) Ltd in 1970.

In 1964 Alan Keen was selling advertising space on the *Daily Mirror* when it was suggested to him that he should contact Philip Birch, who had just arrived at the J Walter Thompson advertising agency from America. He made the phone call and went to what sounded like a very mysterious meeting in a London hotel room, during the course of which Philip Birch said that he was opening a radio station and would Alan Keen care to get involved. It was a heavyweight operation, this one, and a great deal of effort went into the new station for months before it got on the air. In fact over £200,000-worth of advertising had been sold before

On 1st January 1964 Jimmy Savile introduced the very first *Top of the Pops*.

the first transmission was made, but just before Christmas 1964 a group of extremely excited gentlemen gathered round a radio set listening for something only a handful of people knew would happen. At precisely 11.00 a.m. they heard the tuning whistle from the transmitter aboard a ship in the North Sea and two days later the voice of Paul Kay put Radio London on the air on 266 Metres, the first of a highly professional team of disc jockeys to work on the station. The only untried voice on Radio London's original line-up was a young lad whose first big impression on the listening public came as one half of the Kenny and Cash duo – Kenny Everett.

Ken Evans' career on pirate radio had begun with Radio Atlanta (later to merge with Caroline) in December 1963. Australian born, Ken Evans had worked on radio in his native land for a commercial station in Sydney, 2CH, and in 1962 was working in London on an interview assignment. It was here that he happened to meet Alan Crawford, the man who started the North Sea goldrush, and Ken Evans found his way on to pirate radio when Caroline went on the air on Good Friday, which in 1964 fell during March, predating Radio London by some nine months.

Stuart Henry had been born in Edinburgh in 1942, and had always been determined to be an actor. A three-year course at Glasgow Drama College won him a contract with the BBC in Scotland and he worked for a number of years in theatre, radio and television. But in the early sixties, as the pirate radio ships began to multiply in number, Stuart found himself attracted by radio and particularly by the emergence of the new offshore rebel, Radio Scotland. Being a disc jockey was not a prime ambition in Stuart's life until then, and neither was it a job for which he was especially well-qualified either by experience or training, but nonetheless he made an audition tape and sent it to the station. The story of Stuart Henry's involvement with radio may well have ended there had it not been for the fact that Stuart had persuaded his mother to buy him a tape recorder for his thirteenth birthday. Not just any old tape recorder, this one was a Ferrograph, and although perhaps not of professional broadcast quality it was definitely a major advance on the low-speed items which were only then beginning to grace domestic living rooms. By virtue of this machine and his experience with it Stuart says that, while he may not have been an especially good disc jockey, his audition tape was immaculate – thanks to some judicious work with a razor blade and a roll of splicing tape. He got the job, and immediately took to the ocean waves as a pirate disc jockey.

However there was one major flaw in this proceeding; Stuart suffered from violent and almost incurable seasickness. Despite cramming himself with just about every kind of proprietary medication available, he was unable to do anything about this particular handicap and his future on the radio – at least the oceanic variety – began to look rather limited.

The whole affair was not helped very much by conditions on Radio Scotland. Like most of the other pirate ships the atmosphere on board

The young Stuart Henry with optional budgerigar.

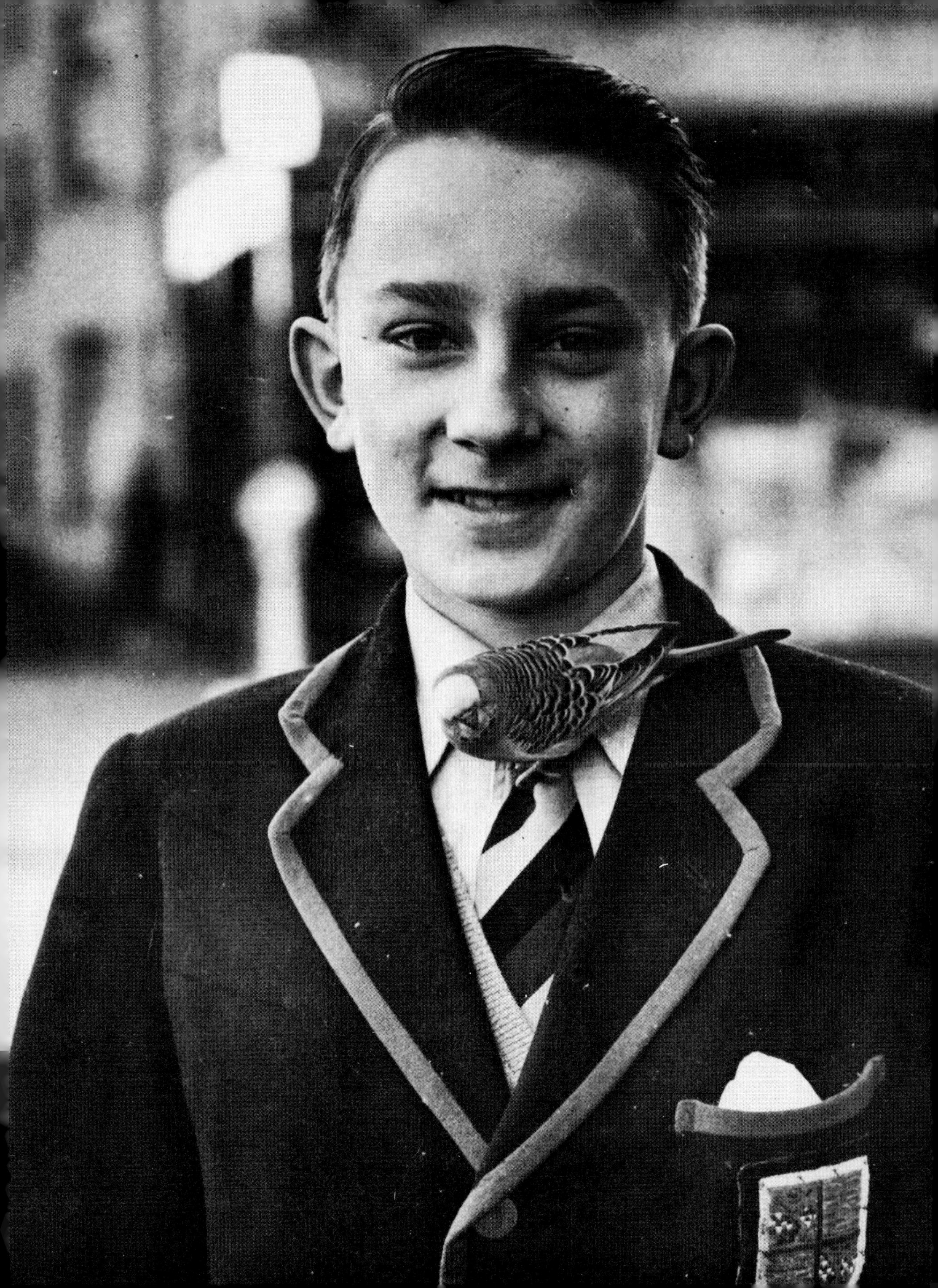

was far removed from that of a cruise liner. The ship, Stuart recalls, was condemned in about 1920, or if it wasn't then it should have been. The studio was roughly the size of a small broom cupboard in which there was just enough room for the DJ to sit behind the control desk. The door to the studio was immediately behind the disc jockey's chair, and if both people were small and slim then there was occasionally room for one other person, standing, to squeeze in behind. There was no actual ventilation in this cell-like arrangement, which meant that it was hardly the sort of place in which to be sick. Other DJs didn't appreciate Stuart all that much, but before too long he was saved from this predicament by the very thing which caused it and against which the entire armoury of medical science (and a hypnotist) had been powerless.

Back on dry land, a failed pirate disc jockey, Stuart was again approached by Radio Scotland. The ship they operated from was anchored in a spot which suffered from notoriously bad weather, a snippet of information with which Stuart was intimately acquainted. Because of this, conditions in the studio were unstable and unpredictable and it was hard to persuade people to work on the ship. Those who did, on three-week tours, often stayed longer than intended simply because bad weather prevented them from leaving. Likewise, it was hard to persuade pop stars who were touring Scotland to visit the ship and be interviewed, because no one could say with any certainty whether they'd be able to get off again or whether they'd be stuck there for weeks on end.

Because of all this Radio Scotland had decided what was called for was a land-based studio in Glasgow, and it was in this that Stuart Henry began to work. At the same time he began, with Tam Paton, to run one of the first mobile discotheque outfits in Scotland – an insignificant enough step which would have important results for Stuart in the future. It brought him together with another Radio Scotland DJ, Mark Wesley, who had begun his pirate career at about the same time, starting on Radio Essex in 1965 before going on to 270. Mark Wesley was on Radio Scotland at the time of the Marine Offences Act and went from there to Radio North Sea International before coming ashore in 1970 to join yet another ex-pirate who had just left Radio Caroline.

Born in Oldham in 1944, here was yet another disc jockey who had never intended to become one. In fact his first idea was to become another sort of jockey altogether, and he and Willie Carson went seeking their fortune together. Willie Carson stuck it out, but his stablemate turned to the music business when Ringo Starr (then playing drums for Rory Storm and the Hurricanes) suggested he enter the talent contest at the Butlins holiday camp the ill-fated band were working at. The result of that was another two years on the road, this time as a singer with The Jasons, who were pitting their talents against The Hollies, Billy J Kramer and the Dakotas and Freddie and the Dreamers in the pubs and clubs around Manchester. When they packed it all in their lead singer went on with another band, and one night when they were working at the Top Rank in Bristol the resident disc jockey failed to show up. The

Tony Prince with famous friends, Linda and Paul McCartney.

manager of the place asked the band's lead singer if he'd take over for the evening and Tony Prince at last found what he'd been looking for.

After a period with Top Rank Tony moved on to compere *Discs-A-Go-Go* on the commercial TV channel in the Bristol area, introducing artists like Tom Jones, Marianne Faithfull, Sonny and Cher, and a disc jockey from one of the pirate ships trying to make a career for himself as a singer. It was he who gave Tony Prince the telephone number of Radio Caroline's offices and when the TV series was over Tony Prince auditioned for a job at sea, eventually staying two years and having more success as a disc jockey than Tony Blackburn had as a singer.

While Tony Prince was discovering that he enjoyed being a disc jockey another northerner was also talking his way into a dancehall as a disc jockey. Born in Birmingham in 1945, he'd left school after failing eight O levels and had trained as a car mechanic, eventually being promoted to car salesman at a Solihull garage. While working at this during the day he persuaded the manager of the local Locarno ballroom to employ him as a disc jockey. Operating the Locarno's one turntable earned him a staggering £1 8s. a night and might have led nowhere had the newspapers not mentioned that yet another pop pirate was going into action in the North Sea – Radio England. Once they'd heard his audition tape they gave Johnnie Walker the midnight to 6.00 a.m. slot, which he filled for 18 months before moving on to Radio Caroline in October 1966.

Most of the DJs on the pirate ships were roughly the same age and had been brought up listening to Radio Luxembourg throughout the fifties, all were possessed of an urge to be involved with entertainment in some way. None of them had thought of being disc jockeys until it happened – the lucky, almost accidental, break seems to be a feature of all their stories. And at about the same time as they were leaving school Tommy Vance was being thrown out of his, which made little difference since he was almost never there anyway. After a brief spell working in a London hotel Tommy Vance joined the merchant navy and ran away to sea. Two years later, back in London, he called into Hertford Street looking for work and achieved a remarkable lack of success.

After a succession of jobs around Britain Tommy followed the lady of his dreams back to her homeland, which happened to be Canada. It was there that his ambition to work in radio, probably inspired by the fact that his father, an electronics engineer, had given him a giant Short Wave receiver when he was only 12 or 13, was finally gratified. Tommy began a lengthy and rather confusing career on the American continent; confusing because he worked at first free of charge on two radio stations (which were 35 miles apart) while at the same time having a full-time job during the day.

Eventually he managed to get a real job in radio which would support him as well, and gravitated gradually to KHJ in Los Angeles, the number one station in that sprawling city. But bad news wasn't far behind and when the draft caught up with him he had to skip town, leaving Los

Angeles 50 minutes before he was due to join the army. His fare was paid by a friend because his own bank account had been frozen, and the girl he'd followed to Canada (now his wife) was left behind because he couldn't afford two plane tickets.

Tommy Vance arrived at Heathrow airport just before Christmas in 1964. Fresh out of sunny California, working for the number one radio station on the West Coast, he was now cold and jobless, with £40 in his pocket and no sign of any more money coming in. He rang Caroline, but it was Christmas and no one was working. The £40 was just enough to find a hotel and eat until the holiday period ended and then Tommy Vance was straight round to Caroline's offices. They listened to his demo tape and put him straight on a train to Felixstowe. All in all, the journey from Hollywood to the North Sea took five days, and Tommy Vance was now at sea with Robbie Dale, Tony Blackburn, Johnnie Walker and Dave Lee Travis.

Also arriving in the North Sea to join Radio Caroline came Tony Brandon, but unlike the others he was working backwards, because before Caroline Tony Brandon's job had been on the English Service at Radio Luxembourg. He had been out in Aden before that, doing concerts and theatrical work for the British troops stationed there but had returned to Britain in March 1966 and within days found himself in Luxembourg alongside Barry Alldis (who would shortly return to London), Stuart Grundy and Colin Nicholl. Tony Brandon's first show – sponsored, like many of the others – was a 15-minute item, *Disc Drive*, which was followed by the taped Jimmy Young show, which Tony Brandon had to sit through in order to carry on with his own programmes afterwards. All the time a taped programme was being broadcast the announcer who followed it would have to be in the studio in case of some form of mechanical disaster. Sometimes the disasters weren't mechanically caused but were the result of human error, especially one involving a breakdown in communications between the English-speaking announcers and the Luxembourg-speaking engineers.

The situation in the studio at Villa Louvigny was still the same as it had always been. The announcer sat on one side of a glass wall, the engineer on the other side. The engineer played the records, the announcer did the announcing. That way everything was nice and straightforward and everybody, including the unions, was happy. In theory at least. The situation was complicated by the language barrier, also by the fact that the Gents' toilet was down two flights of stairs – more than the length of one seven-inch single away, even at jogging speed. It was not always possible to convince engineers that they should play two records back to back, in the approved segue fashion, and many of the announcers finished their programmes twisted in agony. This problem was temporarily relieved by Dave Christian in the seventies, when he supplied a yellow plastic potty for the English Service studio, but the facility was only used once, during a live broadcast, from the top of a pair of stepladders, by an off-duty DJ who had difficulty staying on his feet, never mind the rungs of his ladder, and who shall remain nameless.

Tony Brandon's major problem, though associated with the Luxembourg engineering staff, was slightly different. Just before Christmas 1966 Tony was in the studio doing a live programme before a sponsored show went out on tape. The engineer, Charlie, was well-liked if unconventional, and always began to be slightly unreliable in about the second week of December – the glorious twelfth, as a rule – and remained so until the Christmas and New Year festivities were over. His briefcase was crammed throughout this period not with technical manuals, but with endless bottles of the local wine, and after two or three of these his English, always fractured, couldn't have been saved by a plaster cast and a prolonged bout of traction.

Minutes before the taped programme was due to begin Tony Brandon introduced a record and then sprinted for the Gents. When he came back the record was just ending and Charlie was lying on the floor of the control room swathed in hundreds of feet of inextricably knotted tape – *the* tape – assuring anyone who would listen that everything would be fine. Unable to leave the studio Tony Brandon summoned help by telephone, and the day was saved when another of the English Service announcers, who fortunately happened to be in the building, grabbed a pile of records and rushed up to the studio, getting behind the microphone with only seconds to spare. Doubtless his experience in America helped the subsequent, extreme ad-lib performance, but Tony Brandon is still grateful to Tommy Vance.

Tony Brandon left Radio Luxembourg to move on to the pirate Radio London in February of 1967, roughly the same time that Tommy Vance went back to Caroline. His original stint at sea had lasted about three months and was far from ideal. Apart from the discomfort of bobbing around in the North Sea two weeks out of four, Tommy's wife was still in America. 'Communications,' said Tommy Vance, 'between the North Sea and Hollywood are not too good.' Even had she been in London they would have met only infrequently, since the two weeks' shore leave each month was largely taken up with doing live gigs around Britain. Tommy Vance applied to Radio Luxembourg for the second time in his life and this time was given a job by the same person who had turned him down the first time.

Living in Luxembourg was not a problem to Tommy Vance the way it had been and would be to other people who had lived mostly or completely in Britain. He'd been many places in the world and settled down in the Grand Duchy with few problems. But his wife still wouldn't leave Hollywood to join him, and Ronan O'Rahilly, the public face of Radio Caroline, kept trying to tempt Tommy Vance back to sea, and eventually, after about a year of steadily increasing temptation of the green folding variety, he left Luxembourg for the North Sea. And although he went back initially to Caroline he soon moved to Radio London. This was because, like many others, he could read the writing

Following page left
Stuart Henry with studio guest Charlie Watts.
Below
Mark Wesley and producer Ken Evans sort through some of the Luxembourg mail.

on the wall rather clearly, and what it said, in big letters, was 'Marine Offences Act 1967'.

It hadn't happened yet, but it was clearly coming. Right from the beginning it had been on the cards, but now it was almost inevitable. The Establishment had never approved of the pirates but had not yet felt ready to take them on properly. The Labour government, elected in 1964 to end '13 years of Tory misrule' had been given only the most slender of margins in Parliament and it never felt strong enough to move straight into a head-on conflict with the pirates, mostly because of their enormous national popularity. Even people who weren't too keen on the music acknowledged their statement of independence on behalf of what they perceived to be a good cause with some pleasure, if not actual pride. The British have always husbanded a sneaking admiration for those who steal from the rich and give to the poor. In this case the pirates were stealing air, which is an inexpensive commodity not generally regarded as falling under monopolistic control, and almost everyone was on their side.

However there was a second General Election in 1966 which returned the Labour Party with a much stronger majority, without which they would never have moved against the pirates. But even then they were provoked, when disputes over the ownership of a pirate radio station located on a Martello tower in the Thames Estuary resulted in a shooting in which one person died. Here was real piracy, and at last it was something which the Establishment could rightly legislate against. Within a very short time the Marine Offences Bill had been formulated, and even before it had been passed up to the House of Lords for rubber-stamping large numbers of people working on pirate ships were looking around for new jobs.

Ken Evans was one of them, and he arrived at Hertford Street in February 1966 to take over production of the EMI shows. Like all such producers before him he was employed by EMI and not by Radio Luxembourg, and under his banner came the largest team of disc jockeys working for a single sponsor – David Jacobs, Muriel Young, Alan Freeman, Jimmy Young, Simon Dee, Pete Brady, Mike Raymond and ex-Caroline jockey, Tony Blackburn. Ray Orchard, who had been producing and presenting shows made in London when Muriel Young first started on *Dance Party* in 1961, was still there and at first Ken Evans worked with him, but when Ray Orchard returned to Canada Ken Evans was left in sole charge of the EMI shows and he stayed on doing just that until March 1968 when the situation changed again.

By that time the Marine Offences Bill had been to the Upper Chamber where it had been greeted with unqualified approval, despite clear and continued evidence that the majority of people in Britain felt that pirate radio was a Good Thing. This has never been known to deter the government (any government), however, and may even have acted as some form of inducement. Beyond doubt the government of the day sought the opinions and advice of the BBC – and their attitude to any broadcast material which audiences enjoyed without reservation is well-

Following page right
Until this moment, on 15th August 1967, the Radio London pirate DJs hadn't realised how popular they really were. After 'Big L' shut down, the train bringing them to London was mobbed at Liverpool Street station.
Below
Mark Wesley in charge of the desk in the self-op studio at Villa Louvigny.

FOX
Album
SIX GUN MACHINE
DRIFTERS
BAY CITY ROLLERS
HAPPY XMAS
JOHN LENNON
Listen To This Sticker.
BUS STOP
SKY HIGH
Capitol
The Sensational
ALEX HARVEY BAND

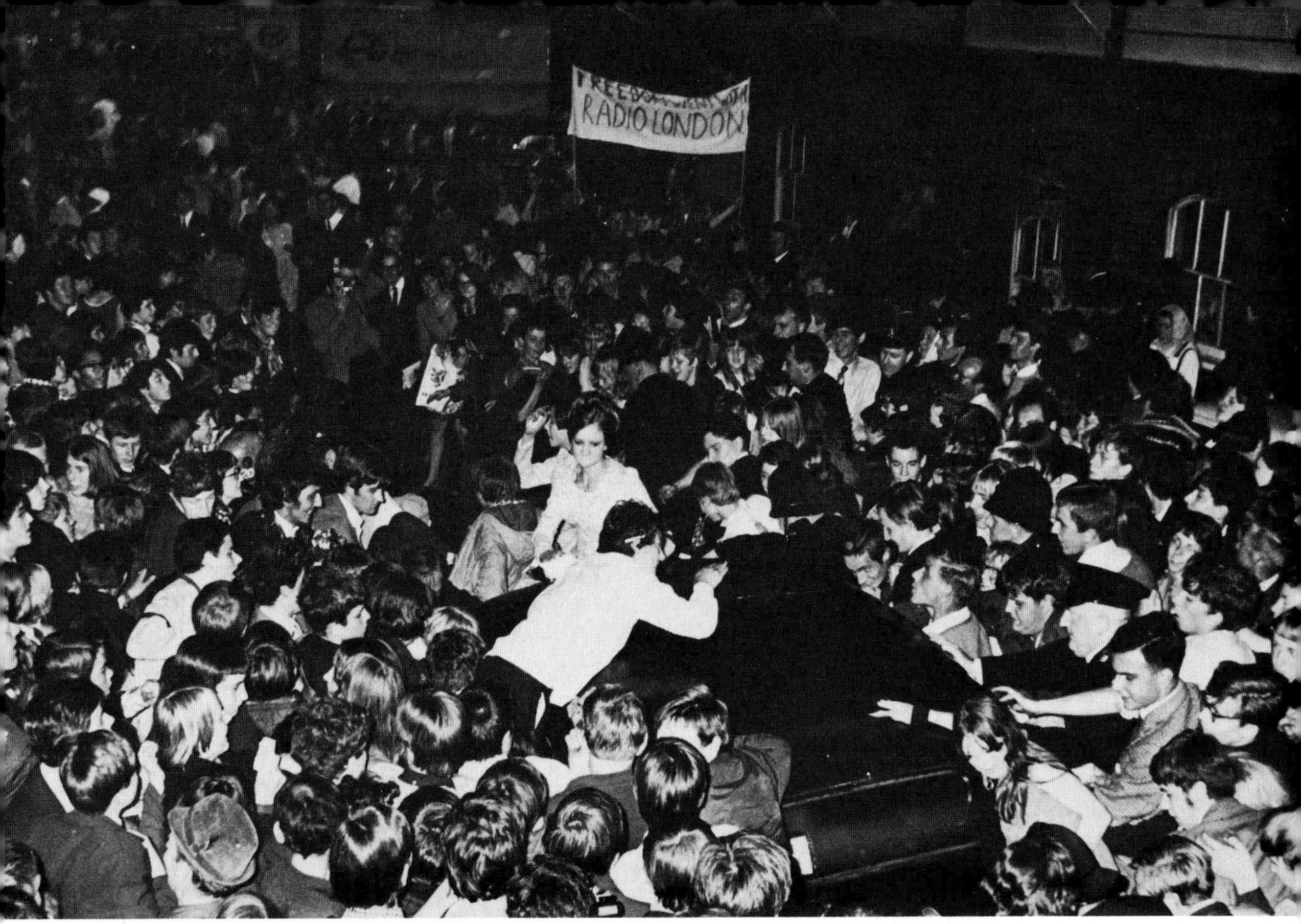
RADIO LONDON

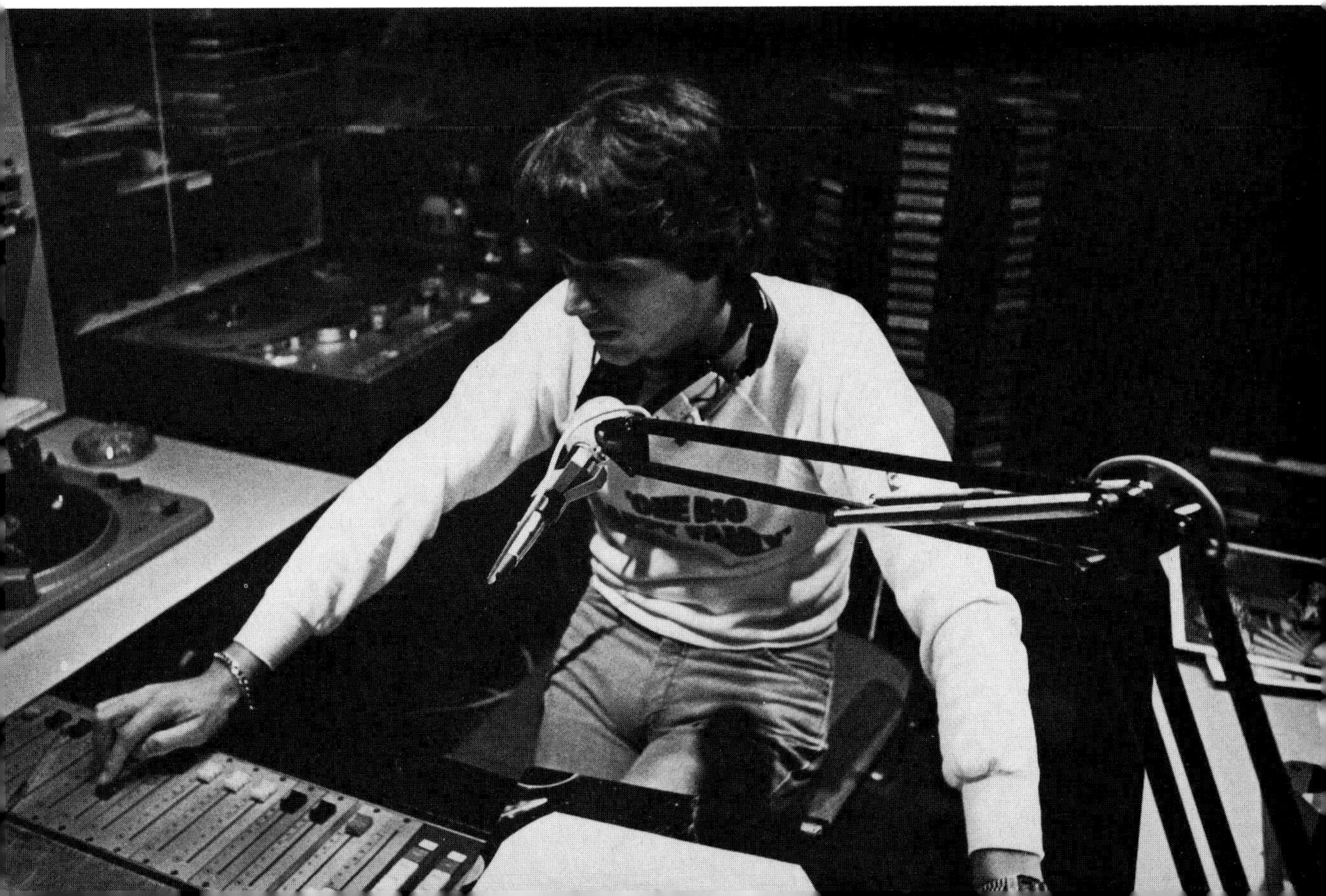

known. In the early twenties it had been 'unconsidered trifles of the lightest type'. Now, in the course of parliamentary debate, this dismissive view of popular entertainment was expressed somewhat differently. One member of the House put forward the view that allowing the public to have what the public wants represented democracy in action. 'It is not,' said one who should have known better, 'it is pandering to populism.' Inevitably the Marine Offences Bill became the Marine Offences Act in 1967 and, like the commercial stations fleeing before Hitler's jackboots in 1939, the pirates went off the air one by one. At first it looked as if Radio London may have found a way round the Act by broadcasting from France, but the French government were not prepared to face out the situation as they had in the thirties with Radios Normandy, Toulouse *et al*, and so Tommy Vance's transfer to Radio London had been in vain.

Radio London went off the air one wet afternoon at three; Caroline, who had already announced their determination to carry on throughout any adversity, was playing the peace anthem 'We Shall Overcome' as the Radio London news bulletin ended with the words 'The time is now three o'clock and Radio London is going off the air,' followed by complete silence.

The BBC plans for a replacement service to fill the gap left by the now-absent pirates made a mockery of all the political posturing which had been used to justify the ruthless eradication of the pirates. The government was quite prepared to 'pander to populism' but only when such indulgence was conducted under the umbrella of the BBC monopoly. Radio One, the new service to emerge from the BBC shake-up which changed The Light Programme, The Third Programme and The Home Service into Radios Two, Three and Four respectively, was born in September of 1967. The first voice heard on Radio One was that of ex-pirate, ex-Radio Luxembourg disc jockey Tony Blackburn. Almost all of his colleagues came from the pirate ships and the BBC swallowed up Kenny and Cash, Dave Lee Travis, Johnnie Walker, John Peel, Stuart Henry and others.

In the interim period they had all been employed on The Light Programme, doing things like *Mid-day Spin* and *Pop North*; now they were part of a bastardised service which duplicated much of its programming with Radio Two. It was years before Radio One finally grew away from this crossover, and in the meanwhile many ex-pirates passed via Radio One on to Radio Two. And at the same time the expansion of BBC radio output meant that there were now many jobs going spare, filled by large numbers of presenters who had once been the mainstays of Radio Luxembourg's sponsored output from London. Tony Blackburn was one of them, Jimmy Savile another, Alan Freeman, Pete Murray, David Jacobs, Barry Alldis, Stuart Henry, Don Moss, David Gell, Tony Brandon, Teddy Johnson – the list was almost endless.

Even so Radio One, in its early period, hardly represented a realistic alternative to the pirate stations. During the daytime at least it was the

1967, and a nervous-looking Cliff Richard presents Simon Dee with a budgerigar in the London studios after Simon was seen on TV thumping a budgie cage to make its inhabitant talk.

The cast of a BBC Light Programme pantomime in December 1965 and there's only one non-Luxembourg face in the line-up. From the left in the back row: Simon Dee, David Gell, Alan Dell and David Jacobs. In the front row are: Don Moss, Keith Fordyce, Pete Murray, odd man out Bill Crozier and Brian Matthew.

only alternative, but Radio Luxembourg once again had the evening ether to itself; the government had wiped out the competition and the BBC, presented with the gift of a vulnerable opening, had once again elected to ignore it completely. They knew what was good for their audiences and they were going to make sure the audiences got it, no matter what other people thought. In the Grand Duchy, and in Hertford Street, the thinking was less naïve.

The BBC was definitely not keen on the idea of its presenters on the brand-new Radio One appearing on programmes broadcast on Radio Luxembourg, even if they were only employed by sponsors. In fact the whole idea of radio broadcasters being involved with commercial organisations is anathema to the BBC. Tony Blackburn's association with EMI and Radio Luxembourg thus ended in 1967 when Radio One began. He had been friends with Richard Swainson (an ex-Caroline employee) and Ken Evans (also ex-Caroline) who were both now associated with Radio Luxembourg, so it was no surprise that he made his first brief sojourn on 208. He even liked the Grand Duchy and at one time quite fancied living there, but by the time Radio Luxembourg got round to offering him a job he was already settled into Radio One's breakfast show – then and ever since their biggest-rated spot of the day. He never got around to live broadcasting from the Grand Duchy until 1973, when Britain joined the EEC. Then, for one day, he and several colleagues (Jimmy Young was one of them) broadcast on BBC from Luxembourg, occupying during the day the studios which by night beamed the Radio Luxembourg programmes to Britain.

In late 1967 Radio Luxembourg faced a changing situation. The pirate radio ships had given them the first really serious opposition they'd ever encountered, and while healthy competition had its advantages – the pirates had undoubtedly increased public awareness of radio, with obvious spin-off advantages for Luxembourg's sales team – it had also made inroads into their night-time audiences. Now the pirates were gone but Radio One threatened. Immediate BBC plans for the future left Luxembourg with a clear field in the evening, but no one knew for how long. And public (and industry) clamour for commercial radio meant that the station would soon be presented with another night-time threat, although perhaps not for a few years. Plans had to be laid at once and would have to allow for the fact that BBC Radio One (and even Two) was draining their resources as far as London-based presenters were concerned. Once again it was time for a change.

8: LIVE, IF YOU WANT IT

The big change-round in the Grand Duchy began in 1968 and was the first radical shake-up since the switch to Medium Wave in July 1951. When Ken Evans first began producing shows for EMI in 1966 he had been handling about 14 hours of programming each week, all of which had previously been mixed in with the live presentation from the Grand Duchy – and that was just one of the many sponsors. In the fifties this pre-recorded material had made up the bulk of Luxembourg's output but ever since the advent of ITV that proportion had been shrinking. By the early sixties it was down to 50 per cent and still shrinking slowly. But aside from the drop in revenue from this type of sponsor there was another problem. After the pirates, the 208 format sounded dated; it had been dated for a while, but now it *sounded* dated.

The pirate ships had employed an entirely different formula to achieve commercial success; their shipboard studios were operated by the disc jockey, and all the advertising material was presented in short inserts played from tape by the DJ, rather in the form of the 'Natural Breaks' which had first appeared on ITV. In its early days ITV's advertising material had always been shown during what was captioned as a Natural Break beforehand, presumably in order to give unsophisticated audiences a chance to realise that what they were about to see represented a commercially-inspired encouragement to buy a product for which they may previously have felt no need. This, of course, did not happen but even so the Natural Break persisted for some time. The policy stipulated that advertising material should only be shown during what was clearly a *natural* break in a programme. As it was explained by Muriel Young, this meant that adverts could not interrupt a whodunnit immediately after the discovery of a corpse if the very next scene was of the anxious discoverer(s) still bending over the cadaver. The programme *could* be broken into at the moment of discovery, however, if the scene which followed the break did not immediately follow the scene before the break – if the discoverer(s) of the aforementioned stiff were by now removed to the police station or to a courtroom, for example. What this shows, principally, is that although the audiences were perhaps unsophisticated, the advertisers were not terribly far ahead of them. Translated on to radio, the 208 habit of sponsored programmes with subtle mentions of the product in question were somewhat less hard-sell than straightforward blandishments to rush out and buy something, but were perhaps faintly more insidious because of that.

There had been, right from the very beginning of commercial broadcasts in 1934, opportunities for advertisers to buy short spots on Radio Luxembourg. The very first Wireless Publicity rate card had quoted sums in the region of £75 for a 200-word message, which would have occupied a great deal longer than the short 30-second commercials modern audiences are more familiar with. In spite of what may now seem like rather a good deal, sponsors preferred the sponsored show as a format all along, and had shown no signs of wishing to deviate from it until TV changed their thinking. The pirate ships had pioneered the new system swiftly and efficiently and derived two noticeable benefits from it.

The first thing was that it allowed advertisers on to radio at very sensible prices, and put them directly in touch with the young singles who are generally reckoned to be the largest group with the biggest disposable income: they buy things. The second was that the format allowed the radio programmes thus produced, direct and continual access to the youngsters. This was the 'strip' formula by which radio today still operates and throughout which the adverts, in short breaks, are as unobtrusive as they can be to the overall programme.

It was this style of operation which Radio Luxembourg adopted in 1968, and from March of that year began to phase in as swiftly as possible. Not surprisingly it involved a number of line-up changes, and here Luxembourg made great use of a number of ex-pirate disc jockeys who were familiar with this method of working and who could help blend it into Radio Luxembourg as smoothly as possible. At the same time they took a step forward in another direction which they so far had been ignoring but to which communications technology could now admit them wholeheartedly – news gathering.

This was only a small part of the overall change, but it was an important one, if only because Radio Luxembourg had never done it before, and also because the original plan for news gathering involved the return of Don Wardell from the Grand Duchy to take over this innovation. He arrived in the Hertford Street offices in 1968 to start up the new service which was scheduled for a March/April launch, alongside the other changes.

Don Wardell wasn't alone in the brand-new department however, and one of the new boys came to Luxembourg via a rather tortuous route involving a public school in Shoreham and an 18-month spell in the Royal Navy which included a superb grounding in electronics. From there it was a short step to getting a job with Radon Electronics, who built a lot of the new mobile disco equipment which had recently become so popular. 'Road-testing' the gear on Worthing Pier alongside big bands like Geno Washington, Jimmy James and the Shondells and Showstoppers Anonymous soon turned into the job of warm-up DJ before live gigs by various top names from Radio Caroline, Radio London and, latterly, Radio One.

Tony Windsor – TW to his audience – had been immensely popular during his years as a pirate disc jockey, but when the Marine Offences Act put most of them out of action he came to London and was now working as assistant to the 208 Programme Director Tony McCarthy. So, when the young DJ who had warmed up the audiences for him on Worthing Pier showed up at Hertford Street looking for audience research figures to use in a thesis about commercial radio, TW pushed him in front of a microphone in Studio B for a voice test. Dave Christian started work for Radio Luxembourg the following Monday, initially as a newsreader on the service which was about to go into action. The original intention was that news would be read live in London and landlined out to the Grand Duchy, but yet again this all fell through, and the Post Office once more refused the facility. So plans were changed again, and Dave Christian was sent out to the Grand Duchy to read the news from there. The idea was to write the bulletins in London and simply send them across by telex. Dave arrived in Luxembourg in January 1969, a few months after two new disc jockeys who had joined Radio Luxembourg on the same day as he had – David Jensen and Noel Edmonds.

This was the all-live format to which Radio Luxembourg was gradually moving as the sponsored shows taped in London were slowly phased out – although they still played a part in 208 broadcasts and continue to do so. This is partly because the lack of that vital landline link between the United Kingdom and Luxembourg makes it unavoidable, and partly because the output of all radio stations includes a percentage of pre-recorded material to accommodate the travel schedules, not only of recording artists coming into the station to be interviewed, but also of disc jockeys who are constantly on the move between the studio and live gigs. Also the inclusion of shows taped abroad allows the station to play a great deal of music which might perhaps otherwise be unavailable for weeks or months to European listeners. Only the recent advances in satellite technology have affected this to any great degree.

In the late sixties and throughout the seventies 208 featured a number of these taped shows which served them very well indeed. When Johnnie Walker finally abandoned Caroline (he was one of the last to leave, along with 'Admiral' Robbie Dale) he worked on Radio One for a number of years, departing eventually for America in late 1974. Living in San Francisco he made a taped show each week in a small studio in Sausalito and airmailed it to the Grand Duchy, providing British audiences with a glimpse of the West Coast which they may otherwise have waited months for, or never heard at all. Johnnie Walker had been widely respected for his integrity when it came to music – at the height of the Teenybopper fads in Britain he continually made it quite clear that there are vast tracts of popular music in the Bay City Rollers vein which he disliked intensely and only played because he was obliged to. His tapes from America were, therefore, a valid contribution to radio in Europe at a time when the BBC still operated the 'playlist' system on Radio One and gave the disc jockeys very little personal control over the music they played.

Much the same was true of Emperor Rosko who, having been involved with 208 since 1966 and the end of his pirate days on Radio Caroline, sent tapes over to Luxembourg from Los Angeles for years, playing the type of West Coast music which appealed to him. Nowadays, of course, things are slightly easier in the communications field, allowing

Dave Christian in the 208 studio at Villa Louvigny.

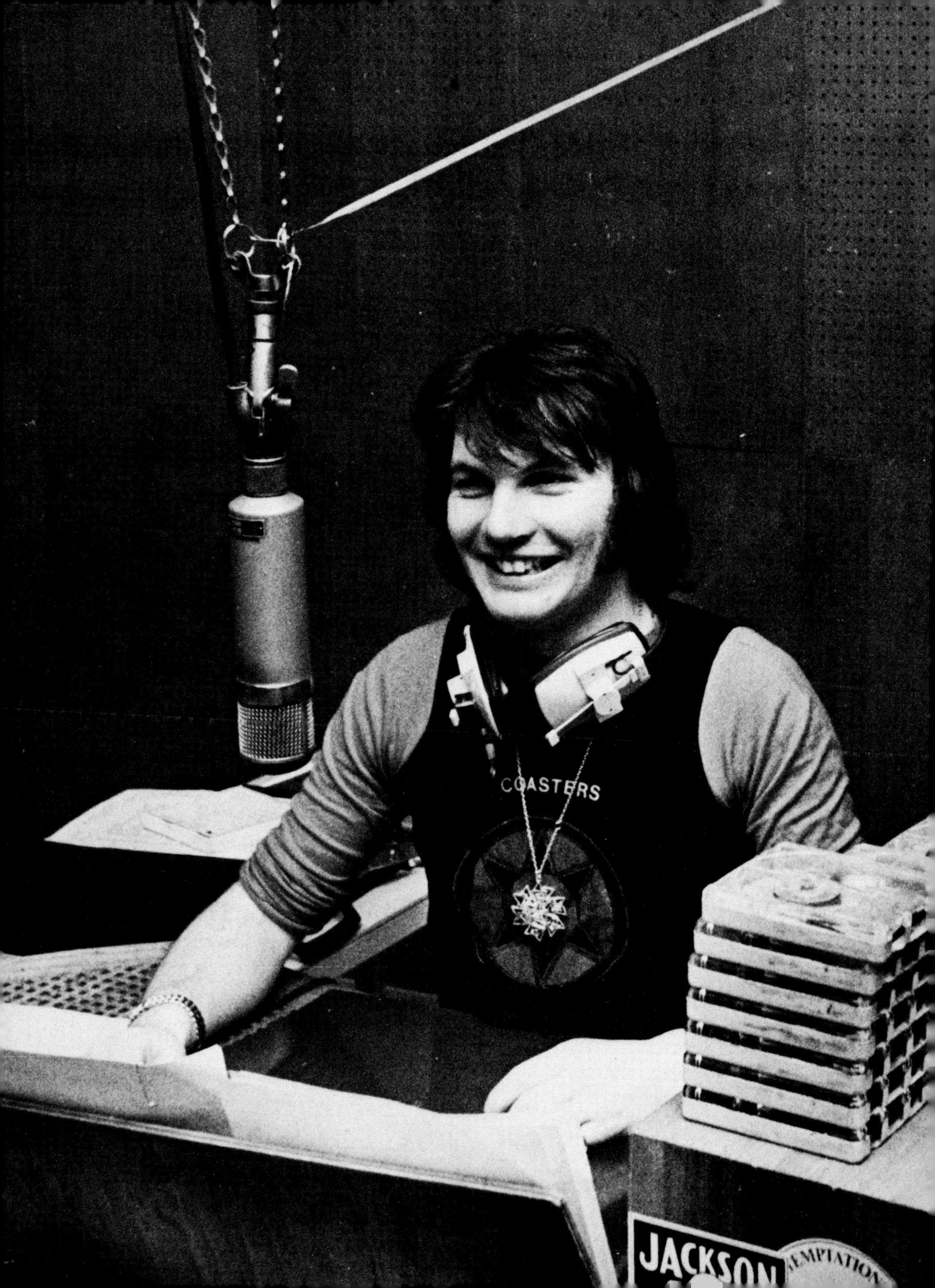
COASTERS
JACKSON

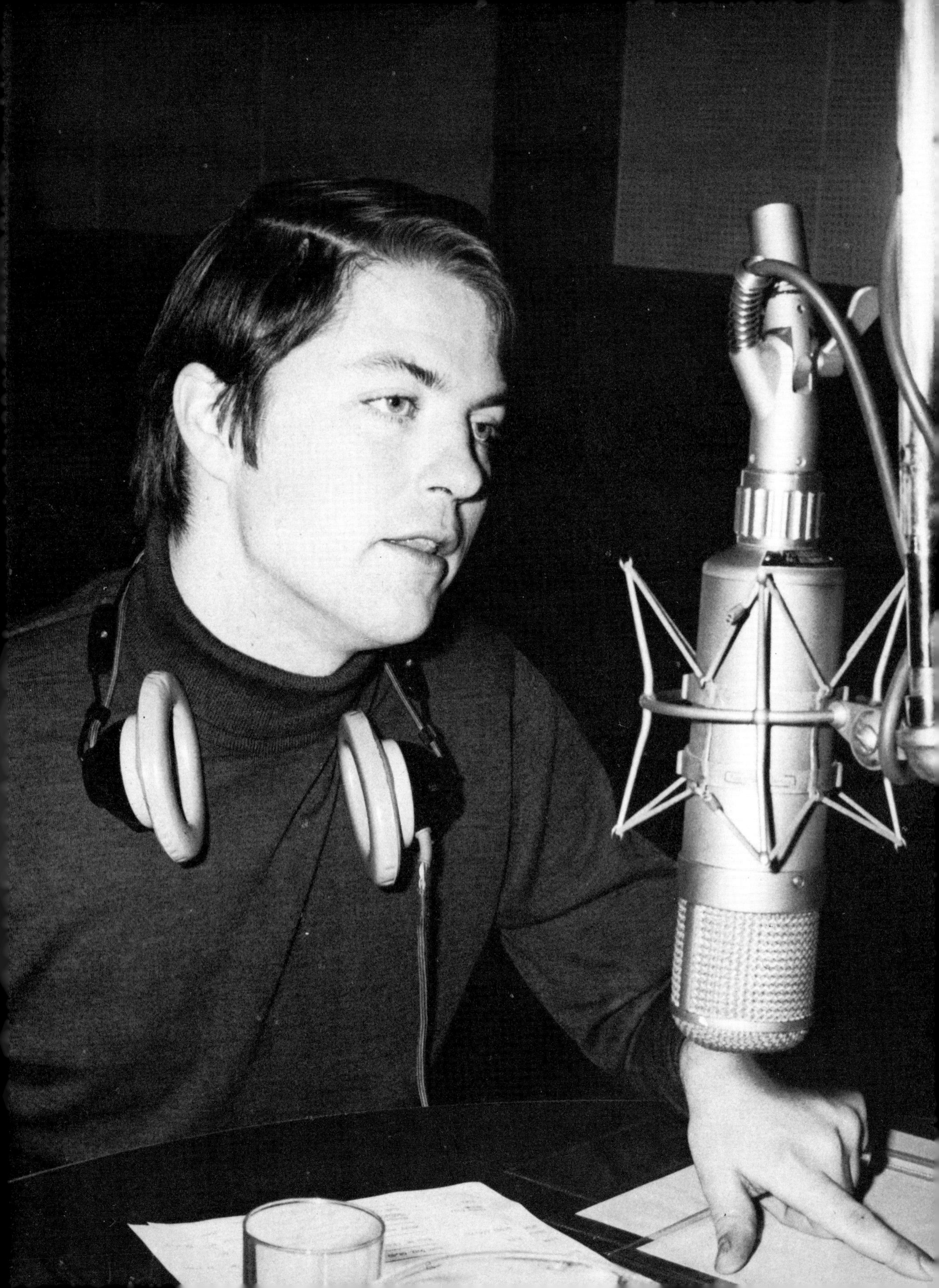

Bob Stewart to do his country marathons live from Nashville thanks to an obliging satellite – without it a taped show would be the only other way to handle it.

So although the new format for 1968 was officially recognised as being 'all-live' that will never really be true of any radio station. But the DJ team out in the Grand Duchy was now bigger than it had ever been before and was a far cry from the days in the thirties when there had just been one continuity announcer in Luxembourg. Now there were lots of them – many from pirate ships – Tony Prince, Bob Stewart, Paul Burnett, Noel Edmonds and David Jensen, joined after a few months by Dave Christian.

Noel Edmonds was a fairly unique character at Radio Luxembourg when he first started. From public school in Essex he'd been offered a place at university which he didn't really want; had there been schools, colleges or university courses in broadcasting then Noel would have attended one of them, but there weren't. Instead he sent audition tapes to every pirate radio ship floating around Britain and was offered a job just in time for the Marine Offences Act, which meant that he never set foot on a pirate ship.

It was a whole year before Tony Windsor, by now at Hertford Street, called Noel and suggested that Radio Luxembourg could use him. To begin with the job consisted of being trained in broadcasting by Radio Luxembourg, the first time the station had attempted such a thing. Noel worked in the London studio, watching, listening and learning as established presenters recorded what would be among the last of the taped shows for broadcast on 208.

Inevitably Noel made his own tapes in the studio, and coached by Tony Windsor, improved to the point where he began to tape shows for the Decca label. But once again Noel Edmonds was just behind the mainstream of events, and his Decca work started at almost the same moment as Radio Luxembourg began to phase out the taped shows. On 2 November, though, he was on his way out to the Grand Duchy to begin live presentation, initially as a newsreader.

This appeared to be something for which he was singularly unqualified, and he demonstrated the fact on his first ever broadcast. The cause of the problem was a news item which should have been very serious; a typhoid outbreak in Italy is no joking matter, after all. Several people had died and several hundred were seriously ill in hospital. All this information Noel Edmonds relayed to the 208 audience in perfect solemnity. Then came the last line which, Noel says, is still branded on his memory word for word: 'Authorities believe they have traced the source of the outbreak to an ice-cream vendor who has been washing his utensils in the Po'... Gales of helpless laughter were swiftly followed by a personal letter to Noel Edmonds from Geoffrey Everitt, who was somewhat less than amused by the whole performance.

After such an auspicious start Noel settled into life in the Grand Duchy reasonably easily, although not completely happily. He'd gone

Pete Brady behind a Radio Luxembourg microphone in Hertford Street.

there expecting it to be a more glamorous version of pirate ships, which in a lot of ways it was but, unlike the three weeks on, one week off routine of the shipboard life, it was five months before Noel had a chance to visit Britain. There were other compensations, though, for at a time when schoolmasters were telling sixth-formers with A levels that if they got a job bringing in £20 per week then they were set up for life, the DJ team on Radio Luxembourg were earning a minimum of three times that amount.

And there was little to do with the money other than get out and have a good time with the other DJs. Tony Prince was already in the Grand Duchy when Noel Edmonds arrived there; after the Marine Offences Act he'd quit Caroline North, sent audition tapes to the BBC and Radio Luxembourg and gone back into the discotheque trail to await results. His decision to leave the still-broadcasting Radio Caroline had been made on the basis of a survey of his fans, which may seem strange. But when Tony had first gone to Caroline he'd only lasted a week before being sacked; the Programme Controller who employed him had left almost the same day as Tony had started and his replacement had felt that Tony Prince was wrong for Caroline. Hundreds of outraged letters to Caroline had forced Ronan O'Rahilly to overrule his Programme Controller and reinstate Tony Prince, so when the decision about whether or not to carry on had arisen Tony had asked the listeners their opinions. The bulk of them had been in favour of an onshore legitimate life, so Tony resigned.

Radio One thought that Tony would be certain to get work on the station 'soon'. Radio Luxembourg offered him a job straight away. For an ex-pirate radio jock working the club circuit there could have been no choice at all. Within a few months of joining the station Tony brought in another new recruit. Luxembourg were looking for more presenters as they moved into the all-live format and it was Tony Prince who suggested that they should listen to Bob Stewart. Caroline North served the northern part of Britain and was never heard in London, so most of the DJs were unknown outside of their own small area, and without Tony Prince's recommendation probably no one south of Manchester would ever have heard of Bob Stewart.

In fact if Bob Stewart had been left to his own devices then we probably would have been without one of the best-known and most instantly recognisable voices on radio. On worldwide short wave radio Bob Stewart is the voice of Radio Luxembourg. On 208 metres Bob can be heard all over Europe as his rich tones, usually described as 'deep brown', cut through the very worst static and hash. No matter how bad the weather or the fade, or how small and cheap your transistor radio may be, you'll still hear Bob Stewart, even if you can't hear anything else.

It was ex-Beatles drummer Pete Best, whose replacement had pushed Tony Prince on to the stage, who made Bob Stewart take his first crack at being a DJ, even though Bob himself felt that he had neither the knowledge nor the expertise to handle the task. Fresh out of the army,

Above
'Baby' Bob Stewart before his radio career began.
Below
Bob Stewart in the studio, circa 1972.

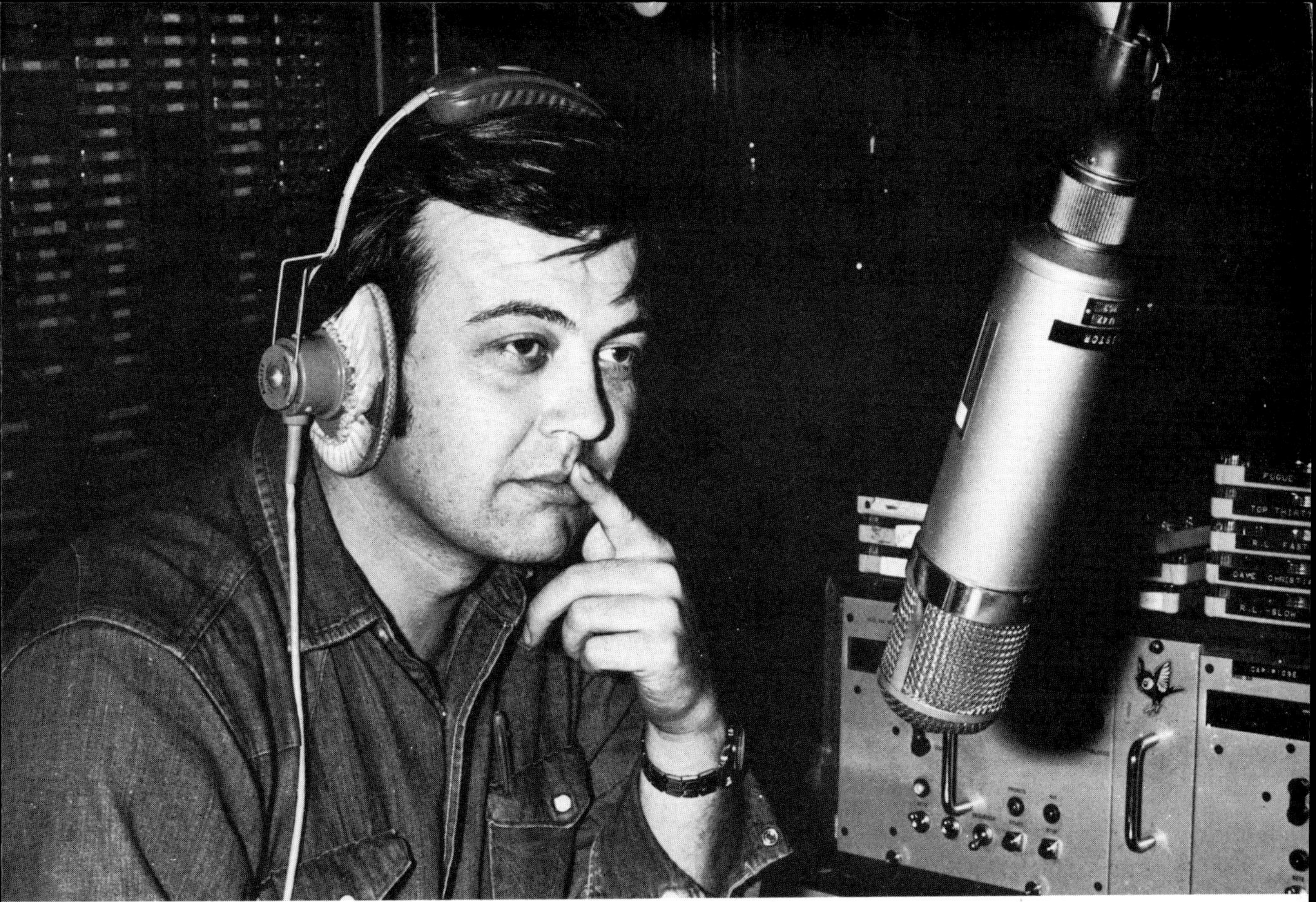

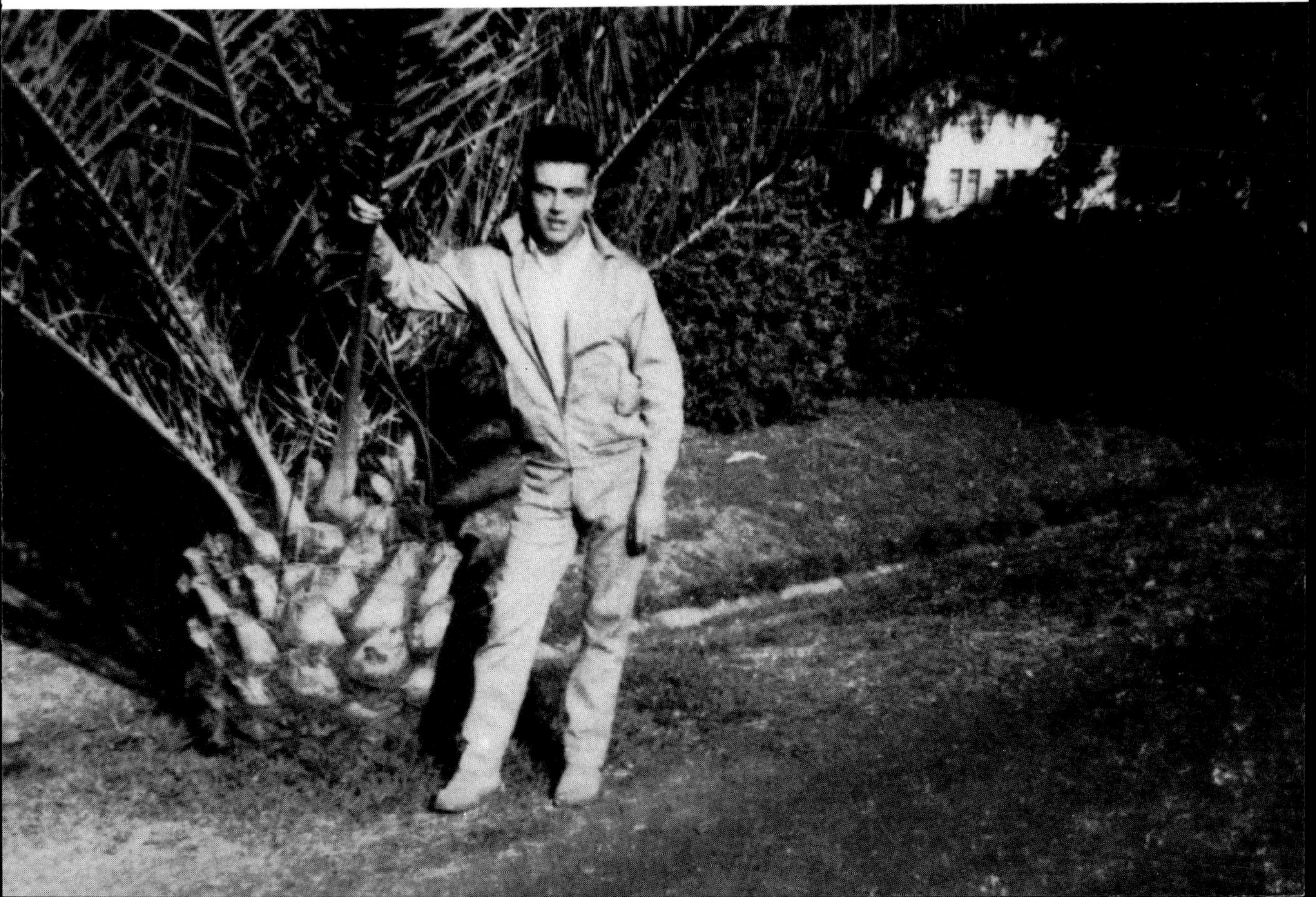

and back in his home town of Liverpool at the height of the Merseybeat boom, that may or may not have been true, but the first club owner who heard the voice insisted that Bob come and work for him. From there it was his friends who insisted he should aim higher, and persuaded him to try for pirate radio, and Bob joined Caroline North and built the audience for the *Baby Bob Stewart Show* up to around four million a day.

Like Tony Prince he came ashore at the end of 1967 and was clubbing it when his ex-colleague recommended him to 208's Tony McCarthy. At first Bob Stewart didn't want to go to Luxembourg, but after frequent calls from Tony Prince he sent a tape to Hertford Street and signed for Radio Luxembourg almost immediately, joining Tony Prince and Paul Burnett out in the Grand Duchy.

Paul had been the very first of the all-live team to arrive in Luxembourg, joining Don Wardell, Colin Nicholl and Norman St John in the art of putting on pre-recorded tapes of people like Sam Costa, Jack Jackson, Jimmy Savile and Tony Blackburn for the first six months, in a programme format which only went 'live' after about 11 p.m. at night.

Paul Burnett had gone into radio in the RAF in Aden and moved to Manx Radio on his return ashore from Radio 270. It was there that Pete Murray heard him and suggested he should send a tape to Geoffrey Everitt. Pete Murray also made sure that Geoffrey Everitt knew the tape was coming and when he heard it Paul Burnett was offered a job on Radio Luxembourg. He and his car, a white MGB, were loaded on to a Bristol aircraft at Lydd and flown to Le Touquet, from where Paul drove into Luxembourg, arriving on a bright sunny day just a month before his 24th birthday. He'd never been on the continent before and initially didn't rate it all that highly, but it slowly got under his skin as it had with so many other people before him.

Eventually the other live presenters began to arrive and the social scene which is so much a part of being a Radio Luxembourg DJ began to evolve. A great number of people who went out to Luxembourg, especially the younger ones, throughout the past 50 years, express very similar points of view about the place. Luxembourg is a very affluent country, the presenters are all well-paid and they are all shuffled into the limelight fairly quickly. Both Tony Prince and his wife Christine say the same thing – it made them very worldly very quickly. Paul Burnett says that going to Luxembourg was a crash course in sophistication. Luxembourg, where it is impossible to eat poorly, has a thriving night-life and none of the licensing restrictions which exist in Britain. Cut off from the bulk of the local population by language, working till very late, it's hardly surprising that a nocturnal lifestyle develops swiftly and becomes packed with entertainment and good humour.

At the time Radio Luxembourg was riding the crest of yet another wave. After the pirate ships had closed down the radio listeners had severely limited choice if they wanted to hear pop music – and the pirates had conclusively proved that they did. During the daytime there was no real alternative to Radio One, although during the afternoon it began a progressive merger which turned it into Radio Two by 5 p.m. After that there was nothing until 7.30, when Radio Luxembourg came on the air. The BBC and Radio Luxembourg had their respective sections of the audiences to themselves and Luxembourg was still the only real all-pop station available.

As time went on the station staff were getting better at what they did. After the end of the sponsored shows they were selling time to record companies – so much for two minutes – during which a record would be played as part of an overall programme which included music from all the different labels. This was the 'top and tail' approach (necessary because very few singles are less than three minutes long) which Alan Keen hated and changed after 1970.

And there were still some taped shows – Alan Freeman kept his running for much longer than anyone else. And Paul Burnett, as well as being a 'live' presenter, also taped shows with Pete Murray. Paul was returning to Britain for live gigs on a regular basis and while he was in London would tape a programme called *Peter and Paul* for Clark's Shoes which was a sort of *Family Favourites* affair. Without the landline between London and Luxembourg it had to be taped in Hertford Street with Paul Burnett pretending to be in Luxembourg. Only once was the tape accidentally erased before transmission, and Paul had to fly back to London to tape the show again. This was a long trek, because it still involved a flight to Brussels first, although it was no longer necessary to catch a train from there to Luxembourg – the journey could be flown in a prop-driven Fokker Friendship. In fact Paul Burnett said he was frightened of flying until he started working on 208, when he had to accept it or stop working. He nearly stopped work altogether at that time, though – he flew between London and Brussels every other week, and luckily for him it was one of the other weeks when his regular flight – the 5.15 Trident – hit the ground just after take-off. There were no survivors. The near miss is a dubious honour Paul shares with colleague Bob Stewart, who had a ticket for a Turkish DC10 which crashed after take-off from Paris killing everyone on board. Bob Stewart switched flights at the very last minute.

The youngest member of the 1968 team was David Jensen. And it was Noel Edmonds, who had already experienced a name-change himself, who thought that David Jensen ought to have some sort of nickname which recognised his extreme youth. He started off with 'Boyo', but it eventually metamorphosed into 'The Kid', and within a few months everybody knew him simply as Kid Jensen and the name stuck so hard that 12 years later he's having trouble getting away from it. Muriel Young, who worked with him all those years ago admitted, in early 1983, that she didn't know his real name and was quite surprised to discover that a new generation of radio listeners were getting to know David Jensen on Radio One.

Kid Jensen wasn't that much younger than the rest of the team in the Grand Duchy – only a couple of years, in fact – but he was the youngest

Following pages
Bob Stewart interviews Paul Burnett. What is Mark Wesley doing?

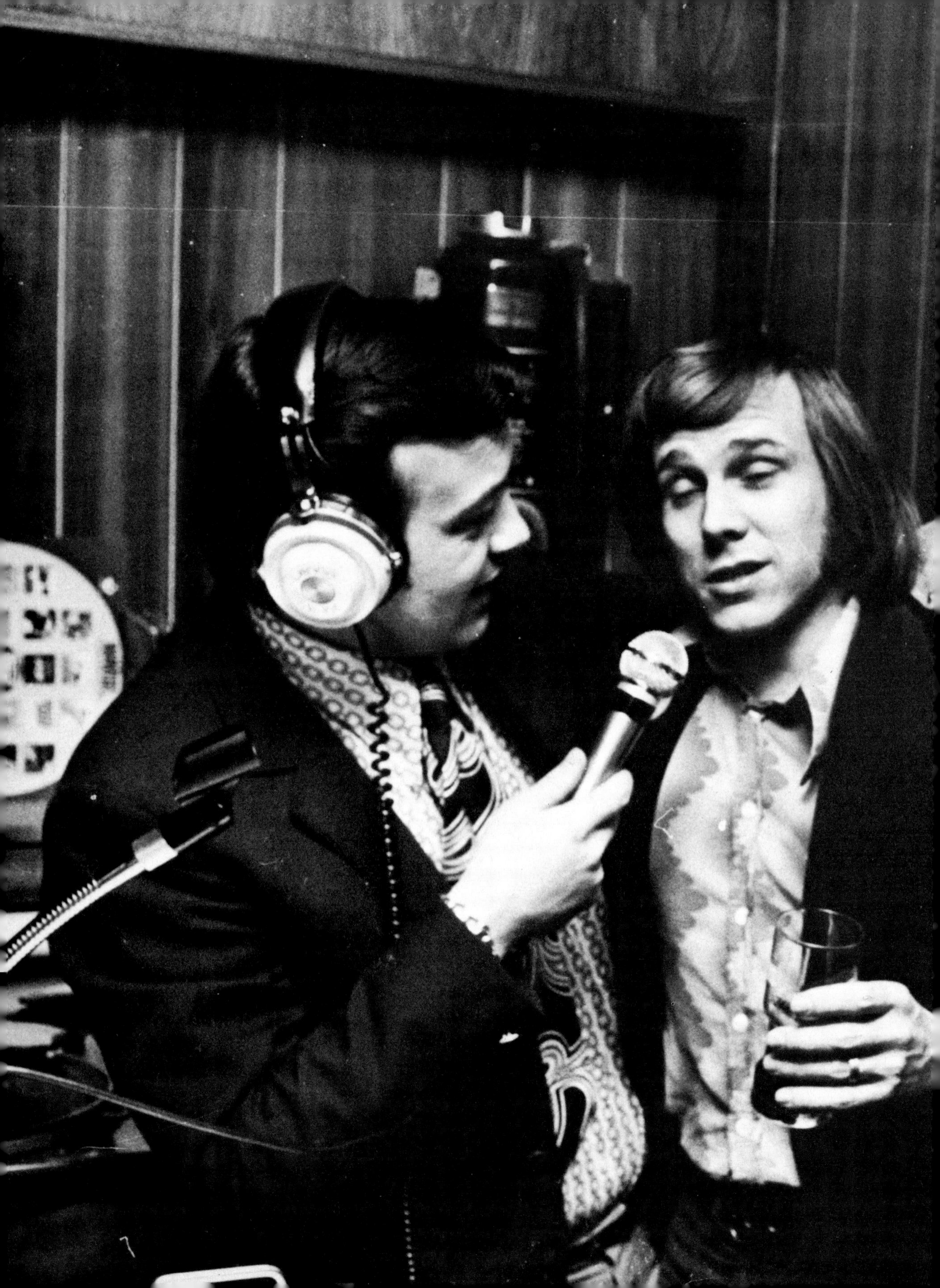

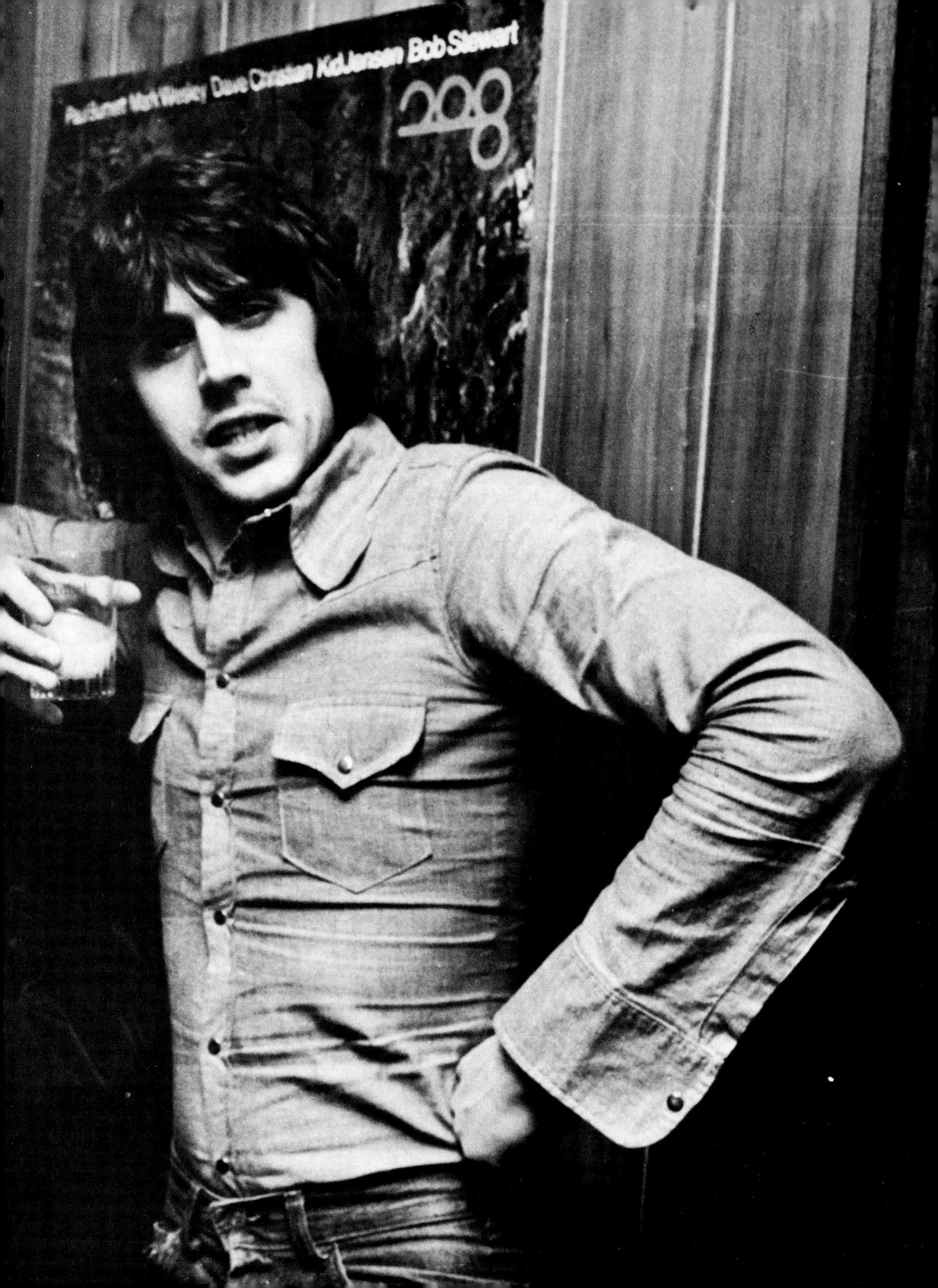

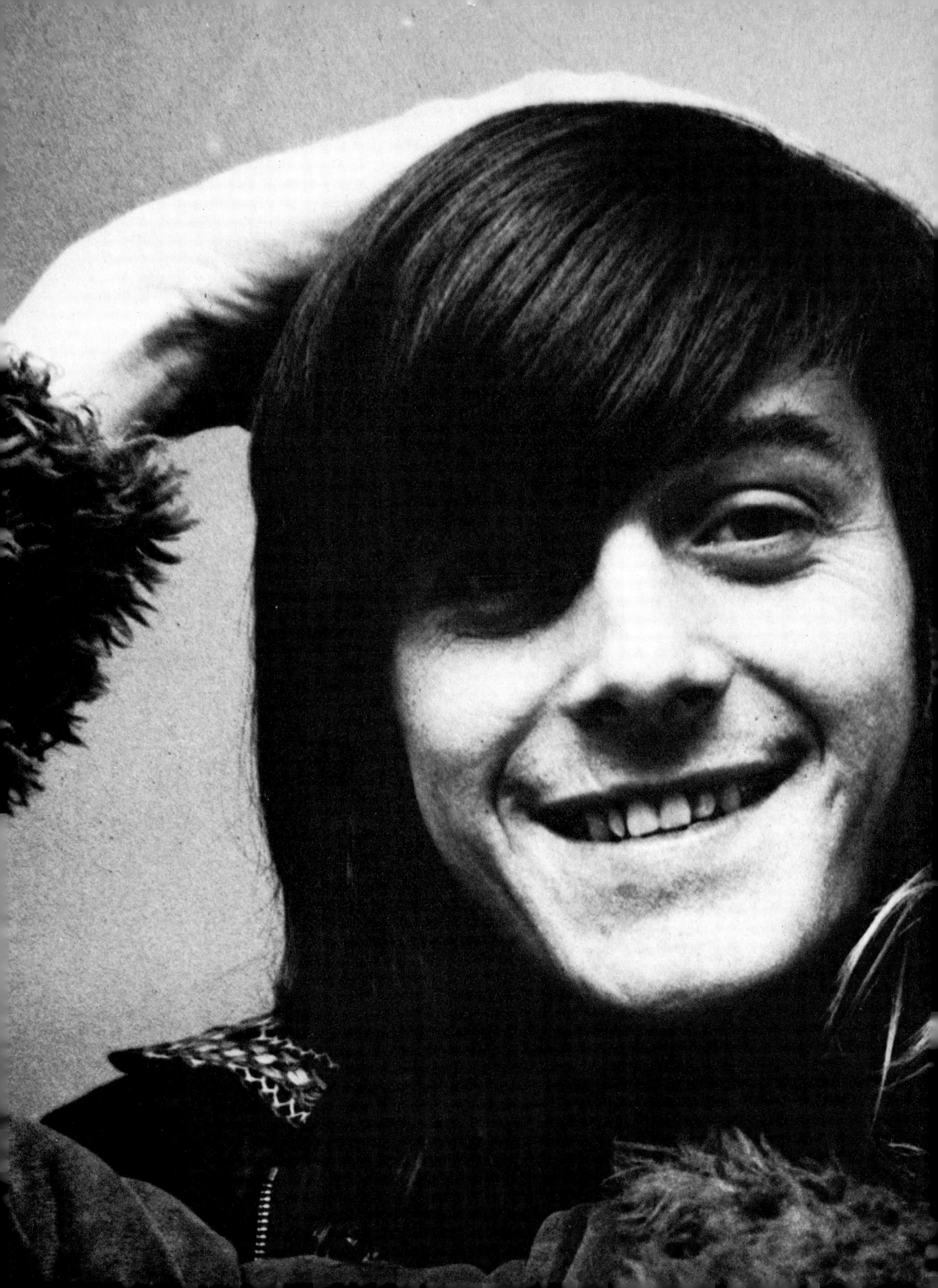

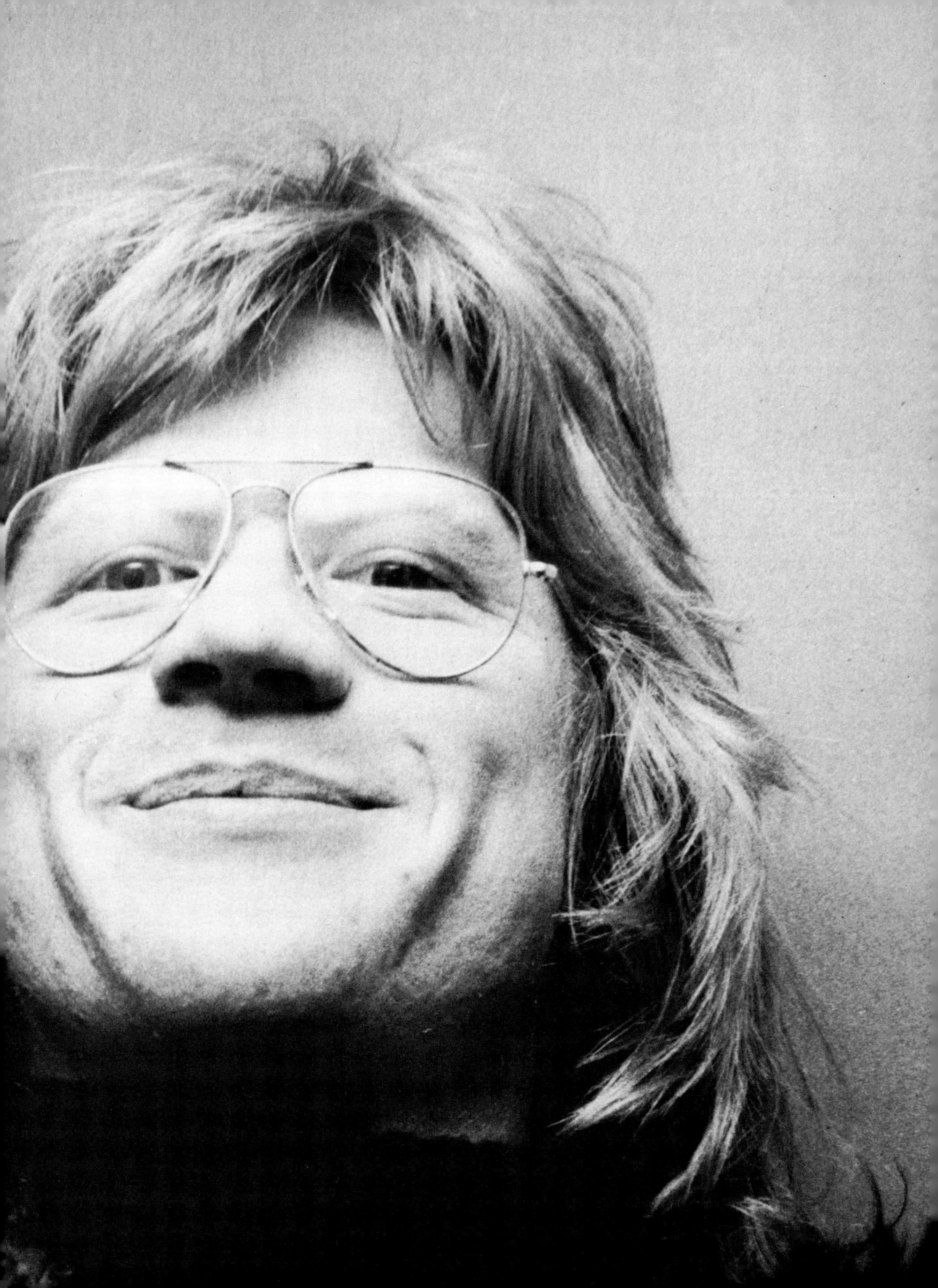

DJ working on radio at that time. Born in Vancouver, Canada, in 1950, he'd been fascinated by radio all his life, and was working on a Canadian station part time by the age of 16. Then an ex-jock from Caroline South (Steve Young) showed up with stories and pictures which sold the extremely young Dave Jensen on the glamour and excitement of pirate radio – which had, of course, just closed down. Undeterred David Jensen wrote to Radio One and to Radio Luxembourg. The BBC sent back one of those 'sorry, but we'll keep your name in our files' letters and Radio Luxembourg replied saying that if he could be there within 96 hours they'd got a job for him.

David Jensen abandoned his musical studies, sold his trumpet and his motorbike and arrived in Europe with little money, a small brown suitcase containing his possessions and a job on Radio Luxembourg waiting for him. He arrived in the Grand Duchy on Paul Burnett's birthday and 'Oh, what a different sort of place' he found. On air late at night, he produced his own programme, chose his own music and invited his own guests out to the Grand Duchy to be interviewed on *Jensen's Dimensions*, a very popular and fairly serious programme which was always highly-rated in the industry and by the audiences. Kid Jensen collected a number of awards for this show despite the fact that he was always on the air very late – it was the last programme of the night, finishing at 3 a.m. British time, 4 a.m. Luxembourg time.

After the show the clubs were still open, fortunately, and it was then that the social life took over for a few hours. The jocks were all good friends with each other, they'd go out together (there were even fewer English-speaking people in Luxembourg then than there are now) and have a few drinks. At the time their favourite watering hole was the Black Bess and it was here that the football team (which according to Mark Wesley was stupendously unsuccessful) was founded. All around the many clubs in Luxembourg Ville there are doubtless large numbers of people who remember these days. Aside from the fact that the studio guests who came to appear on *Jensen's Dimensions* were highly prized by all the disc jockeys for their conversational value they were also highly acclaimed musicians. In a period when Kid Jensen's programmes included bands like Wishbone Ash, Steely Dan, Thin Lizzy, Neil Young and Van Morrison, it was not unusual for impromptu groups to take the stage in one of the clubs like Charlie's or Chez Nous. They were generally aided by Mark Wesley (who has always been a keen musician) and anybody else who could 'half play some kind of instrument'. But who wouldn't try – if it was an opportunity to play alongside Van Morrison, or even Jimi Hendrix?

After that it was home to bed in the smallest of the small hours before arising during the afternoon for another night's work. In a way it was an almost entirely nocturnal existence, complicated by a number of different factors. After the advent of this all-live team, with large numbers of people necessarily living in Luxembourg, it was clear that there were more potential problems than the one of communications. In the past the

Previous page
Tony Prince and Kid Jensen, 'just good friends'.
Opposite
Kid Jensen had many visitors in Luxembourg for his *Jensen's Dimensions* show. This is Neil Sedaka.

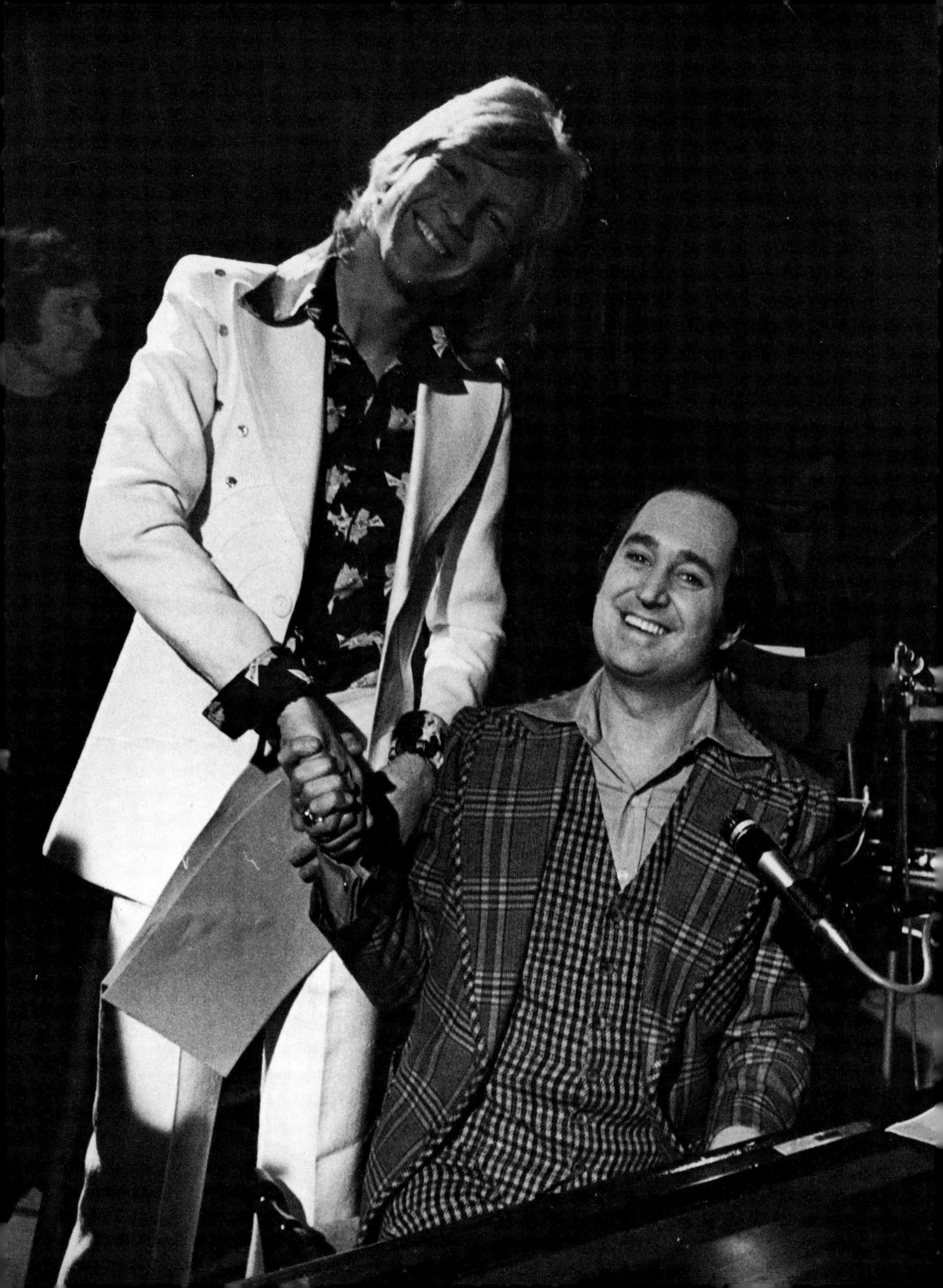

reaction of resident announcers to Luxembourg itself had always been pronounced – they either liked it or hated it, and there seemed to be little middle ground. Now there were more people to take into account, and even the ones who liked it were no longer alone, but had to get on with the rest of the team. As a rule a sort of shared adversity helped cement friendships between the DJs, and a routine gradually became established. New arrivals were always shown round the station and the town by the newest member of the existing team, on the basis that he was best placed to remember the sort of effect it could have on people used to Britain all their lives. Finding accommodation was the hardest part of all this, and once that problem was solved most of the rest of it began to fall into shape a little more easily.

Luxembourg is not like London or other big towns which have a nomadic population and are thus well-equipped with suitable facilities to meet their needs. There is no bedsitterland in Luxembourg and accommodation is both scarce and expensive; living in hotels is fun for a few days but murder after a couple of weeks. On top of all that, it's a foreign country, and although English is probably the second language in just about every country in the world now it certainly wasn't then. The early DJ teams spent almost all their lives in each others' company, which could get a bit stressful at times though problems were generally shortlived.

When Kid Jensen got to Luxembourg, young as he was, homesickness was not a real problem to him in the way that it could be to others; he was many thousands of miles from his native land and thus had a mental detachment which people who are away from home, but still within easy reach of it, cannot always manage. To begin with he shared a rather scabby flat with Noel Edmonds – in fact for a brief while they had only one double bed – which overlooked a graveyard and seems to have been used mostly for sleeping and making beans on toast. When Noel returned to Britain after nine months in the Grand Duchy, Kid Jensen and Dave Christian managed to pull off something in the way of an accommodation coup. They found an apartment each in a large house which also served as a base for a selection of almost totally absentee stewardesses from, of all unlikely places, Air Bahamas.

This was a vast improvement and offered a variety of what smart estate agents would call mod cons, including a lift. Which was very handy on occasions, particularly when Dave Christian broke the only mirror in the place and took his shaving kit out into the hallway, jammed his foot in the lift door and shaved there, using the mirror which was conveniently stuck to the back wall of the lift. Despite mod cons the apartments were still empty more often than full, once again being used mostly for sleeping and eating. By now the culinary arts were second nature to Dave Christian, and he (and Kid Jensen) survived mostly on a diet of coffee, cornflakes and tinned ravioli.

Out in the Grand Duchy the team were having the time of their lives, but they could never have done so were it not for the fact that the music was progressing and so was Radio Luxembourg. At about the same time as the station moved over to its live format the music industry was entering a period of transition which would provide the continental station with yet another opportunity to spot a huge market before anybody else saw it coming. And although the Beatles were not the originators of the new direction it was through their music that its arrival became widely recognised, as their traditional rock'n'roll-based music was phased out by something grown on the West Coast of America.

Flower Power music first gained attention at the Monterey pop festival in 1967 and after a catalytic and cataclysmic collision with Timothy Leary, inspired by his message to 'tune in, turn on and drop out' with the newly-illegal hallucinogenic drug LSD, became acid rock; and as the last of the barriers went down, pop music diversified in a way that it had never done before. Although traditional styles didn't fade away there was now a far greater variety of style than had ever been available to audiences previously. It led indirectly to the foundation of the supergroups, produced Blind Faith out of Cream, Traffic and Family, introduced 'the highest-paid band in the world' – Crosby, Stills, Nash and Young – and allowed the development of a solo career for P P Arnold's backing band, The Nice, who eventually evolved into legendary superheroes as Emerson, Lake and Palmer, bringing as they did so the world of classical music into the rock musician's legitimate repertoire. Composer Leonard Bernstein was so horrified by what they did with his song 'America' that he refused to allow its release. Eventually this diversification created the musical pressures which in part contributed to the final split among the Beatles, who had taken readily to the drug-oriented styles and were by now almost always sitting on an Indian hilltop with their Guru, the Maharishi Mahesh Yogi.

But the influences which arrived at the very tail-end of the sixties were by no means destructive. This was possibly the most productive period rock music ever passed through, and certainly gave rise to the kind of music which Kid Jensen was playing late at night on Luxembourg. Coupled with the in-depth interviews, *Jensen's Dimensions* was without doubt one of the most committed and respected music shows of the time, during a period when the BBC, although still nominally embracing a style and freedom which had begun with the pirates, had still not got to a stage of allowing disc jockeys on their 'all-pop' channel Radio One the sort of individual liberty which they had enjoyed five or six years previously as North Sea pirates.

In the meantime Radio Luxembourg had come to an agreement with Britain's biggest-selling newspaper, the *Daily Mirror*, and all the news output on 208 was supplied by the paper, although it still had to be telexed out to the Grand Duchy. The *Mirror* was the first big daily to relax the total embargo on Radio Luxembourg schedules and information which had been imposed by the Newspaper Publishers' Association in 1933; it had taken 35 years to get off the blacklist. Since then Luxembourg has concentrated on building its links with Fleet Street and

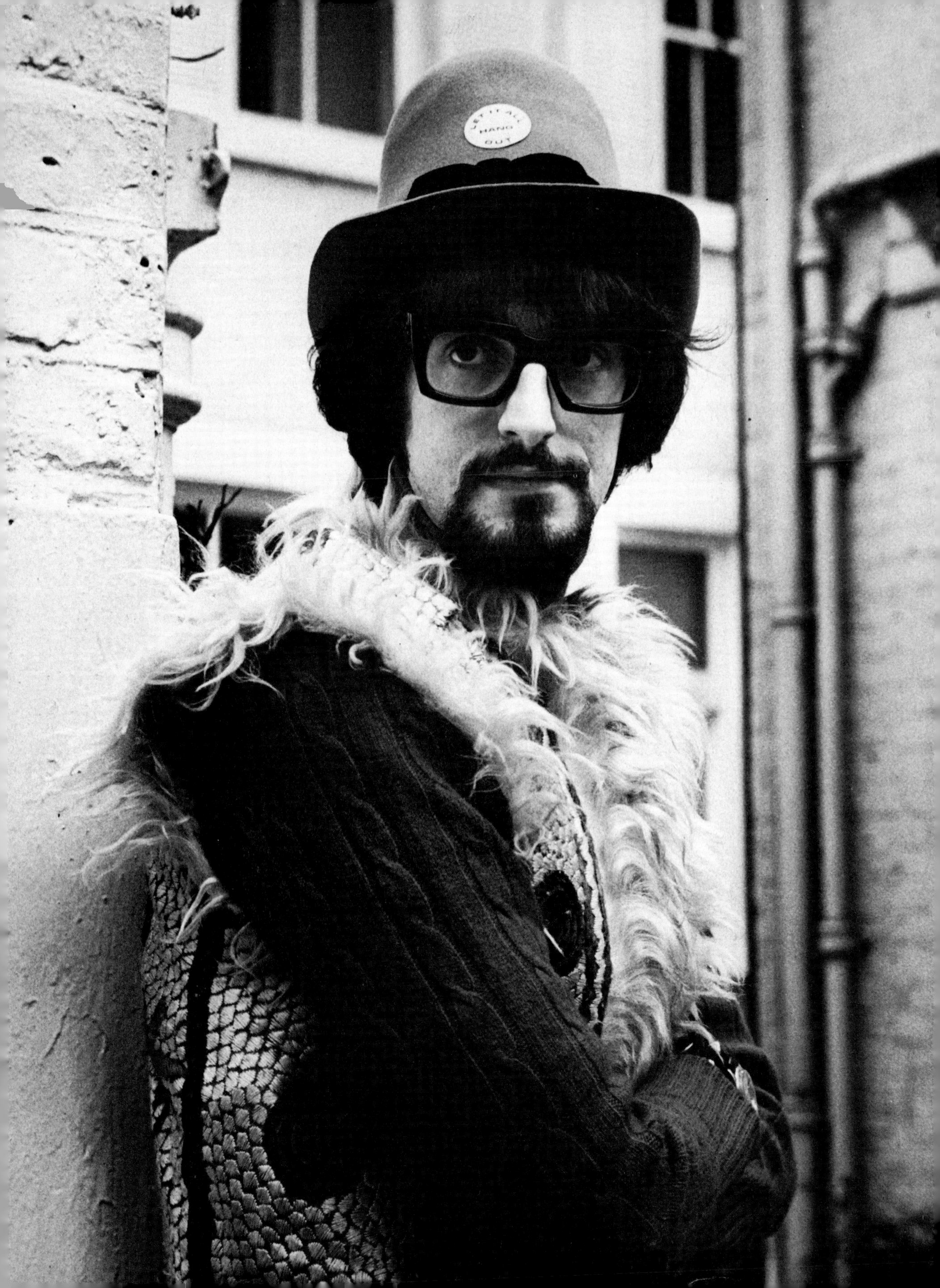
LET IT ALL
HANG
OUT

in 1982 enjoyed more Press coverage than any other radio station.

In 1969 Don Wardell, who had been with Luxembourg for the past three years, left to go into the record industry on the promotions side; today he lives in Los Angeles, ironically promoting the output of one of the bands which he disliked so much in the late sixties that he felt obliged to get away from having to play their music. Then they were Jefferson Airplane, and were to San Francisco what the Beatles were to Liverpool, nowadays they're better known as Jefferson Starship.

Ken Evans had moved from producing for EMI into producing for Radio Luxembourg as the taped programmes were slowly phased out, recording among other things interviews with people like Cliff Richard and Paul Jones and, as the sixties moved on, others like Neil Young. But Ken Evans' career was about to take a turn in an upward direction; he was promoted to Programme Director in 1970 by the newly-appointed General Manager.

By the late sixties the previous Manager, Geoffrey Everitt, was somewhat disillusioned. He'd been at Radio Luxembourg ever since the station reopened after the war, first as a presenter out in the Grand Duchy itself and later, after about seven years behind the microphone, as a producer in the Hertford Street studio. From there he'd gradually worked his way upwards from Chief Producer to General Manager, but he'd been on the station now for almost 25 years. In his own words, he'd lived through what he felt was 'the best period – the early and mid fifties', and was now faced with a music industry of which he was not particularly fond. The standards and values to which he had worked all his life were held in less and less esteem. 'I can remember,' he says, 'a time when if you shook a chap's hand you had a deal,' but it wasn't like that any more, and a lot of the time Geoffrey Everitt was both annoyed and saddened to find people trying to get out of signed contracts or in some cases simply ignoring them. The record industry was very big business indeed by this time and, with that amount of money at stake, and with the fortunes that were there for the making (almost overnight in some cases), it was perhaps not surprising to discover that there were a few unscrupulous people who were more than willing to pull a shady deal or a fast stroke. More often than not it would be the artists who bore the brunt of some incredibly ruthless shaftings, but it worked the other way as well, and at all levels of the industry. *And* it was getting worse . . .

Geoffrey Everitt resigned in 1970, and his replacement, like so many others on the Radio Luxembourg payroll, came from the ranks of the radio pirates. After Radio London had closed down, their Programme Director had gone into music publishing on his own account, but after a two-year absence he returned to radio, and on 1 August 1970, Alan Keen took over as Radio Luxembourg's General Manager.

It was Alan Keen who really pushed the all-live format into reality, dispensing with more and more of the few taped shows that were left on the 208 airways. One of his first tasks was handed to him by Geoffrey Everitt more or less on the day he accepted the appointment, and he was

Jonathan King letting it all hang out in 1970.

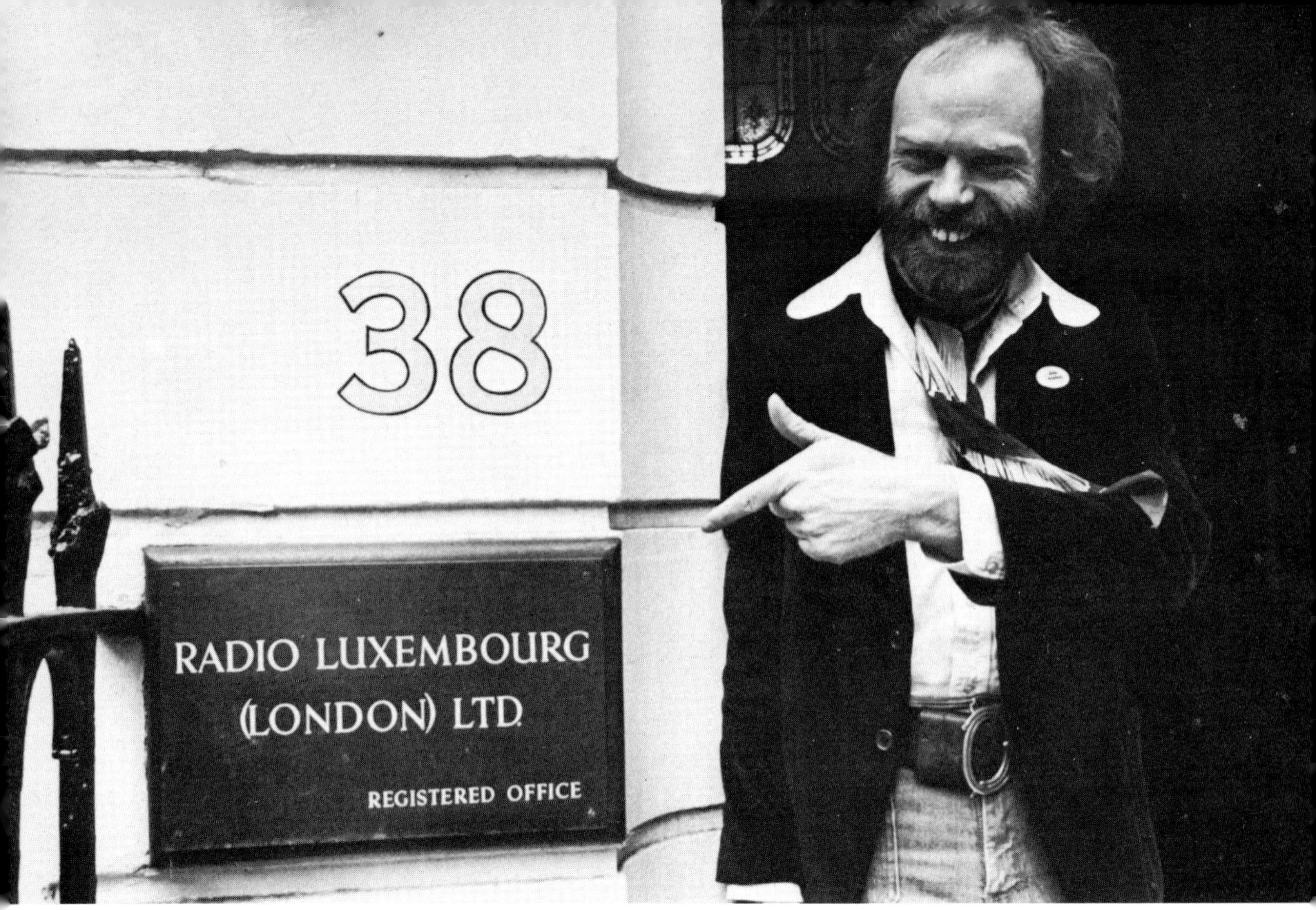
38
RADIO LUXEMBOURG
(LONDON) LTD.
REGISTERED OFFICE

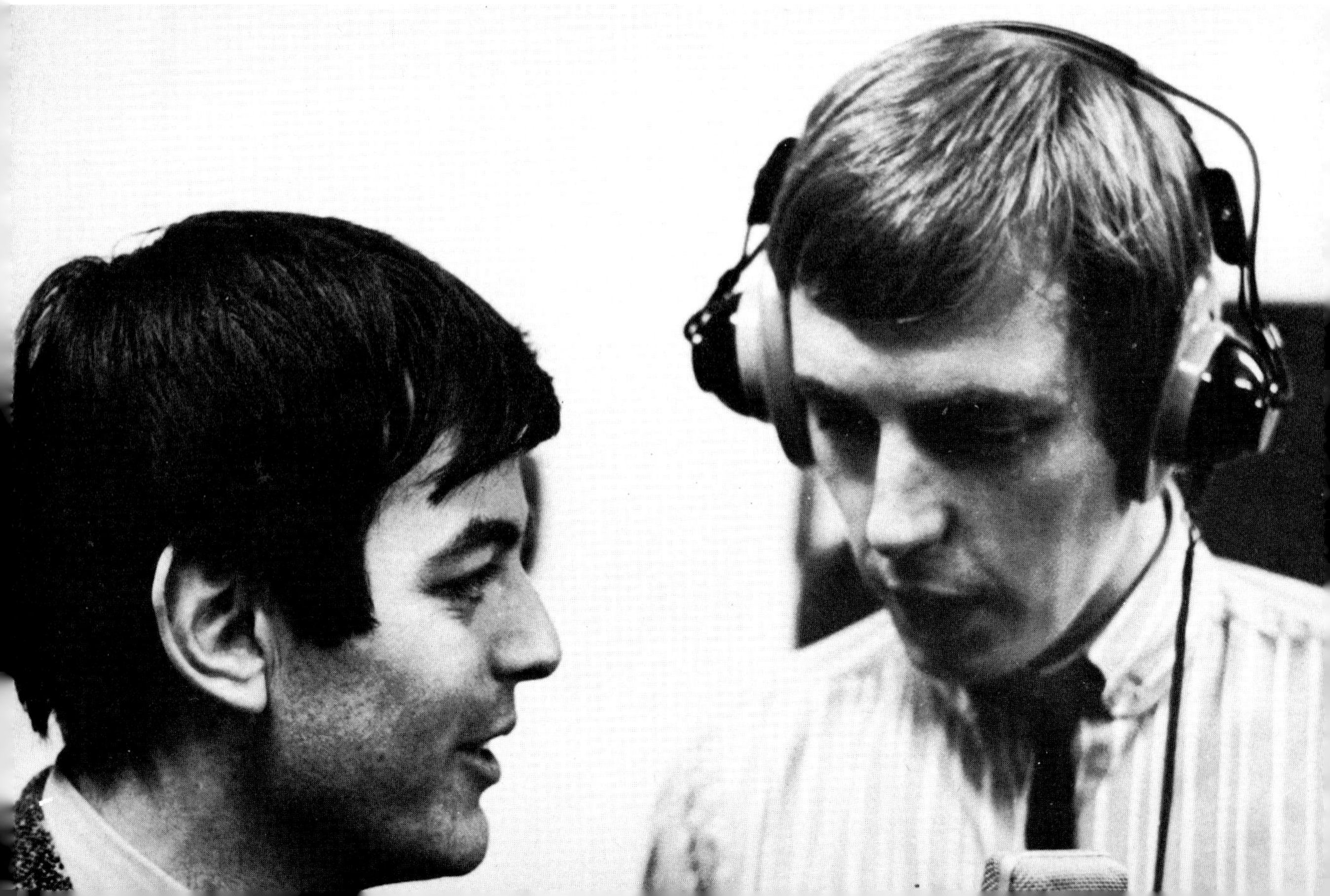

told that he'd have to fire Tony Prince, whose clubland antics in Luxembourg after the show was over were apparently getting out of hand.

Although Alan Keen didn't fire Tony Prince it would not be long before he left the station anyway, in November the same year, heading for America and a bigger world of radio. Alan Keen regarded this as a shame for the same reason he hadn't fired him as suggested – he thought that Tony Prince was too important to Radio Luxembourg to lose him.

Before then, however, one thing Alan Keen did do was to hire Kenny Everett to tape material for transmission on 208. Everett was one of the ex-London DJs who had gone to Radio One when it started and was now a solo performer without team-mate Dave Cash (also at the BBC). However, Kenny Everett was not renowned for his good behaviour on the wireless and had on more than one occasion said things which were not altogether acceptable in the eyes of Authority. This time he had conjectured aloud (and on the wireless) about how much the Transport Minister's wife had paid her examiner to let her through the driving test (which she had just passed). Kenny Everett, highly popular though he was, left the BBC and Radio One within hours of the broadcast, and was snapped up by Luxembourg.

At the same time as Kenny Everett began to record in Hertford Street Tony Windsor, who had introduced Dave Christian to 208 and found Noel Edmonds from among a huge pile of audition tapes, left the station. Noel himself had gone out in early 1968 and only stayed nine months before returning to Britain and a career on Radio One which is sufficiently well documented already. But Kenny Everett would not be around for long. Alan Keen had his first experience of radio with the pirate ship Radio London and even the relatively relaxed Radio Luxembourg (compared to the BBC, at any rate) suffered from what Alan Keen saw as unacceptable strictures as a result of the sponsored shows. He was determined to apply the same formula to Luxembourg as had been so overwhelmingly popular on Radio London. So popular, in fact, that when the station went off the air and the DJs returned to dry land they were mobbed outside Liverpool Street Station in crowd scenes which hadn't been equalled since the early days of Beatlemania (and wouldn't be seen again until Radio Luxembourg discovered The Osmonds). Some of the people on the ship had no idea that they were so popular in Britain until they got off the train from Felixstowe.

The formula had worked so well for the pirates that it would definitely work again, and out went the last traces of taped, sponsored programmes which Alan Keen disliked so much. 'They were awful,' he says now. 'They used to top and tail records,' a process whereby listeners never heard the whole record all the way through – the beginning and the end were missed off entirely. This was because the record companies wanted to get as many of their products as they could on to the airwaves and the only way to do it, because of the large numbers of single releases each week, was by playing bits of records. In this way they could get

Above
'Whispering' Bob Harris, best-remembered as the host of *The Old Grey Whistle Test,* did a short spell with Radio Luxembourg. The engineers in Hertford Street still like to listen to his tapes.
Below
Tony Blackburn and Simon Dee; both have taped shows for Luxembourg and Tony broadcast from the Grand Duchy itself (for the BBC) at the time Britain entered the EEC.

through 36 records in an hour, or at least play parts of 36 records an hour, whereas a hard-working DJ who plays entire records and keeps chat to a minimum can expect to get through 18 singles in an hour, maybe less. In fact definitely less, if he stops for news and has to include advert breaks. Today Radio One gets through approximately 16 records each hour, which gives some idea of the cavalier fashion in which the sponsored shows treated their own (presumably highly-prized) product. But it would no longer suffice. The music was everything to the kids and was also everything to Radio Luxembourg, since they depended upon it for their survival. Only by playing the right sort of music and presenting it in the right way would the station keep its audiences and its advertisers; without one or the other the only result would be closure. Having successfully held off the threat of commercial television in the fifties the inevitable fruit of the union between television and advertising was now looming over Radio Luxembourg's horizon – Independent Local Radio (ILR) throughout Britain on a scale which, if anything, would be even bigger than that of commercial television simply on the number of stations which would appear. And if they weren't enough of a threat to advertising revenue, right alongside them would be non-commercial BBC local radio which would try to steal audiences away from everyone.

Radio Luxembourg had emerged through a mixed field to be a clear winner in the late thirties, had shrugged off the set-backs of the war and done it again, had survived the inroads of ITV, survived the onslaught of the pirate ships and was now faced with the biggest threat of all. Local radio stations would provide a much clearer reception (and in stereo) than the skywave signal which emanated from the Grand Duchy. They would be able to grab peak-time audiences in the morning and evening drive-time slots when Luxembourg wasn't even on the air (this is important, since single-channel loyalty among radio audiences is far more pronounced than among television viewers) and they would still be there late at night after the television stations closed down, moving into a spot which, until now, Luxembourg had been able to keep almost for itself.

On top of that ILR would have a major advantage when it came to reporting local events, weather and traffic conditions, as well as maintaining a local physical presence.

This last was at least something which Radio Luxembourg could do something about, and as a national station it even enjoyed something of an advantage over the local stations. So although they hadn't yet emerged from the depths of bureaucracy, the local stations would have to be fought straight away. There's no advantage quite like being first.

One of the things Alan Keen must have been aware of was the enormous popularity enjoyed by the pirate disc jockeys, of which many of them had been unaware, and which they had, with a few small exceptions, done little to capitalise on. So the Radio Luxembourg Roadshows were conceived. These were little short of national tours organised by the radio station with the object of putting faces to names

Jimmy Savile and Barry Alldis in Hertford Street.

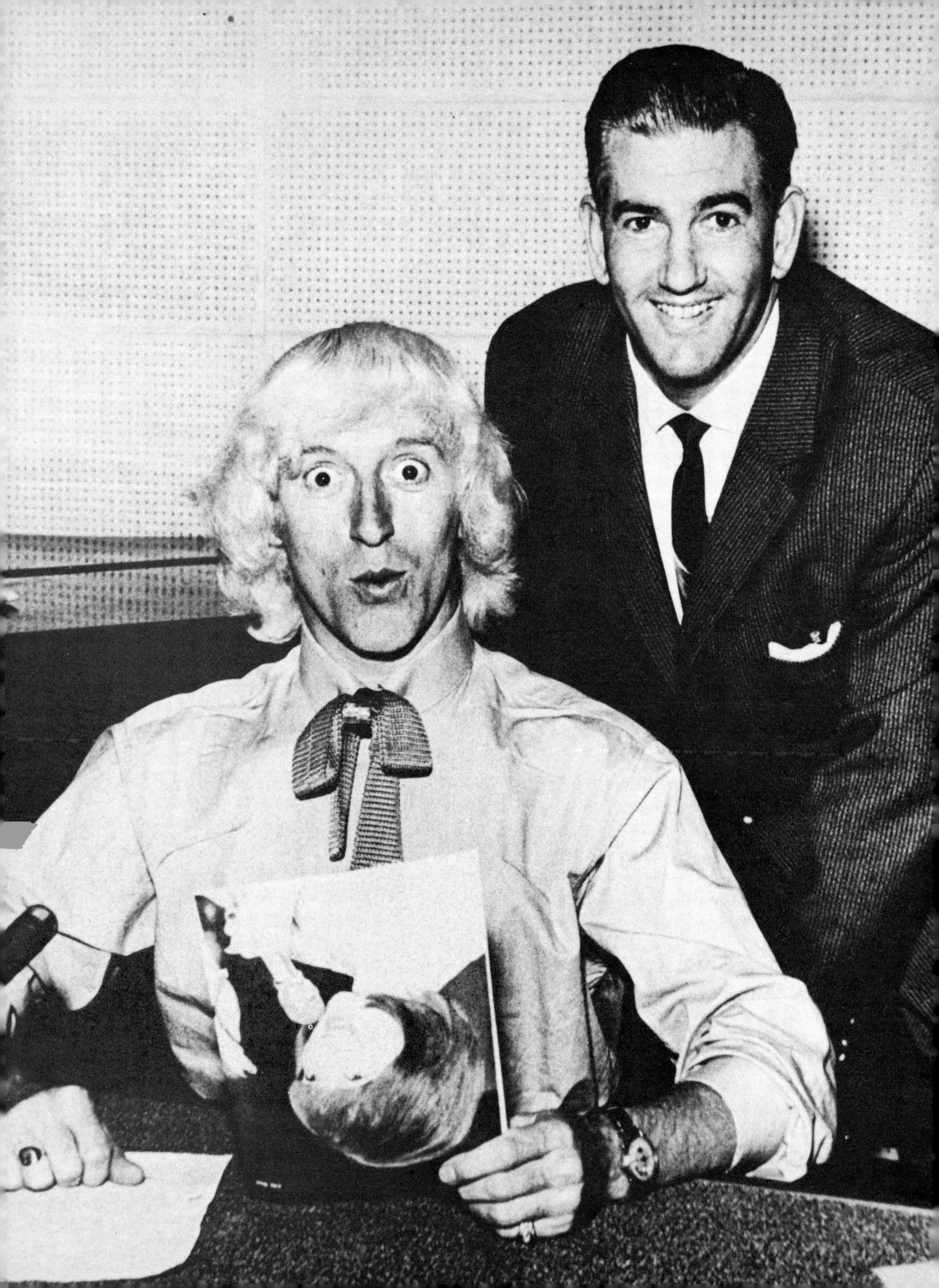

WISHBONE ASH
on mca
CANNED HEAT
FUTURE BLUES
Moody Blues
the taste

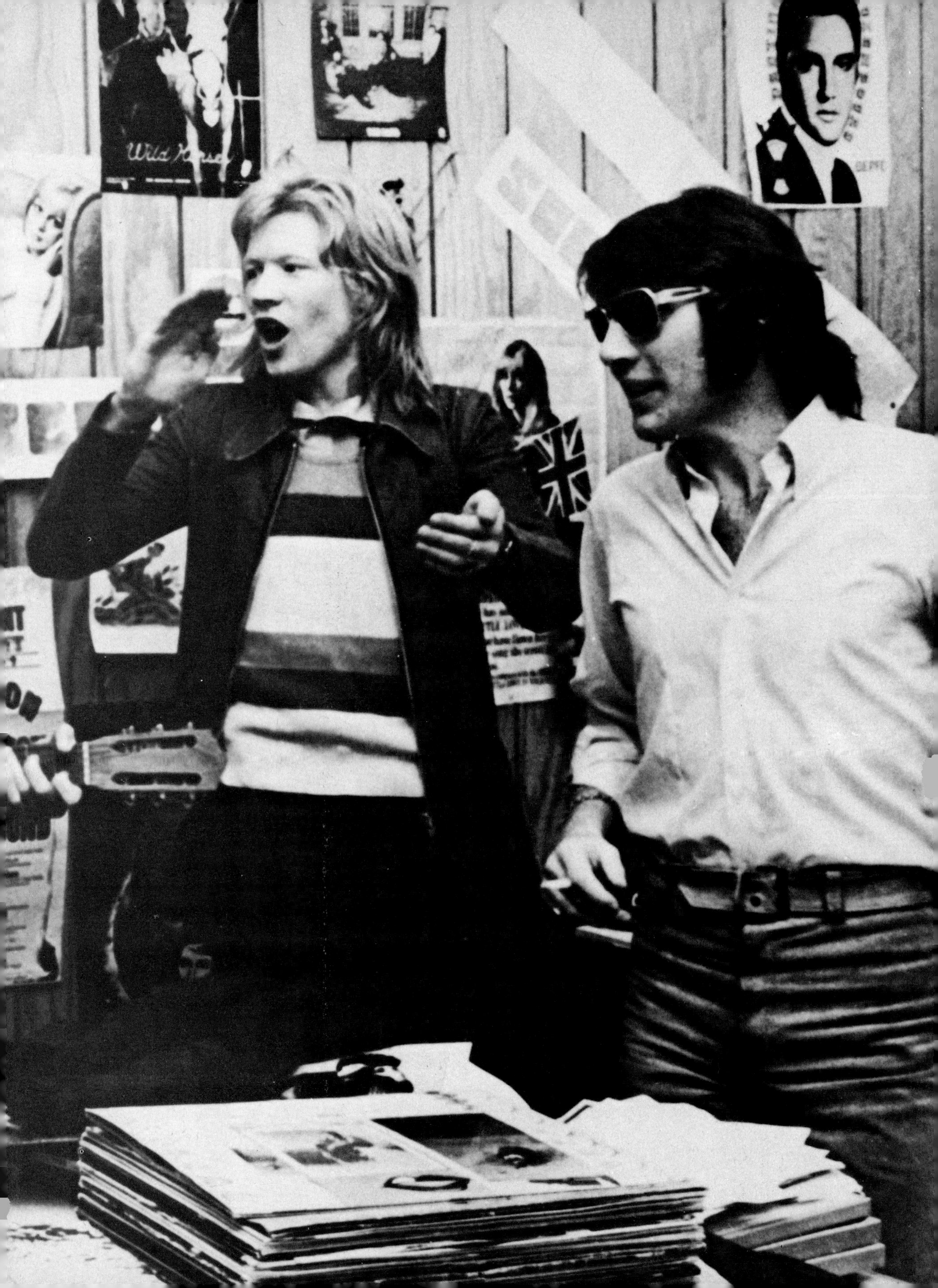
Wild Horses

and putting the radio station physically into local communities. Denied landlines from London, denied transmitters on the British mainland, there was nothing to stop the DJs from making personal appearances. Communications were now such that this was not the logistical exercise it had previously been, and the immense popularity of the taped shows made in the fifties with live audiences showed that it was a sensible move. The addition of sponsorship made it a terrifically profitable enterprise as well; Skoda were the first to act as sponsors, then came Sony and Crocodillo, and the Roadshows served their purpose rather admirably.

One of the disc jockeys who served a full period in Luxembourg and always went down a storm on the roadshows was Mark Wesley. His pirate career finally ended in 1970, long after the Marine Offences Act had closed down most of the ships, when Radio North Sea International abandoned ship in late September. From there he had gone into the record business as a plugger – the first record he handled was Elton John's 'Your Song', a top tenner on both sides of the Atlantic – and things looked fairly rosy for Mark Wesley.

But then came a phone call from Ken Evans, the end result of a rather tortuous set of circumstances. Tony Prince had left Luxembourg in late 1970, almost at the same time as Mark Wesley was stepping ashore from the North Sea, and Radio Luxembourg had announced a competition to find a new voice to replace Tony Prince on 208. Mark Wesley was placed third in the results but the winner had gone out to the Grand Duchy in January of 1971. Sadly it didn't work out, on the air or off it, and within six weeks he was back in Britain – would Mark Wesley care to replace him? On a bright sunny day in March Mark Wesley carried his suitcase out of the Hertford Street office and set off for the Grand Duchy to join Paul Burnett, Kid Jensen, Dave Christian and Bob Stewart. Like so many before him he slipped easily and quickly into the lifestyle of both country and station and stayed for nine years before returning to local radio in East Anglia. While he was out there two of the most important things he achieved were marrying a Luxembourg girl, and becoming a stalwart of the Radio Luxembourg football team – The Black Bess Barflies – who used to practise every Thursday and get slaughtered every Sunday with monotonous regularity (the Decca team smashed them 7-3 on one memorable occasion).

In the studio it was still business as usual. Despite the all-live format the studios were still not self-op, and the engineers lurked as usual behind their glass-windowed control room. In the studio there was still only a table with three buttons (the cough switch, the signal button to tell the engineer when to start the record and, of course, one to operate the famous gong) and a huge microphone dangling from the ceiling. The DJ would write a playlist, give the engineer a copy, and sit alone in the studio, twiddling his thumbs in between records.

Sometimes there were diversions to be enjoyed. Swinging the vast (and heavy) microphone was one tactic employed by visitors and which was only unpleasant if the chap in front of it was not as well co-ordinated

Previous page
The office of the English Service in the seventies; left to right, Paul Burnett, Mark Wesley, Kid Jensen and Dave Christian.

as he might have been. Trying to talk into a microphone doing Edgar Allan Poe impressions isn't easy either, and may have accounted for occasional evenings when the famous Luxembourg fade was slightly faster than normal. And, as Tommy Vance had discovered, the input into the DJ's headphones was tiny, providing little or no volume whatsoever – feeding the Medium Wave transmitted signal into them provided a louder noise but also produced terrible howling feedback if the DJ got too close to the microphone.

And there is an apocryphal tale about one of the younger presenters who was told that the best way to combat the 208 fade was to monitor the output through headphones and lean closer to the microphone and shout loud every time the volume went down in the 'phones. It is said that the ingenue in question performed this ritual for almost two weeks before realising that everybody else was laughing . . .

One person who wasn't laughing resigned shortly after Mark Wesley arrived in Luxembourg. Here was yet another expatriate who missed England and home cooking too much to hold out in the Grand Duchy for more than a very short time. The weather was miserable, the food foreign and all the people foreign also. After a period of deliberation he resigned from the station. The very next day, sitting outside a café under the trees which line the Place d'Armes, in brilliant sunshine, he reconsidered, but it was too late. His replacement went on air at seven that evening, opening up the station entirely unannounced. 'I don't know if you've missed me, but I know I've missed you,' said Tony Prince.

His wife had become pregnant practically on the same day that he'd left Radio Luxembourg about a year or so previously, and their plans to travel round America had necessarily been scrapped. Tony had been working in Luxembourg ever since, waiting for a phone call he knew would come, although he didn't know when.

It was Alan Keen who rang him from London, asking when he'd like to get back on the air.

'Yesterday,' was the characteristic reply, although barring miracles it was clearly out of the question. However he got second best.

'How about tonight?'

9: TEENYBOPPER

The American market had been totally bemused by the Beatles and the succession of Liverpudlian foursomes who'd swept across the country in their wake. The extent of their obsession is obvious enough – even now very few of them have heard of the most popular British entertainer since the war – Cliff Richard. In response to the Merseybeat the Monkees were manufactured in a recording studio and enjoyed a passing, but delirious, success. After that – relative silence until the arrival of the Partridge Family and their success story, David Cassidy.

Tony Prince had flown out to LA to interview the entire Partridge Family on the set of their TV programme and after the end of the series went back again to interview teen heart-throb Cassidy at the beginning of his solo career. After a trip which lasted slightly longer than 24 hours and involved about three hours sleep Tony Prince arrived back in London and staggered into the Speakeasy club to pass some time. By chance he met a friend, Roger Holt, who was in the process of arranging a tour for a group who had enjoyed considerable success in their regular spot on the CBS *Andy Williams Show* on American TV. A bunch of five young kids who neither drank, smoked nor said boo to geese (they all refused to drink Cola because it contained caffeine), the Osmonds, said Roger Holt, would be big news on both sides of the Atlantic. Their new single release, 'One Bad Apple', was a straight rip-off of the hugely popular Jackson Five number 'ABC' and was going to be very successful. Would Radio Luxembourg be interested in a little advance publicity on their behalf?

Tony Prince mentioned the idea to Ken Evans who, to the complete surprise of everyone, and especially Tony Prince and Roger Holt, suggested that 208 record five half-hour programmes with the Osmonds, one for each member of the group (Little Jimmy Osmond was as yet only a baby). Within a short while Tony Prince was on his way to Caesar's Palace in Las Vegas to tape the shows and they went out on the 208 airwaves on consecutive nights immediately prior to the arrival of the group in Britain at the start of their first British tour. After each half-hour interview Tony Prince plugged the tour and told the audience their arrival time at Heathrow, with the result that the Osmonds had upwards of 2000 fans waiting for them at Terminal Three, to give them the sort of reception which hadn't been seen since the Beatles split in 1969.

Radio Luxembourg had discovered the Osmonds, and Tony Prince joined them on their tour, cramming his early evening shows with information about the minutiae of the group's life. It was a tactic which was immediately and immensely successful. Not only had Radio Luxembourg discovered the Osmonds, they'd discovered a whole new sub-teenage audience who would latch on to almost anyone young enough and cute enough to qualify as an idol, no matter what their musical talents may or may not be. By now Radio Luxembourg had discovered something far bigger and more important than the Osmonds. They had discovered the teenyboppers.

They had almost been found by the Monkees, had struggled to emerge during the bubblegum period of the Archies and the Kassenetz Katz Singing Orchestral Choir, had nearly made it for the Partridge Family but by the time the Osmonds arrived they were fully paid-up members of the pop music world and they claimed their heritage with an enthusiasm and volume which not even the Beatles had generated in the early sixties. After the Osmonds David Cassidy came to Britain on tour and, as a consequence of having his arrival at Heathrow mercilessly plugged on 208, he too was met by a barrage of screaming pre-teen girls. The Jackson Five enjoyed the same greeting and eventually the British Airports Authority wrote to Radio Luxembourg asking them to stop the announcements. A barrier collapsed at Heathrow during a particularly hysterical welcome and disaster had narrowly been averted. The Queen's Building at Heathrow had not been constructed to take this kind of onslaught and the BAA were afraid that people may be hurt if the mass turnouts continued. Reluctantly Radio Luxembourg complied with the request, but it was already too late to stop the teenyboppers from becoming the dominant market force. A wave of bands which met with their approval were swept to brief pinnacles of adoration and then quickly replaced, in a fever of excitement which boosted the careers of the Bay City Rollers and the once serious Tyrannosaurus Rex who'd never had a hit until they changed to T Rex and began churning out mindless rubbish in the 'She ain't no witch and I love the way she twitch' mould. Finally it all collapsed in the bickering around the spellbinding Rubettes, a group of allegedly unmusical frontmen who were vilified in the national Press by the man who claimed to have sung the vocal track which launched them to pop stardom for a few weeks.

Out of the whole teenybopper craze only a few bands achieved any musical excellence along with their brief fame. Although the Osmonds managed 25 singles in the British charts in five years, the most lasting influence to emerge from the period was that of Scandinavian Eurovision winners and subsequent supergroup Abba, who have become Sweden's biggest export currency earners and are flattered every year by the number of imitators who hope to repeat the blonde foursome's 1974 win.

But at the height of it all, in the mid-seventies, it was Radio Luxembourg who had spotted the teenybopper market and claimed it as their own. This they did well enough on radio and backed it up with the magazine *Fab 208*, which was more or less the Radio Luxembourg house magazine as well as the publication in which all the endless likes, dislikes, and ambitions of the young pop idols were revealed. Radio Luxembourg was yet again streets in front of anyone else; it was a heady period for the music industry and an exciting time to work on the radio station which was leading the field.

David Cassidy visited Luxembourg at the peak of his fame and was amazed that for the first time in years he could go out to a disco without

Following page
Tony Prince, 'your Royal Ruler', at the height of the teenybop era.

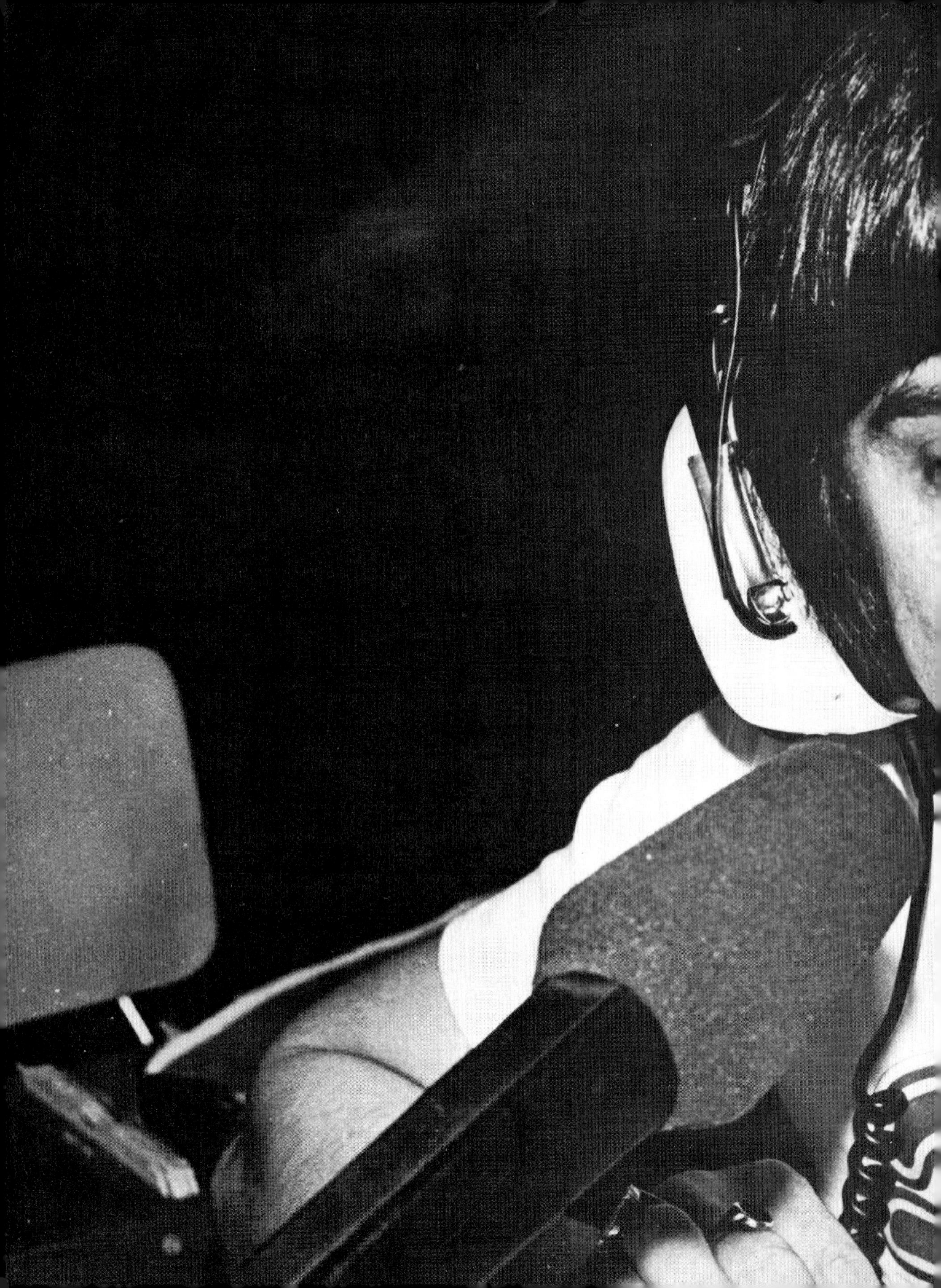

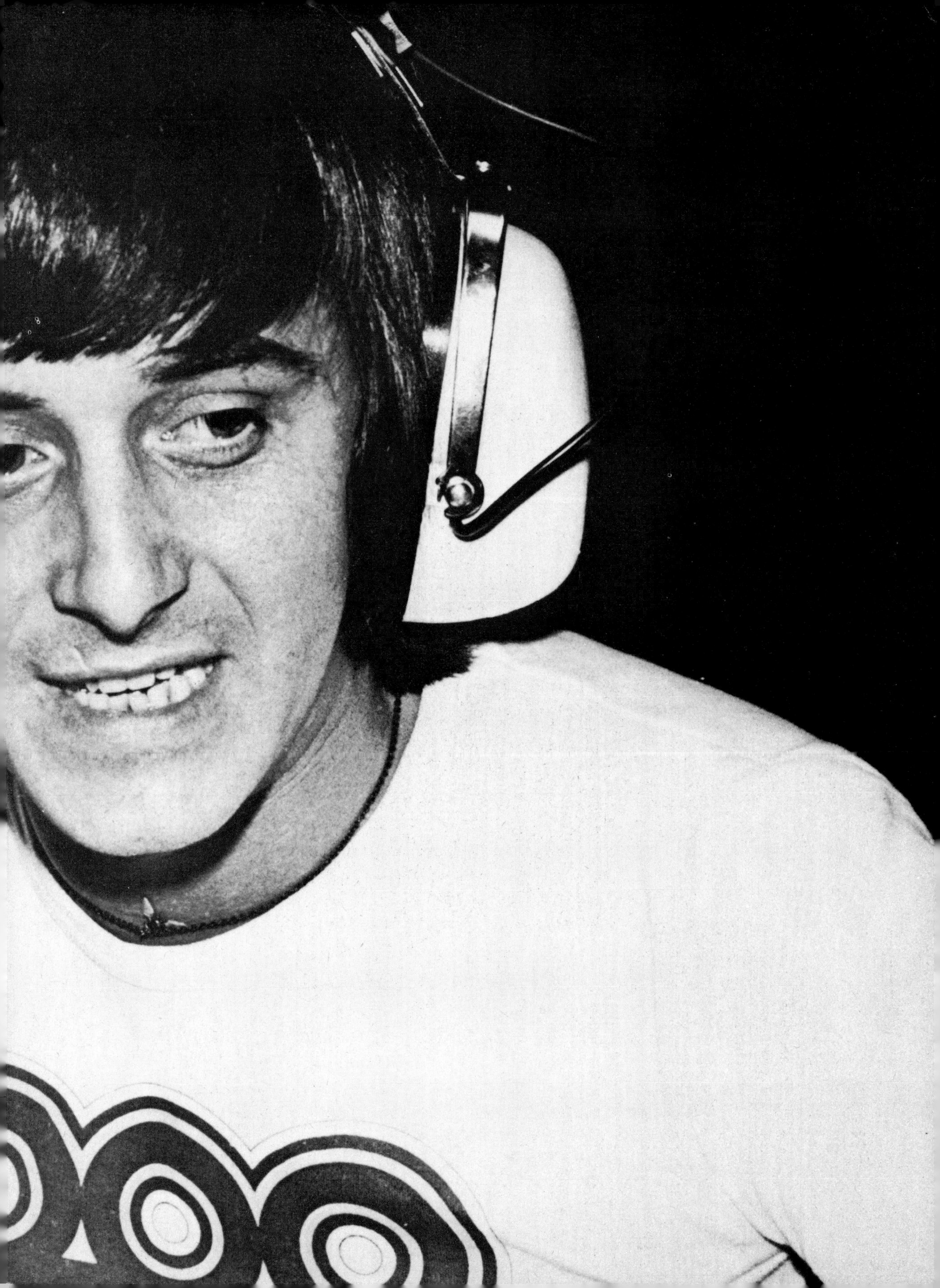

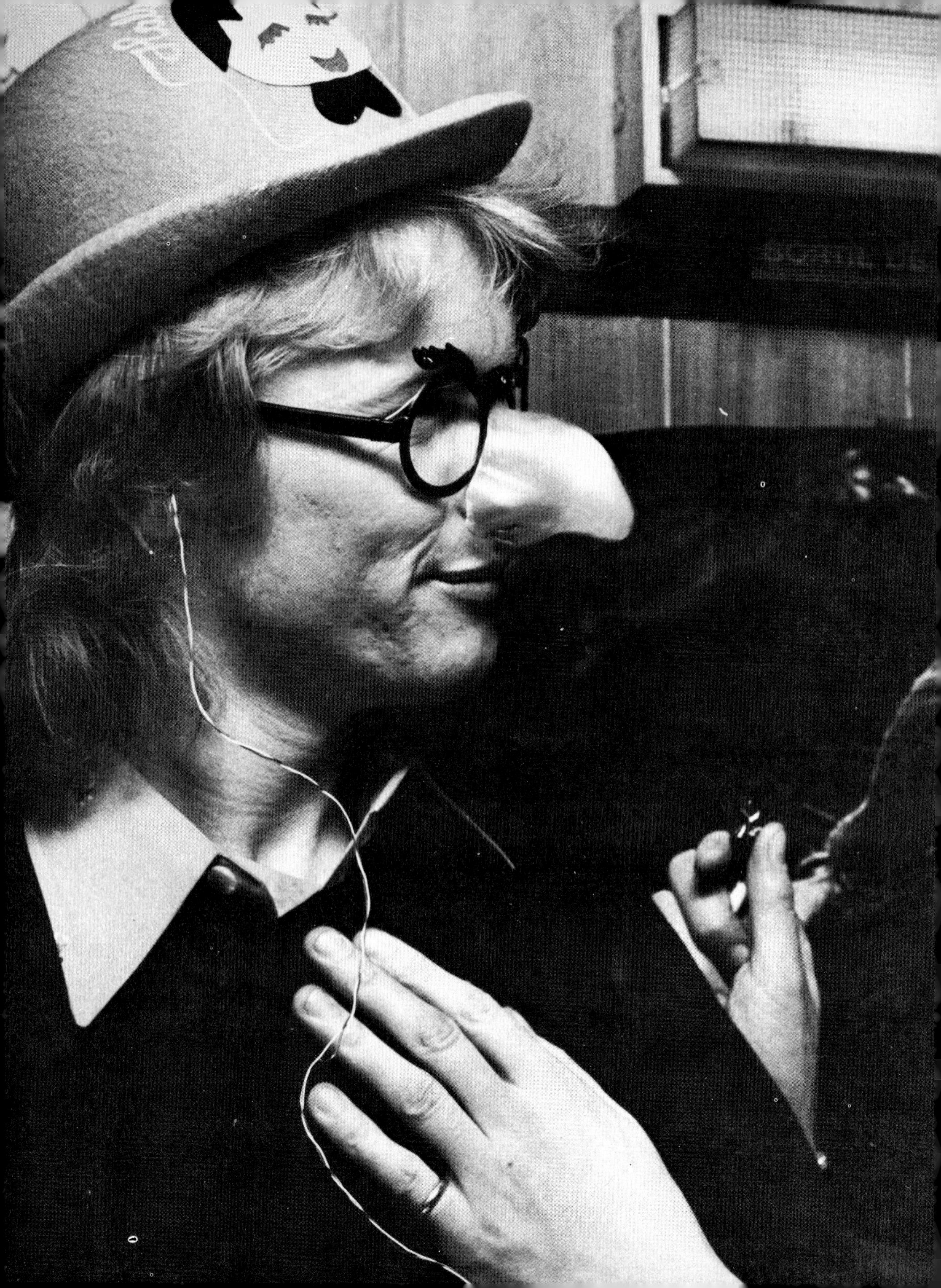

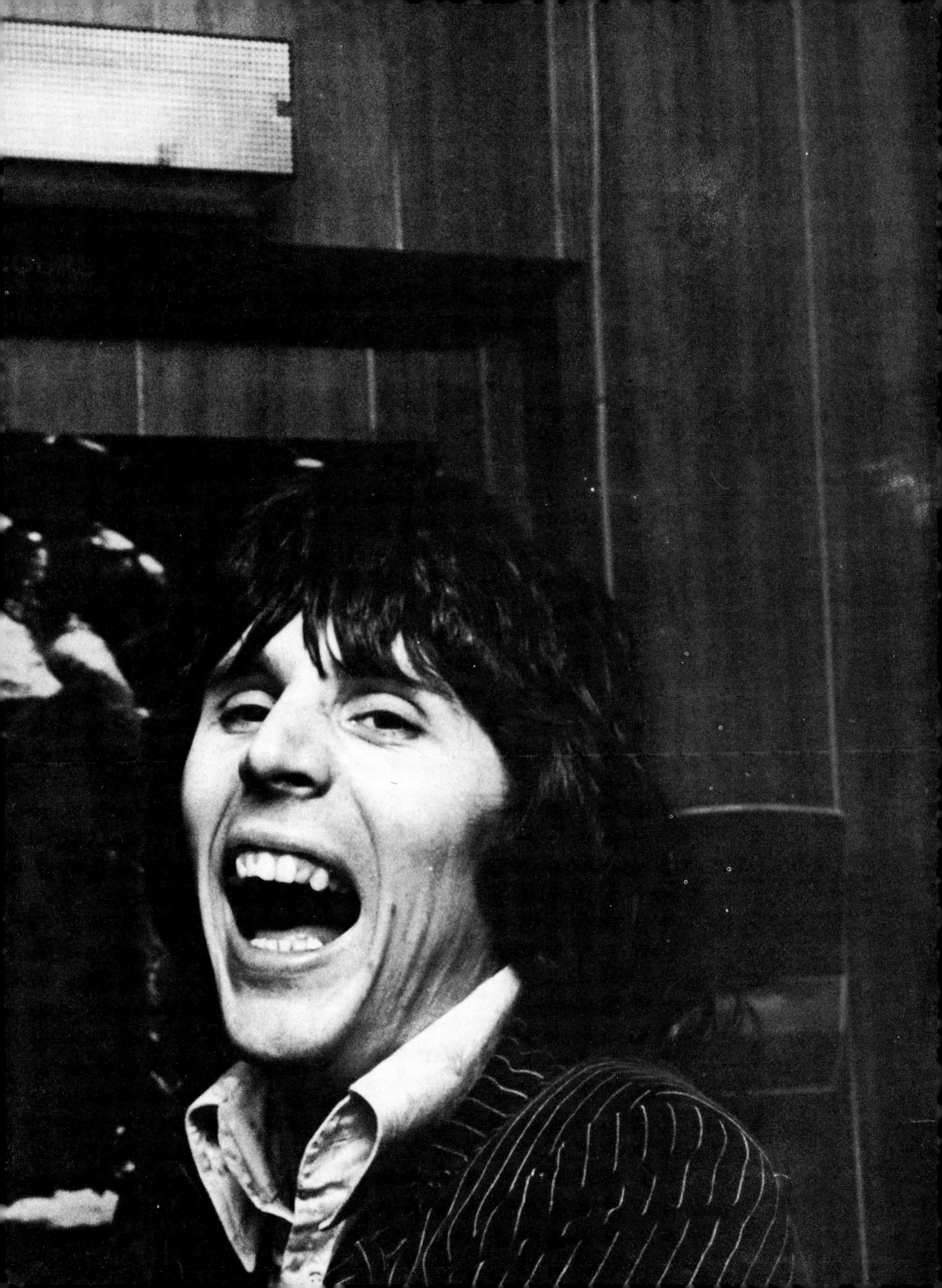

being mobbed. Once off the air the DJs worked their way through a circuit of nightclubs, their numbers swelling every time one of them finished on air and came along to join in the fun. They were the centre of a circle of attention in the Grand Duchy and although that circle followed them from club to club there were none of the mob scenes which would have greeted Cassidy in any disco in any town in Britain. This was always true of any visiting pop star and accounts for a lot of the high jinks which went on in Luxembourg. Most of it would never have happened in Britain because the DJs would have had other things to do and also because they would never have been able to go out in groups and enjoy a relative privacy.

It was this removal from the atmosphere of London and the distance between them and Authority which encouraged the practical jokes and the humorous backdrop to their lives which many of them found very reminiscent of the pirate ships. It was the protracted boredom of the pirate ship life which had elevated the practical joke from a mere prank to an art form and which was now carried on in the Grand Duchy where there were so many ex-pirate DJs who were already well-schooled in the art.

Thus it was that Kid Jensen (always a favourite victim, as the youngest member of the team) came home one night to find the 'blood'-spattered body of a young girl in his bedroom and an apparently dead Noel Edmonds with his head in a reeking gas oven. It wasCed Jensen who was chased through the dark Parc Municipal surrounding the Villa Louvigny one evening by the two gorillas who had that day escaped from the local zoo. It was only when one of them tripped over a low fence while in hot pursuit and gave voice to a most un-apelike curse that the gorillas were revealed as CBS pluggers Lewis Rogers and Colin Fawcett and that Tony Prince's high-pitched screaming was not fear but hysterical laughter. And when a worried-sounding Bob Stewart rang Tony Prince one evening and asked how to put out a fire in a chip pan he was told to put it in the fridge, which he did – but the pan really was on fire.

It wasn't all pranks, though. A friend of Tony Prince heard that he had enjoyed his first fondue but had never had a cheese fondue, so he took him to a restaurant he knew which specialised in the dish. Tony hated it and had a pork chop instead, the round trip took two days – the restaurant was in Switzerland. And in between all that there came what the DJs called 'the Luxembourg blues', a sort of deep depression which might last for a day or two and to which the practical jokes were the best antidote. The unreality of the nocturnal life and the consequent sense of distance from the 'real' world made it hard for the DJs to believe that they were doing what they were doing as well as they were doing it. Had it not been for the increasing number of personal appearances they were each making and the advent of the Luxembourg summer roadshows then they too might have been as cut off as the pirate jocks on the ships who didn't realise they were popular.

Previous page
David Jensen (plus nose) and Mark Wesley, seen here in a quiet moment of relaxation.

It wasn't a life which suited everybody. Noel Edmonds had stayed only nine months before resigning to take up a post with Radio One which was, at the time, entirely fictitious. Fortunately his huge gamble paid off and he did indeed land a small job with the BBC which eventually led on to much grander things, including TV. It's hard to believe that Noel Edmonds would never have made it in broadcasting if he had not started as a trainee on Radio Luxembourg, but speaking 15 years later, in 1983, he echoes the sentiment expressed by practically every single ex-Luxembourg DJ between Charles Maxwell from the thirties and the current eighties lineup when he says, 'I'm grateful to Luxembourg for everything, it was a fantastic apprenticeship.'

Another Radio Luxembourg DJ who thought he'd been in the Grand Duchy so long he'd become a fixture, joined Noel Edmonds on Radio One in March 1974. It had been an ambition of Paul Burnett's to work for the BBC – he recalled the saying that there are three magic numbers in radio – 208 – and three magic letters – BBC – but believed he'd been with Luxembourg too long to change over to what was their major competitor. He'd married a Luxembourg girl and become part of the Radio Luxembourg scene, but after what he called 'six of the happiest years of my life' he moved on to join Radio One for a Saturday morning show which soon grew into other things.

At about the same time as Paul Burnett was speaking to Radio One the person who would replace him was making almost daily train journeys between London and Birmingham, where he had been working on the local station. He was the first capture which Luxembourg made in this way, using the new ILR stations as a source of talent in the same way as both they and Radio One had used the closing pirate ships. The first of many to come to 208 along this route, Peter Powell arrived in the Grand Duchy in April of 1974 after a series of meetings, interviews and pilot shows conducted for and with Rodney Collins, Ken Evans and Alan Keen at long distance. One of 60 applicants, Peter had joined the shortlist of six and then, after five visits to Hertford Street in three weeks, had become the sole survivor of a tough selection process. For Radio Luxembourg it was an important signing, replacing the first of the 'live' team at the height of the teenybopper period; it was critical that whoever they selected would be able to fit into the station straight away and would relate to the kids and their music.

Peter Powell managed immediately, more or less adopting an upcoming Edinburgh band managed by an old friend of failed matelot and now Radio One DJ Stuart Henry, Tam Paton. The Bay City Rollers, with tartan scarves and spiky hair, were as musically creative and adventurous as a bowl of washing-up water, but they were staggeringly popular with young girls all over Britain. Probably the most meritorious of their hits was a re-released Four Seasons number, 'Bye Bye Baby', but that was hardly the point. Using a proven bespoke songwriting team, and with the all-pervading hand of Jonathan King (who had practically invented bubblegum music singlehanded) to guide them, the Rollers

Following pages left Peter Powell. *right* the mid-seventies – Peter Powell and Stuart Henry share a soft drink.

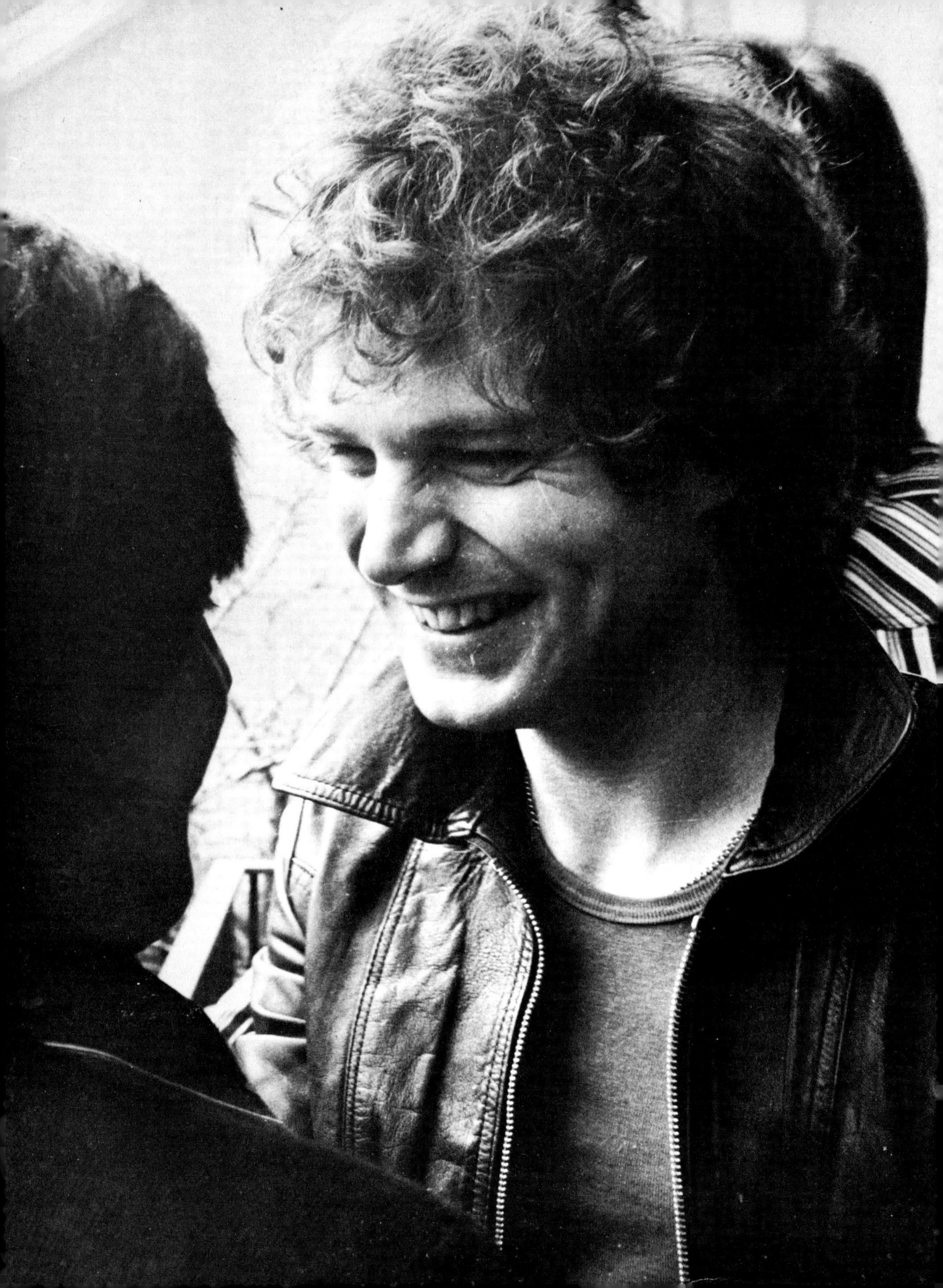

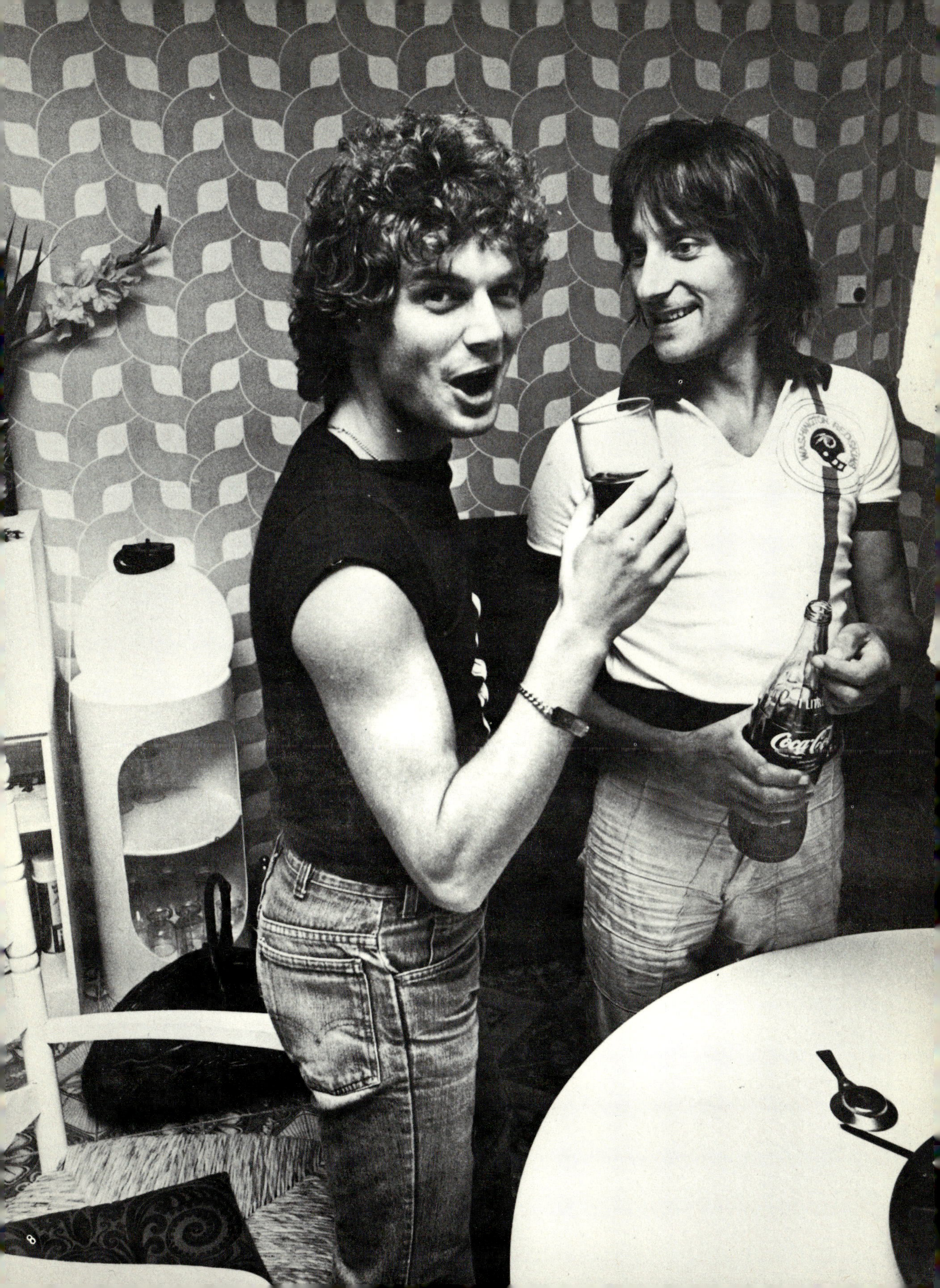
Coca-Cola

were *the* phenomenon of 1975. All of their uninspiring albums went gold and Rollermania was the in craze. It was this wildly popular band which Peter Powell welcomed on their first visit to the Grand Duchy, and continuing contact with the teenybopper audience discovered by Tony Prince was maintained. If anything the hysteria was heightened by deliberately exploiting the huge market with shows like *Battle of the Giants*. This kind of vinyl contest between big-name bands like the Osmonds and the Rollers in an hour-long special was enormously successful and also indicative of the way that Radio Luxembourg was sweeping ahead of the BBC in capturing the young radio audience of the time. It couldn't happen now. Somehow the same format between, say, Culture Club and Duran Duran, isn't the same sort of thing. The music and the market have changed quite dramatically since the mid-seventies. In a way the teenybopper explosion was its own death warrant; all those clean-faced and righteous young bands made the space and created the mood for a reversal of their own trend and made the appearance of punk bands like the Sex Pistols almost inevitable.

Despite the excitement of the period, and despite being at the virtual spearhead of an innovative and successful radio adventure, Peter Powell never really settled in Luxembourg. 'Being signed by Luxembourg was the most important break in my career,' he says now, and like so many others he is still grateful to Radio Luxembourg for the time he spent on the radio station. 'It offered me an enormous amount of freedom and fun, and I learnt radio and the responsibility of broadcasting there,' is how he sums it up, but the continental lifestyle and the nocturnal existence forced on everyone who works in the Grand Duchy never appealed to Peter in the same way that it did to others who stayed longer or, like Bob Stewart, are still there. Peter Powell missed out on pirate radio – in fact he never even got to listen to it, never mind work on it – and Luxembourg was to him what pirate ships were to his predecessors. 'I missed Top of the Pops, Brew 11, home cooking and having a morning paper delivered,' he says, expressing a feeling which echoes that felt by Steve Wright who went to Luxembourg five years later.

Almost a year after Peter Powell joined Radio Luxembourg Dave Christian and Kid Jensen left. Kid Jensen went into local radio in Nottingham before going on to Radio One in the autumn of 1976 – it was a sort of 'cooling-off' period which allowed him to become dissociated from the Radio Luxembourg sound and made his presence on BBC radio rather more acceptable – it's a roundabout route which several people have taken with great success. To replace the two missing bodies Radio Luxembourg took on two people who had hitherto been working for the BBC.

Barry Alldis returned in 1975, bringing his Luxembourg-born wife back home, and stayed on 208 to become their longest-serving presenter until his sad and untimely death in late 1982. At the same time another ex-BBC person was flying out to Luxembourg, so that by mid-1975 the DJ team in the Grand Duchy was Tony Prince, Bob Stewart, Mark

Barry Alldis, Luxembourg's longest-serving presenter until his untimely death in 1982.

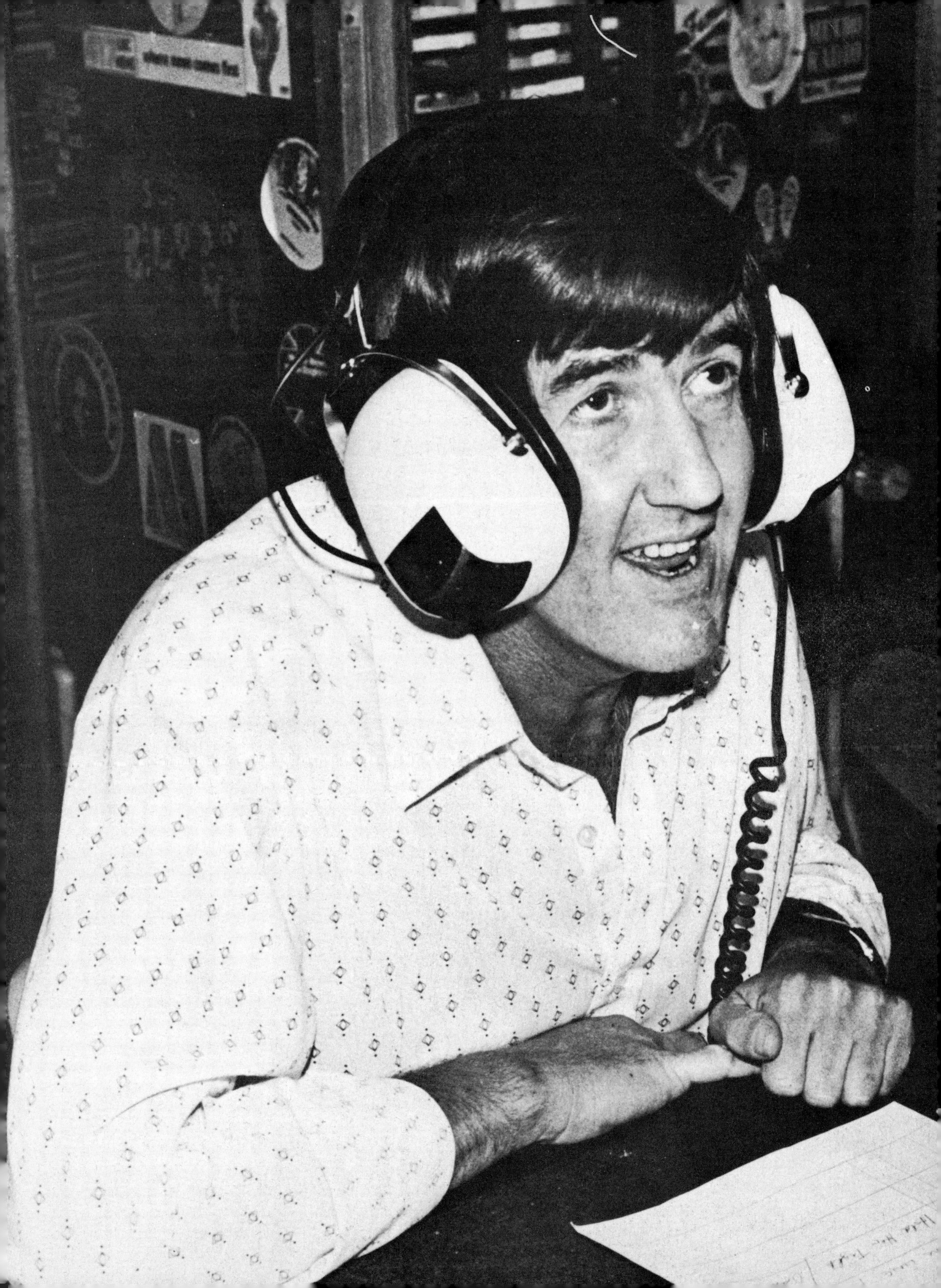

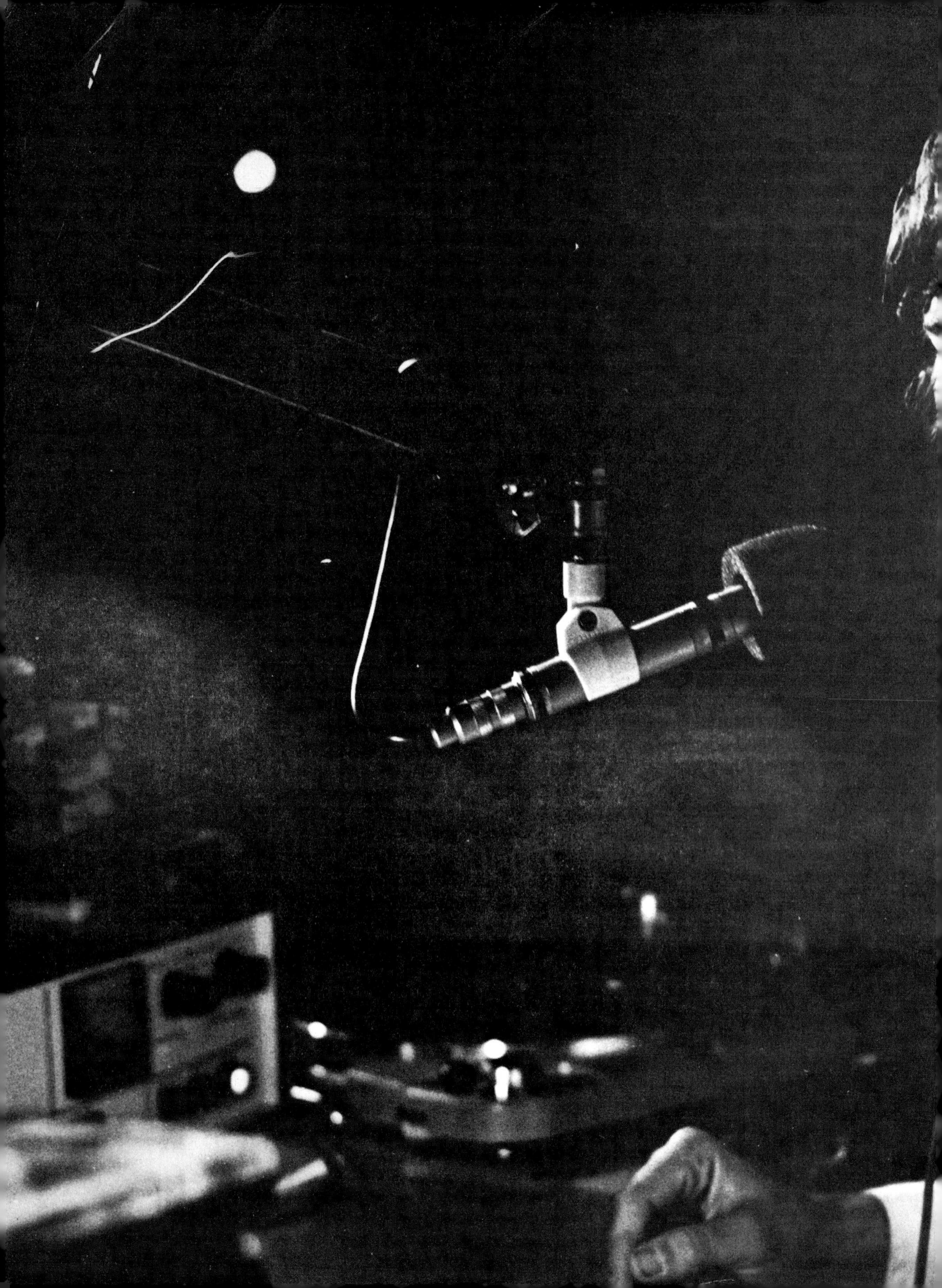

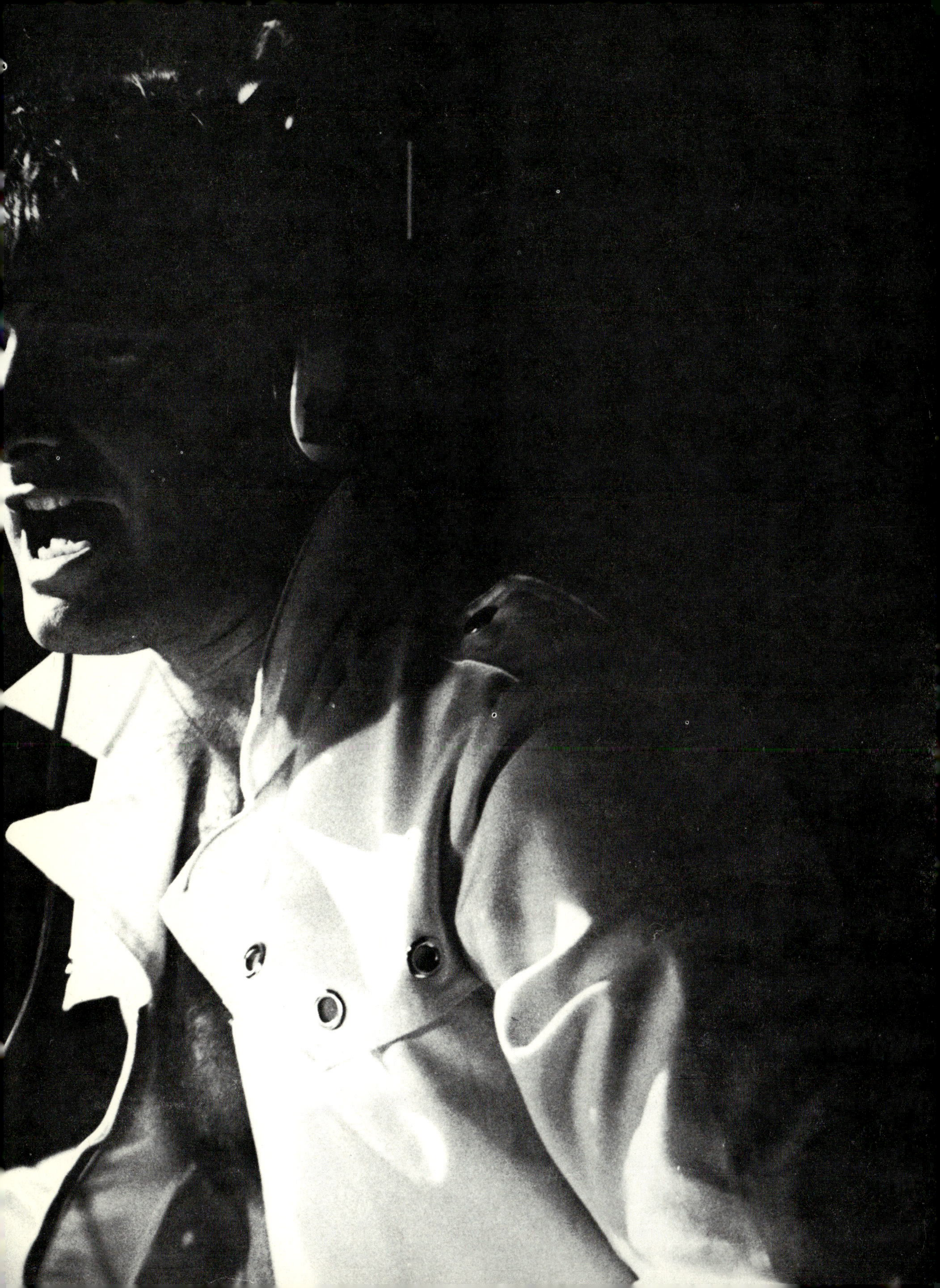

Wesley, Peter Powell, Barry Alldis and Stuart Henry.

Stuart had become part of the original team who opened Radio One in 1967, going from *Mid-Day Spin* to *Sounds of the Seventies* and then the *Radio One Club*, a series of outside broadcasts from colleges and universities all over Britain. After parting with Radio One in 1974 Stuart and his then girlfriend Ollie decided to retire from the radio business and take off for somewhere sunny. Living off the rent from their flat in Hampstead, they planned to be beach bums somewhere 'where you can be a rich man on twenty quid a week'. But it was not to be. Stuart had what he considered a very fine arrangement with his accountant – 'I never talked to him, and he never talked to me'. Once a year Stuart would visit the accountant at his London flat. It was a very nice flat, with lots of nice paintings and the walls painted a deep blue colour – 'very restful,' Stuart calls it. After half an hour admiring the decor and chatting about art Stuart went home. Eventually the taxman caught up with Stuart and, just as he was planning retirement, he found himself forced to get a job – a most fortunate misfortune, as it turned out.

Rodney Collins, who had been at the BBC and was now working for Radio Luxembourg, approached Stuart and offered him a job on 208, and in 1975 he arrived in the Grand Duchy to work for a radio station which was still operated by the engineers from a separate control room instead of by the DJ and still had what Stuart described as 'a post-teenybop' playlist. Stuart's first reaction was one of instant dismay; he disliked Luxembourg and hated the playlist – 'never in my entire life has anybody said "you *will* play this, followed by this" to a disc jockey – and calls it 'a hangover from the spots and pimples era featuring no-hope would-be teenybop bands, a list of myriad nonentities that we've all forgotten about.' His first reaction was to get out and go home as soon as possible. But before he'd arranged that everything started to change.

The first difference was a three month experiment in self-operating studios which was arranged simply by putting a microphone in the engineer's control room and presenting the programmes from there. This worked well enough for the system to be adopted and purpose-built self-op studios were constructed – and are still in use. Even now Radio Luxembourg's English Service is still something of an innovation, and the great percentage of the studios are still built the old way, although the studios in Paris are an exception to this rule; they were changed by the French Service's biggest hero, Emperor Rosko. It was he who saved the French station from what seemed like certain extinction, and did so almost singlehanded. He managed to get a self-op studio built in the corridor of the Paris offices and his popularity rose to such heights so quickly that, within weeks of his first broadcast, there were queues of young fans outside the building waiting for their turn to file down the corridor, squeeze past the makeshift control desk and watch the Emperor himself at work.

Then, in the search for something to replace the teenybop craze, Radio Luxembourg became an all-album station, which was a short-lived

Previous page
The man who turned the tide for RTL France, Emperor Rosko hard at work.

experiment, abandoned after about six months when they moved back into chart music. The station had changed in a year, and Stuart stayed in Luxembourg and married Ollie. Both decisions were exceptionally fortunate. Shortly after his arrival in Luxembourg the strange illness which had been affecting Stuart's balance and gait was finally diagnosed as Multiple Sclerosis. It was, he says now, a relief to have a name to put to it, but it was also a relief to be in Luxembourg and not stranded on an isolated beach in the Seychelles. It would not be until 1978 that Stuart Henry 'came out of the closet', as he puts it, and told the world about his illness, and at the same time, with the full support of Radio Luxembourg, launched the Stuart Henry MS Appeal. During the intervening period Ollie learnt to drive, so that she and Stuart could get about in the Grand Duchy, and she also learnt how to be a DJ, first on RTL's English-language local radio station for Luxembourg, Community Radio, and later on 208 itself, sharing presentation with Stuart on five or six programmes every week.

Before that there were other changes. Ken Evans moved on from his job as Programme Director at 208 on 31 May 1977 to go into the record industry itself. He thought he'd been producing for long enough – 11 years all told – and it was time to try something else. However it would not be long before he was back in a studio again, and now produces an assortment of shows for BBC Radio Two, including his regular spot with an old-time Luxembourg colleague, David Jacobs.

When Ken Evans left, Alan Keen suggested that Tony Prince move to London and fill the vacant seat, but Tony was quite happy behind a microphone and couldn't visualise himself anywhere else. Bob Stewart tried it for a while, but he didn't like it either, and the set became empty yet again. This time Alan Keen succeeded in persuading Tony Prince to have a go, and after nearly 10 years residency in the Grand Duchy Tony and Christine came back to Britain, although Tony still had a regular show on 208 and was forced to travel regularly between London and Luxembourg, covering thousands of miles each year just on that one return journey. It was under Tony Prince that the album format was dropped and for a little over a year Luxembourg became a disco station. This came at the height of the 'Saturday Night Fever' era and served its purpose admirably, especially as the only other musical trend still seemed to be leaning to the rather unmelodic punk bands. In fact the move away from the teenybopper audience had been orchestrated by Tony Logie, who spent only two years with Radio Luxembourg, between 1977 and 1979. It was Logie who realised that the teenybopper market, although vociferous, had little or no financial potential, especially in the eyes of advertisers. He identified the 18–24 age bracket as the target and the station went for it wholeheartedly and with immediate (and pronounced) success – the poor ratings at the end of 1978 had been turned into very good ratings by the end of 1979, and by the end of 1982 Radio Luxembourg could count on 1.75 million listeners every night. The disco format eventually gave way to Luxembourg's return to its original

Following page
Mike Read on the road for 208.

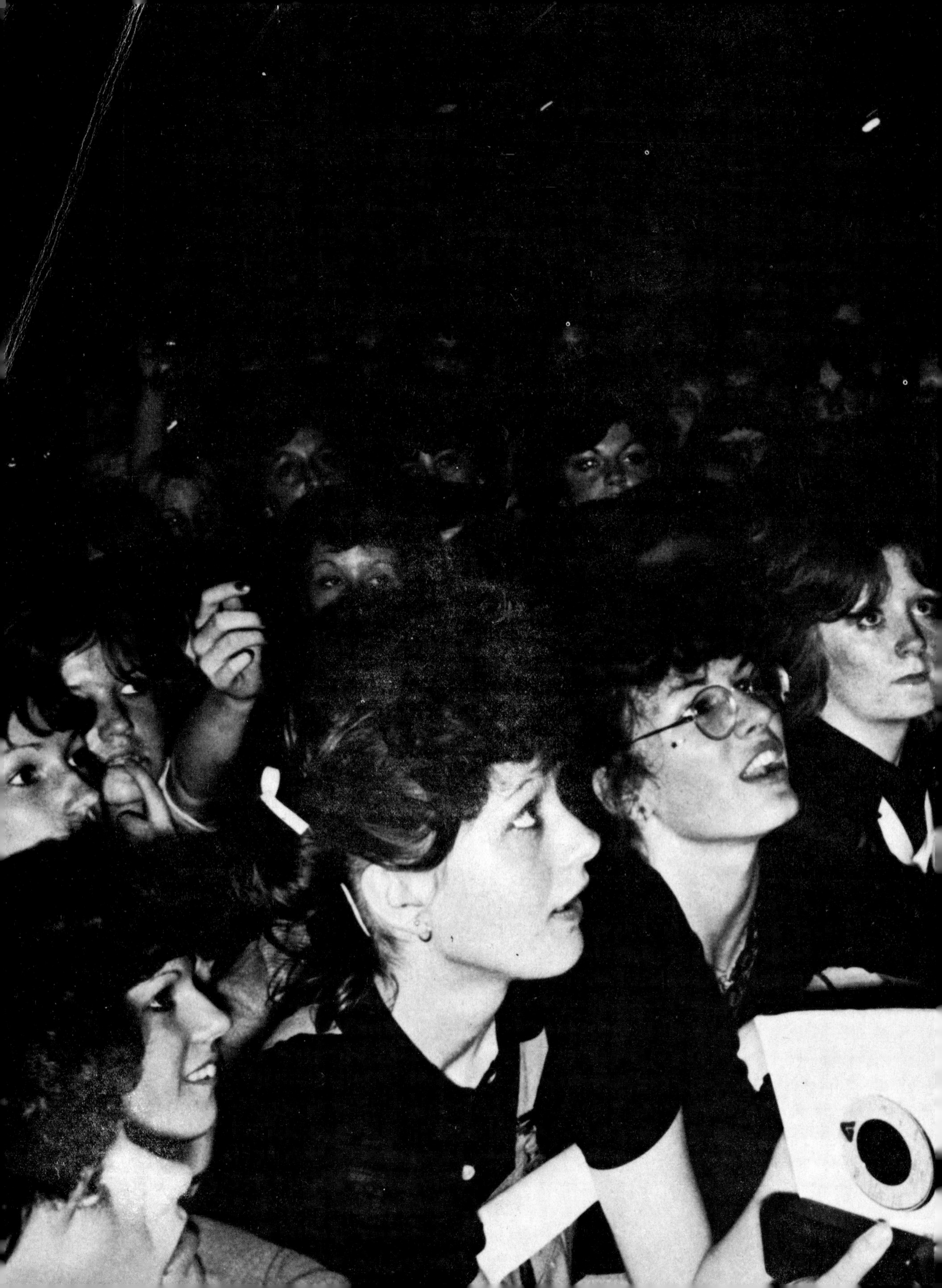

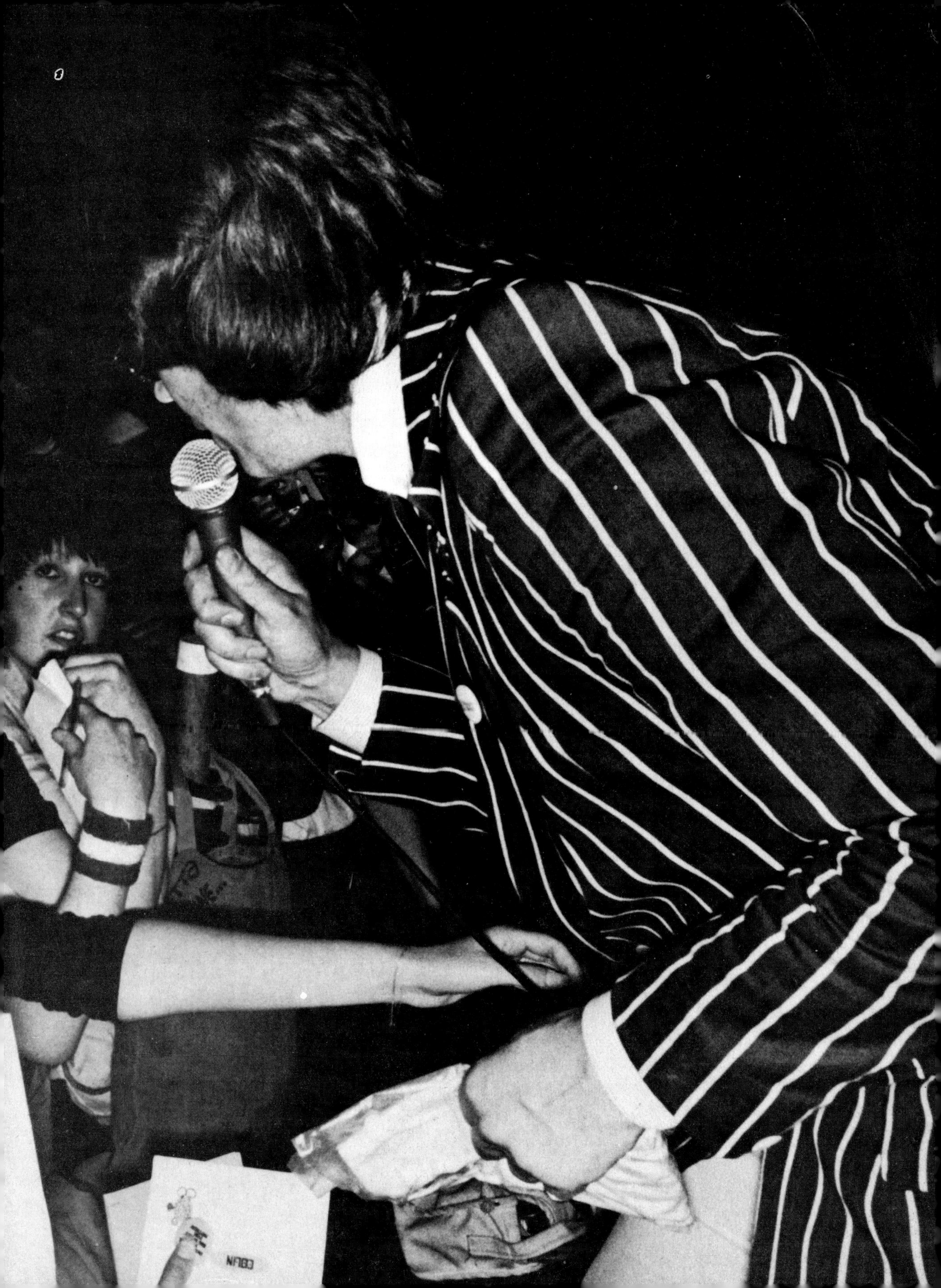

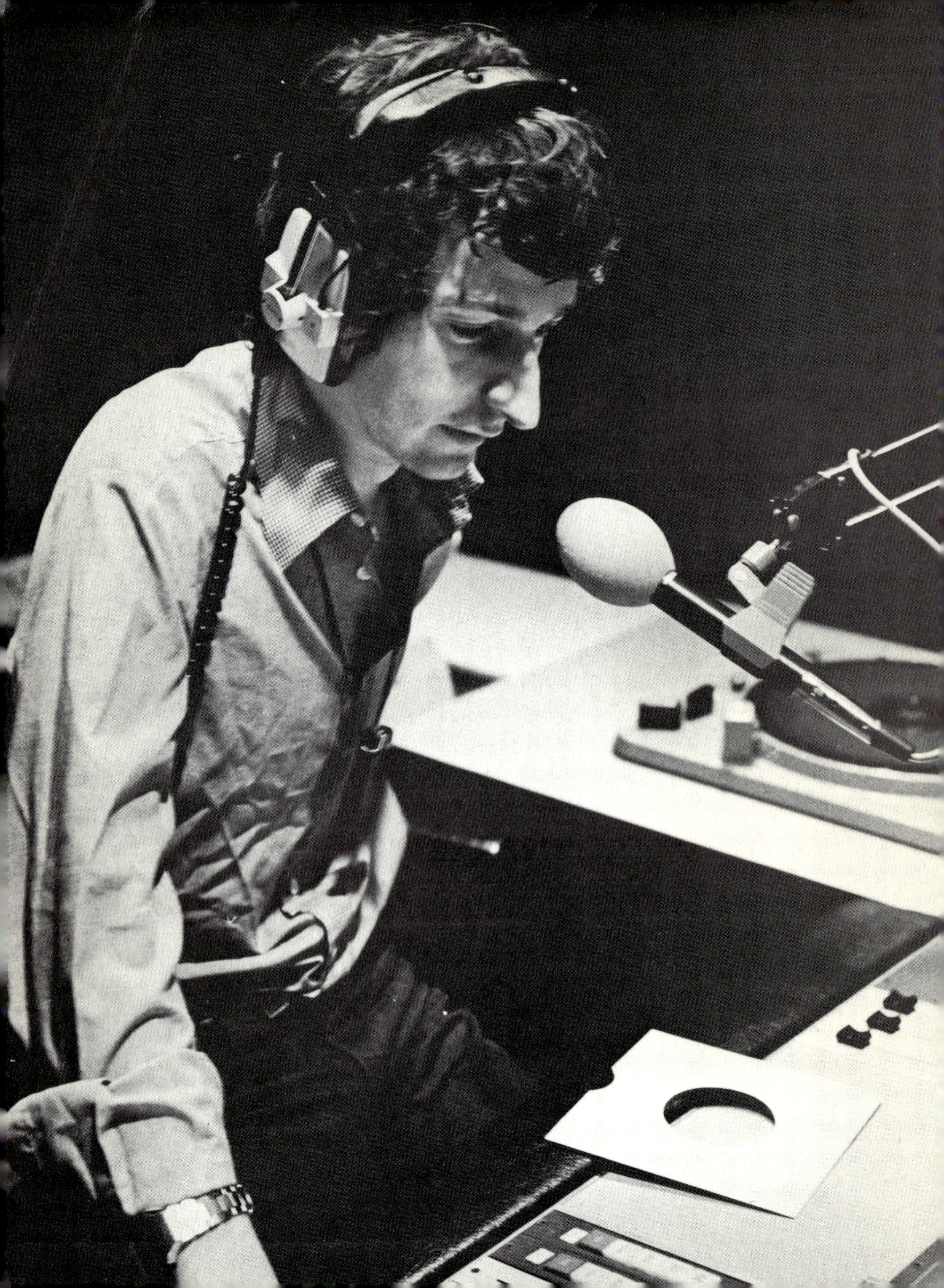

format which had started the whole thing off 50 years ago and which it still sticks to today – solid chart music liberally sprinkled with the classics of the past, competitions (in which the total value of the prizes is staggering), and of course Bob Stewart's regular diet of country music.

Bob Stewart never used to like country music, but he spent a great deal of time in the company of a large American Sergeant of Marines who doted on it, and Bob recalls it could be dangerous to say you didn't enjoy it. After a while you get used to it, then it grows on you, and now Bob himself is a dedicated fan, and his weekly broadcasts from Nashville, relayed live by satellite, are a regular feature of the 208 programme output.

But that wasn't until after Peter Powell departed for London in the October of 1977, a few months after Ken Evans had left. Peter returned to London and the BBC, and never lost his feel for the younger end of the audience; he has consistently remained in touch with the new bands and the new tastes, a successful pattern first learnt on Radio Luxembourg and for which Radio One has ever since been the richer.

As Programme Director it was Tony Prince who had to fill his own shoes out in Luxembourg and also the gap left by Peter Powell, and to do the latter Rob Jones arrived from Liverpool's Radio City. Rob was training to be an accountant when he landed a job on Merseyside's brand-new commercial station, on the condition that at the same time he keep up with his studies. However, it was accountancy which fell by the wayside, and Rob made himself a successful career in local radio. Three years later he was sitting in the studio when the phone rang halfway through the programme: 'What do you want?' he asked the caller rather abruptly, and was somewhat chastened to find that what he wanted was Rob to go down to London for an interview. Still, 'Nobody seemed to mind,' he says, and he got the job anyway, arriving in Luxembourg at about the same time as another DJ who had just come from commercial radio, in this case Radio 210 at Reading. This was Mike Read, Cliff Richard lookalike and walking pop music encyclopaedia, whose time in the Grand Duchy was as short as Noel Edmonds' had been and whose subsequent career has followed a similar enviable course. When he left, his replacement was also drawn from 210, because ex-210 staffer Richard Swainson, who was now working in Hertford Street, played a tape of Steve's 210 breakfast show to Tony Prince, who in turn played it to Alan Keen.

Steve Wright was not at all keen on Luxembourg – 'I missed Rich Tea biscuits, *Coronation Street* and the *Evening Standard*,' he says. Unlike Noel Edmonds, Steve was unable to invent a suitable payola system to cover the deficiency. Noel had found that tea and bacon were the things he missed more than anything, and regular packages of the same used to arrive in Luxembourg courtesy of a record company not totally unconnected with Micky Most's brother Dave. That doesn't mean that their records received any favouritism but 'they certainly got noticed'.

Without these few home comforts Steve Wright was not at all keen on

Steve Wright.

the Grand Duchy. Like Peter Powell he enjoyed the radio station – 'it had a good ambience, an exciting sound and a nice feel to it' – but still Steve didn't feel at home in Luxembourg. He sent an audition tape to Stuart Grundy and was soon on his way to Radio One, sad to leave behind the people on Radio Luxembourg, but glad to get back to watching TV 'and being British', something he couldn't manage even with his regular weekly trips back to London, some of which had been of only a few hours' duration. He used to catch the morning flight into Heathrow, soak up London, and catch the evening flight back to Luxembourg.

Another DJ who never got into the swing of Luxembourg was media enigma Simon Dee. Long after his fall from grace he surfaced in Hertford Street, told Tony Prince he was anxious to get back to work again, taped four very good shows, missed his next studio booking completely and was never heard from again.

Someone who did fit into the 208 'ambience' very easily arrived in the Grand Duchy after Steve Wright returned to London. A large (15 stone) Texan, Benny Brown went to a high school party in South Carolina at 15 years old and saw WCOS radio DJ Chris Kraft in action. It was 'an instant glamour trip' for Benny and he pursued a career in radio with a dedication and singlemindedness unusual in many of Luxembourg's top names. His career took him through radio in Texas, Kansas and Hawaii and then to Vietnam before arriving in Europe in the mid-seventies. He worked with Wolfman Jack as his sound engineer in 1975 and 1979 and spent a great deal of time on the road. He eventually arrived at Villa Louvigny in March 1980, but the Benny Brown Roadshow is still a big part of his life, and whenever he's not on 208 he's generally on his way to or from somewhere in Europe for a live gig – much of the work in Germany, stemming from his time there on the American Forces Network.

And almost at the same time that Benny arrived in the Grand Duchy Alan Keen left Radio Luxembourg after 10 years, going back to his original career in newspaper advertising, this time with the *Guardian*. His place was taken by Patrick Cox, who has now assumed another role when, after almost 15 years with 208, Tony Prince resigned in March 1983 to pursue his own career with his Disco Mix Club as well as recording a weekly show for 208 much in the way that his predecessors would have done in the fifties and sixties.

Out in the Grand Duchy that left only Bob Stewart of the original 1968 'all-live' lineup, along with Rob Jones, Benny Brown, Stuart and Ollie and newcomer Mike Hollis – who has traditionally been allocated the very latest of the late shows. Dave Christian's back in the Grand Duchy as well, back at Villa Louvigny working for RTL but not on the English service. Multilingual in the extreme, Dave Christian is just as happy in French or German and broadcasts in three languages from the Grand Duchy – an ambition which the Compagnie Luxembourgeoise de Radiodiffusion started out with when it was formed in 1929.

Even today Radio Luxembourg still doesn't have a landline between

Above
Benny Brown sometimes doubles up with Rob Jones on phone-ins.
Below
Stuart and Ollie behind the microphone together at Villa Louvigny.

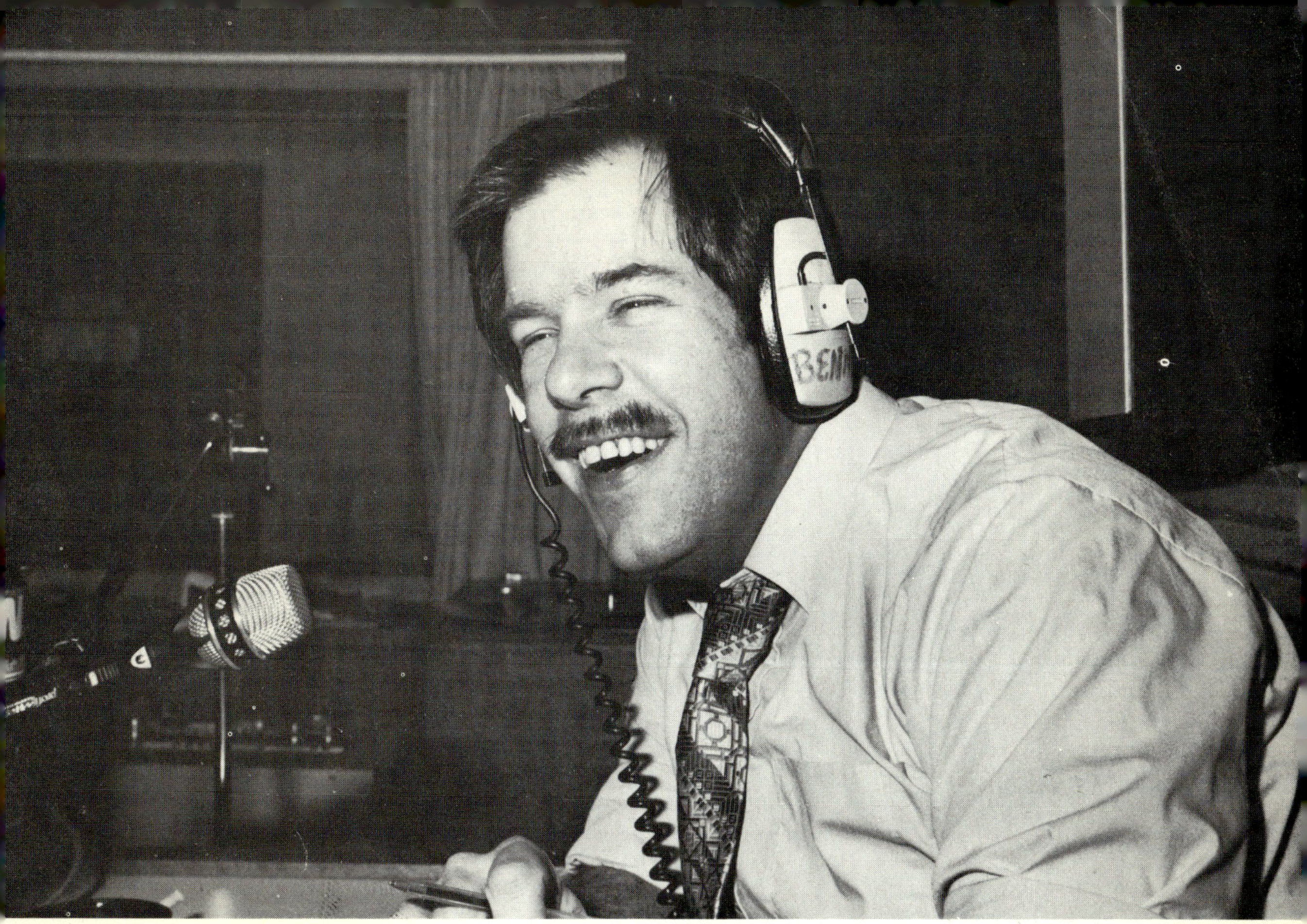

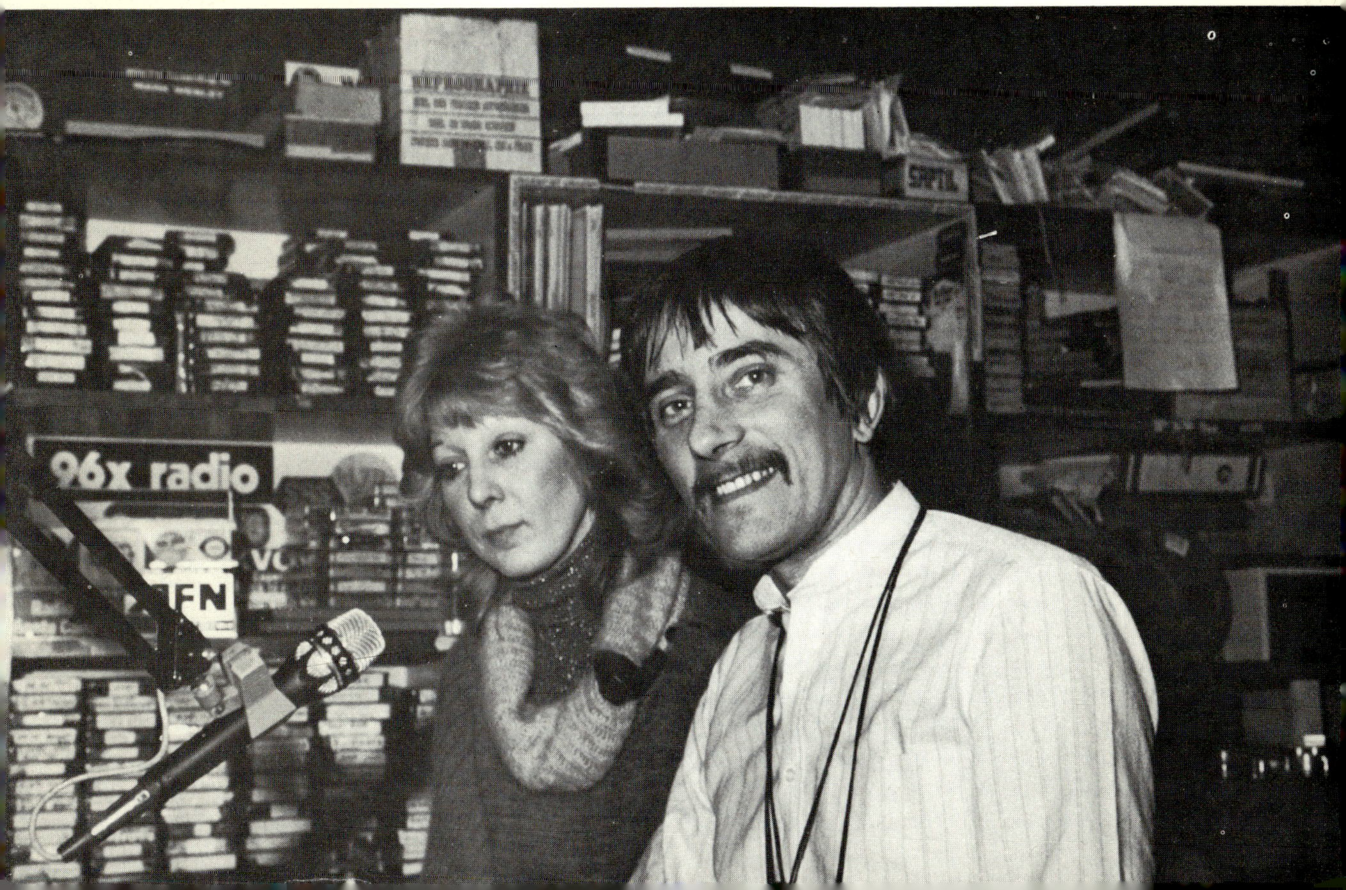
96x radio

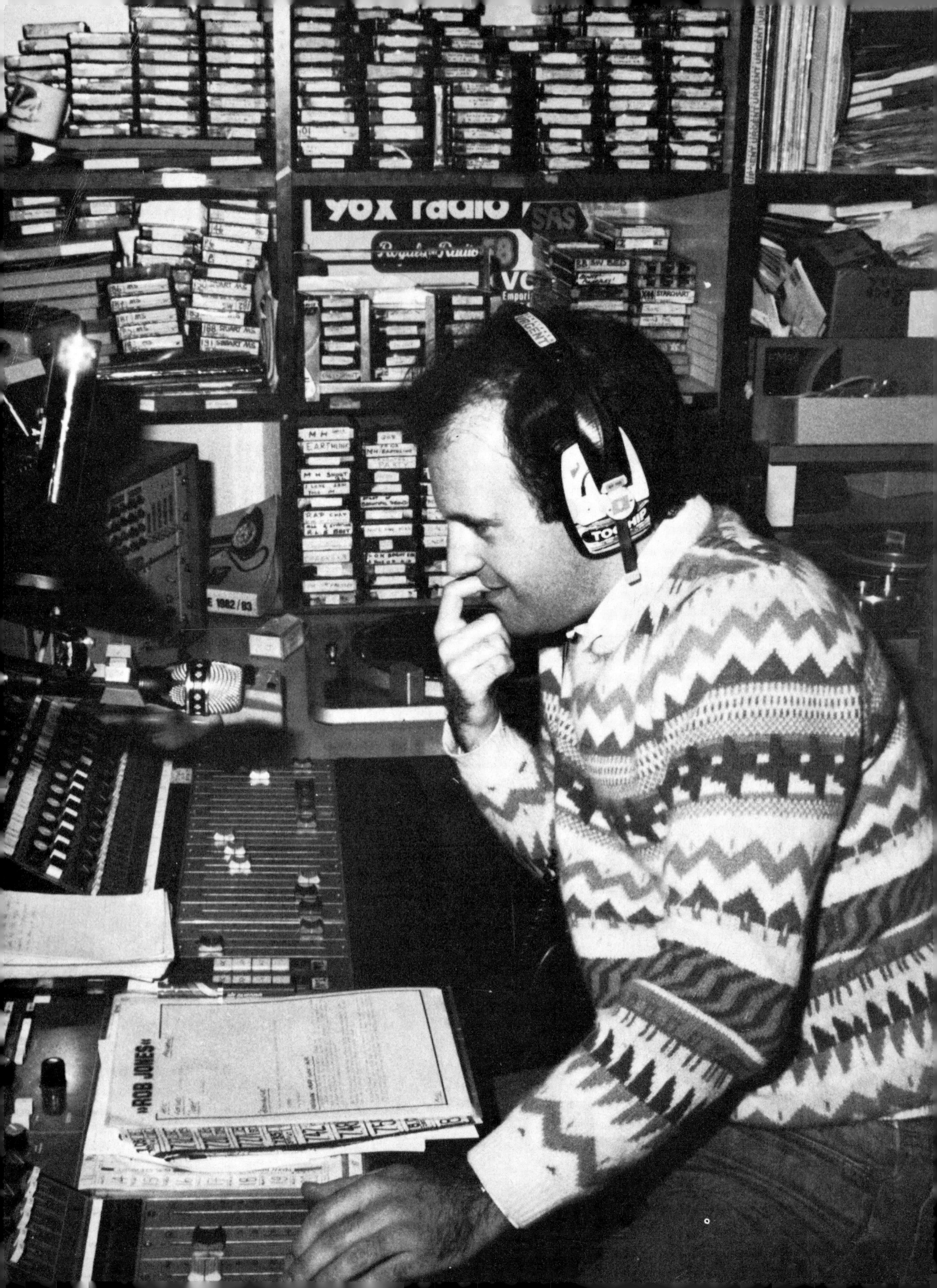
SAS
ROB JONES

London and the Grand Duchy and the chances are they never will, although the technology exists. In fact RTL France does have precisely that privilege, which it uses frequently for live TV broadcasts to France from Britain. And when the French radio service want a landline back to Paris they get one, although they have to use the facilities of London's commercial station, Capital Radio. The truth is that the resistance to the English Service of Radio Luxembourg, which was formed in prejudice 50 years ago, is still as real as it was then, and it is clear that Radio Luxembourg will never gain acceptance by the broadcasting 'establishment' in this country.

This is even more obvious when the station's attempts at diversification are examined; ever since the advent of ILR, Radio Luxembourg has been trying to gain involvement with local radio stations in Britain but has never been successful, and it is unlikely that the situation will ever change.

Recent advances in satellite technology have meant that this need not be a handicap. The possibility that RTL would launch their own geostationary satellite over Europe has been debated for a number of years and at one stage it looked certain that they would go ahead. But then the more recent arrival of cable TV in Britain has offered what may turn out to be a more practical alternative. Most cable TV companies also pipe radio into the homes they serve and there is no reason why one of the stations thus delivered could not be Radio Luxembourg. In the early months of 1983 it was not clear which of these two possible choices would be the most sensible and economically viable. RTL delayed their decision, but the message is still clear. As Patrick Cox explains it, 'One way or another, we'll still be here in 50 years' time, whatever it costs.'

When a similar sentiment was expressed in 1933 nobody really believed it, and perhaps they may be forgiven. But now that Radio Luxembourg has achieved exactly what it set out to achieve, and has used the medium of radio to cross international boundaries of art, culture and mutual understanding, now that RTL is the largest commercial organisation of its kind in the world, it is impossible not to believe that in another 50 years' time they'll still be here, doing what they do best.

Rob Jones is supposed to *ask* the questions on the phone-in shows.

INDEX

Advertisers' Weekly, 22, 43
AFN (American Forces Network), 61
Aldrich, Ronnie, 86, 93
Alldis, Barry, *84*, 86, *87*, 95, *96*, 97, 101, 104, 117, *118*, 119, 129, 134, *161*, 176, *177*, 180
Alldis, Fernande, 97
Allen, Patrick, 86
Ambrose and his Orchestra, 45
Andrews, Eamonn, 86
Andrews, Stanley, 65
Anen, Francois, 13, 121
Anka, Paul, 92, *106*
Arden, Neil, 42–3
Atwell, Winifred, 86

Baby Bob Stewart Show, 146
Bailey-Watson, Monty, 80, 81
Barker, Charles, 38
Batchelor, Horace, 8
Battle of the Giants, 176
Bay City Rollers, the, 173, 176
BBC, 11–20 passim, *21*, 22–39 passim, 43, 45–6, 47, 49, 50, 52, 54–65 passim, 74–7 passim, 83, 85, 86, 88, 94, 98, 100, 101, 103, 104, 111, 116, 117, 119, 120,123, 131, 134, 137, 140, 147, 152, 155, 159, 173, 176, 180, 185; local radio, 160; Radio One, 134, 137, 139, 140, 144, 146, 152, 159, 160, 173, 176, 180, 185, 186; World Radio, 20
Beatles, the, 8, 102, 113–14, 116, 120, 123, 155, 159, 166, 167
Beery, Wallace, 37
Berry, Roy, 82
Billy's Banjo Show, 101
Birch, Philip, 123
Black Bess Barflies, the, 164
Blackburn, Tony, 123, 128, 129, 131, 134, 137, 146, *158*
Bolton, Derek, 65
Brady, Pete, 131, *142*
Brando, Marlon, 79, 82
Brandon, Tony, 129–30, 134
Brent, Tony, 93
Bringing Christ to the Nations, 102
British Forces Network, 85, 101, 114
Brown, Benny, 186, *187*
Brown, Bob, 114
Bruck, Jean, 25
Burnett, Paul, 143, 146, 147, *148–9*, 152, *162–3*, 164, 173

Cameron, Don, 93
Campbell, Pat, 109
Candid Mike, 80, 86
Capital Radio, 81, 189
Carpendale, Vice Admiral Sir Charles, 15, 16, 19, 45
Carr, Pearl, 62, 100
Carson, Willie, 126
Cartmel, Marie, 111
Carver, Peter, 101

Casalis, Jeanne de, 31
Cash, Dave, 124, 134, 159
Cassidy, David, 166, 167, 172
Cavendish, Lady Charles, 35–6
Christian, Dave, 129, 140, *141*, 143, 154, 159, *162–3*, 164, 176, 186
Churchill, Winston, 53, 59
Clapham and Dwyer, 32, 36
Cliff Richard Show, The, 101–2
CLR (Compagnie Luxembourgeoise de Radiodiffusion), 14, 19, 22, 24, 25, 26, 42, 45, 59, 104, 186
Collins, Rodney, 173, 180
Costa, Sam, 86, 98, 102, 146
Countdown, 116, 119
Cowboy's Lullaby, 75
Cox, Patrick, 186, 189
Crozier, Bill, *136*

Daily Mirror, 82, 88, 94, 123, 155
Dale, Robbie, 129, 140
Dance Party, 8, 111, 113, 131
Dan Dare, 82, 85, 102
Daniels, Billy, *72*
Danvers Walker, Bob, 16, 50, 52, 80
Dee, Simon, 131, *135*, *136*, *158*, 186
Dell, Alan, *136*
Denning, Brook, 101, 104, 114
Dennis, Chris, 119
Det Nye, 117, *118*
Discotheque, 111
Disc Drive, 129
Double Your Money, 86
Duc, Jean Le, 13, 14

Earthlink, 8
Edmonds, Noel, 140, 143–4, 147, 154, 159, 172, 173, 185
Elrick, George, 93
Etienne, Henri, 13, 14, 16, 19
Evans, Ken, 123, 124, 131, *133*, 137, 138, 157, 164, 166, 173, 181, 185
Everett, Kenny, 123, 124, 134, 159
Everitt, Geoffrey, 64, 65, 67, *69*, 70, 71, *72*, 75, 79, 85, 101, 143, 146, 157
Everly Brothers, the, 92, 102, 109

Family Favourites, 98, 111, 147
Fernandez, Raoul, 13, 15
Fields, Gracie, *34*, 35, 55
Five o' Clock Club, 111
Fordyce, Keith, 85, 86, *87*, 88, 94, 95, *96*, 111, *136*
Formby, George, 55
Frankau, Ronald, 32, 33
Freed, Alan, 79, 86
Freeman, Alan, 86, *89*, *90*, 98, 102, 131, 134, 147
Fury, Billy, *105*

Gell, David, 85, 86, 88, 94, 134, *136*
Gillette Sports Parade, 80
Goebbels, Joseph, 30, 53, 55

Good, Jack, 86, 92, 100
Green, Hughie, 71, 86
Green, Phil, 62, 65
Grundy, Stuart, 129, 186

Hall, Henry, 36, 94
Harris, Bob, *158*
Harris, Phil, *78*
Hearne, Big Bill, 119
Hector Ross Radio Productions, 80, 81
Henry, Ollie, 180, 181, 186, *187*
Henry, Stuart, 124, *125*, 126, *132*, 134, 173, *175*, 180, 181, 186, *187*
Hitler, Adolf, 49, 53, 57, 134
Hobley, MacDonald, 93, 102
Hollingdale, Paul, 104
Hollis, Mike, 186
Holloway, Stanley, 31, 36
Holly, Buddy, 102, 114
Holt, Roger, 166
Horlicks Teatime Hour, The, 36, 45
Housewives Choice, 75–6, 85, 98, 100, 117, 120

IBC (International Broadcasting Company), 15, 16, 18, 19–20, 24, 26, 27, 28, *29*, 33, 36, 38, 39, 40, 43, 50, 59, 65, 70
ILR (Independent Local Radio), 160, 173, 189
Infra-Draw Method, the, 8
Irish Half Hour, 66, 75
Italy Sings, 86, 102
ITV (Independent Television), 83, 93, 94, 95, 111, 138, 160

Jackson, Jack, 35, 71, 86, 146
Jackson Five, the, 166, 167
Jacobs, David, 71, 80, 86, 131, 134, *136*, 181
Jamboree, 86
Jensen, David ('Kid'), 39, 140, 143, 147, *150–1*, 152, *153*, 154, 155, *162–3*, 164, *170–1*, 172, 176
Jensen's Dimensions, 8, 152, 155
Johnson, Bryan, 86
Johnson, Teddy, (a.k.a. E. Victor Johnson, Edward V. Johnson), *60*, 61–2, 65–6, 67, 70, 71, *72*, 73, 75, 76, 77, *78*, 82, 93, 100, 117, 134
Jones, Phillip, 66–7, *69*, 71, *72*, *78*, 79, 83
Jones, Rob, 185, 186, *187*, *188*
Jones, Spike, 55
Joyce, William ('Lord Haw Haw'), *52*, 53–4, 57, 59, 76
Junglinster Long Wave Transmitter, the, *10*, 15, *17*, 19, 20, *23*, 28, 32, 39, 48, 50, 52, 55, 57, *58*–9, 70, 104

Karibian, Leo, 111
Kay, Paul, 124

Keen, Alan, 73, 123, 147, 157, 159, 160, 165, 173, 181, 185, 186
Kelly, Barbara, 78
King, Jonathan, *156*, 173
King, Ted, 101
Kirkham, Ken, 93

L'Antenne, 13
Late Night Luxembourg, 114
Lee, Frank, 65, 66, 74
Lift-Off, 111
Logie, Tony, 181
Lucerne Conference, 24, 25
Lynn, Vera, *6*, 55, *56*

McCarthy, Tony, 139, 146
McCartney, Paul and Linda, *127*
McCullough, Derek ('Uncle Mac'), 40
Madren, Peter, 76, 79, 85, 97
Marconi, Guglielmo, 9
Marine Offences Act, 131, 134, 143, 164
Masterspy, 86
Matthew, Brian, *136*
Maxwell, Charles, 42, 43, 50, 52, 65, 173
Mid-day Spin, 98, 134, 180
Midnight on Luxembourg, 102
Miles, Michael, 86
Mitchell, Guy, *69*
Monday Spectacular, 111
Monkees, the, 166, 167
Moran, Johnny, 119
Moss, Don, 134, *136*
Much Binding in the Marsh, 70, 75
Muckslow, Arthur, 100, 111
Murdoch, Richard, 74, 86, 93
Murray, Pete, 66, 74-5, 76, 79, 80, 81, 82, 83, 85, 86, 95, 97, 100, 134, *136*, 146, 147
Music for Everyone, 66
Music for You, 80
Music of the Stars, 80
Music Makers, 42

Nicholl, Colin, 129, 146
Norton, Dick, 79, 85, 95

O'Dee, Barry, 101, 104
O'Rahilly, Ronan, 130, 144
Opportunity Knocks, 8, 71, 86
Orchard, Ray, 86, 102, 111, 131
Osmonds, the, 166-7
Ovaltinies, 8, 47
OWI (Office of War Information), 58-9
Oxley, Mel, 85, 86

Palmolive Concert, 36
Paramor, Norrie, 92, 93
Partridge Family, the, 166, 167
Paton, Tam, 126, 173
Patton, George, 57, 59
Payne, Jack, 35, 45, 61, 62, 65
Peel, John, 123, 134
People Are Funny, 80
Peter and Paul, 147
Phillips, F. W., 15, 19

Pilkington Committee, 103, 104
Plomley, Roy, 50, 52
Plugge, Captain, 14-15, 16, 22, 26, 38
Pompeian Beauty Preparations Programme, 35-6
Poste Parisien, 18, 22, 26, 39, 52
Powell, Peter, 173, *174*, *175*, 176, 180, 185, 186
Presley, Elvis, 92, 93, 94, 102, 108, 109
Prince, Christine, 146, 165, 181
Prince, Tony, 123, 126, *127*, 128, 143, 144, 146, *150-1*, 159, 164, 165, 166, *168-9*, 172, 176, 181, 185
Princess for a Day, 8, 80, 86

Radio Caroline, 123, 124, 126, 128, 129, 130, 131, 134, 137, 139, 140, 144, 146, 152
Radio London (pirate), 123, 124, 130, 134, 139, 159
Radio Luxembourg Book of Stars, 108
Radio Luxembourg London Ltd (originally Wireless Publicity), 83
Radio Luxembourg Roadshows, 160, 164
Radio Lyons, 18, 39, 46, 47, 52
Radio Normandy (later Radio International), 15, 16, 18, 22, 27, 28, 33, 35, 39, 46, 47, 50, 52, 55, 59, 134
Radio North Sea International, 126, 164
Radio One, *see under* BBC
Radio Pictorial, 35, 88
Radio Revue, 48
Radio Scotland, 124, 126
Radio Toulouse, 13, 18, 22, 26, 39, 47, 52, 134
Rathbone, Basil, 86, 102
Rawitzki, Herr, 16
Raymond, Mike, 131
Read, Mike, *182-3*, 185
Ready Steady Go, 95, 111
Record Club, 86
Record Crop, 102
Record Roundup, 86
Reid, Beryl, 86, 93
Reith, Lord John Charles Walsham, 11, 13, 15, 20, 45, 46, 57, 61
Richard, Cliff, 86, 93, 102, 108, *135*, 157, 166, 185
Rosko, Emperor, 140, *178-9*, 180
Routh, Jonathan, 80
RTL (Radio Tele Luxembourg), 27, 104, 181, 186, 189

Savile, Jimmy, 86, 102, 109, *110*, 114, *122*, 134, 146, *161*
Sedaka, Neil, *153*
SHAEF (Supreme Headquarters of the Allied Expeditionary Forces), 57-8, 59
Shapiro, Helen, *110*
Shelton, Anne, 73
Smash Hits, 95, *96*
Smith, Ogden, 39, 40

Société d'Etudes Radiophoniques, 13, 14
Somers, Debroy, 36, 45
Spin with the Stars, 102
Sporting Challenge, The, 102, 103
Stafford, Jo, 86, *90*
Stanniforth, Max, 15, 16
Stewart, Bob, 143, 144, *145*, 147, *148-9*, 164, 172, 176, 181, 185, 186
Stone, Christopher, 30, 31, 32, 66
Sunday Pictorial, 88, 94
Sunday Referee, 28, 33, 35, 88
Swainson, Richard, 137, 185

Take Your Pick, 86
Teen and Twenty Disc Club, The, 8, 109
Thompson, J. Walter (agency), 42, 47, 123
Topical Half Hour, 66
Top Twenty Show, 8, 75, 79, 97, 119
Travis, Dave Lee, 123, 129, 134
Tuesday Requests, 86
Tune a Minute, 67
Twenty Questions, 75

UIR (Union Internationale de Radiophone), 11, 12, 14, 22, 24, 25, 26, 30, 39

Vance, Tommy, 123, 128-9, 130, 134, 165
Views on the News, 54
Voice of Prophecy, The, 86

Walker, Johnnie, 123, 128, 129, 134, 140
Walters, Harry, 73, 97-8, 100
Wardell, Don, 114, *115*, 116, 119, 139, 146, 157
Wednesday Requests, 86
Welch, Leslie (the Memory Man), 102, 103
Wesley, Mark, 123, 126, *132*, *133*, *148-9*, 152, *162-3*, 164, 165, *170-1*, 176, 180
What's My Line?, 80
Whitney, John, 80, 81
Williams, Howard, 86
Williams, Stephen, 28, 39, 40, 52, 59, 61, 64
Windsor, Tony, 139, 143, 159
Winifred Atwell Show, The, 86
Winter, Marius B., 45
Wireless Publicity (later Radio Luxembourg London Ltd), 36, 38-9, 40, 42, 43, 64, 83, 138
Wireless World, 15, 18
Workers' Playtime, 57, 98
Wright, Steve, 176, *184*, 185-6

You Lucky People, 86
Young, Jimmy, 86, *99*, 100, 129, 131, 137
Young, Muriel, 111, *112*, 113, 114, 116, 120, 131, 138, 147
Young, Steve, 152